**EVERY DAY, 30,000 FLIGHTS WORLDWIDE
SAFELY REACH THEIR DESTINATIONS**

**ON THE NIGHT OF SEPTEMBER 2, 1998,
ONE FLIGHT WOULD NOT**

The plane's electrical systems began to stop working, one after another, in increasingly rapid sequence. Co-pilot Stephan Loëw was already having trouble controlling the plane when the bright video displays showing his instrument readings may have suddenly gone blank and dark.

The two pilots began speaking simultaneously.

"Swissair one-eleven heavy is declaring emergency—"

"We are between, uh, twelve and five thousand feet. We are declaring emergency now at, uh, time, uh, zero-one-two-four—"

"Roger."

"Eleven heavy, we starting dump now. We have to land immediate—"

"Swissair one-eleven," the air traffic controller responded. "Just a couple more miles. I'll be right with you."

"Roger ... And we are declaring emergency now," one of the pilots said again. "Swissair one-eleven."

"Copy that," the controller said. Just over 10 seconds later, he said: "Swissair one-eleven, you are cleared to, uh, commence your fuel dump on that track and advise me, uh, when the dump is complete."

There was no answer from the plane.

"Swissair one-eleven, check you're cleared to start the fuel dump."

Still, there was ɪ
It was shortly be

D0910704

Swissair MD-11 crashes into the Atlantic

A crippled Swissair flight trying to make it to Halifax to attempt an emergency landing, crashed into the Atlantic Ocean near Peggy's Cove, Nova Scotia Wednesday night.

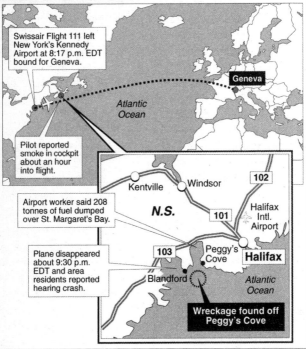

Swissair Flight 111 left New York's Kennedy Airport at 8:17 p.m. EDT bound for Geneva.

Geneva

Atlantic Ocean

Pilot reported smoke in cockpit about an hour into flight.

Airport worker said 208 tonnes of fuel dumped over St. Margaret's Bay.

Plane disappeared about 9:30 p.m. EDT and area residents reported hearing crash.

Kentville

Windsor

102

N.S.

101

Halifax Intl. Airport

103

Peggy's Cove

Halifax

Blandford

Atlantic Ocean

Wreckage found off Peggy's Cove

Sean Vokey - **CP**

FLIGHT 111

The Tragedy of the Swissair Crash

STEPHEN KIMBER

SEAL BOOKS
Toronto

FLIGHT 111/An original Seal Book
First published August 1999

For information: Seal Books, 105 Bond Street, Toronto, Ontario M5B 1Y3

ISBN 0-7704-2840-1

Seal Books are published by Random House of Canada Limited. Its trademark, consisting of the words "Seal Books" and the portrayal of a seal, is the property of Random House of Canada Limited, 105 Bond Street, Toronto, Ontario M5B 1Y3, Canada. This trademark has been duly registered in the Trademark Office of Canada.

Cover photograph by CP Picture Archive (Beth Keiser)
Cover, text and insert design by Janine Laporte

PRINTED AND BOUND IN CANADA

WEB   10 9 8 7 6 5 4 3 2 1

For
Edward G. Kimber
(1914–1981)

Acknowledgements

I knew when I set out to write the human story of the tragedy of Swissair Flight 111 that the book I wanted to write would not be possible without the cooperation of a lot of people who had no reason to answer questions I had no right to ask. I am grateful so many of them did. I am especially indebted to those family members — Peggy Coburn, Mark and Barbara Fetherolf, Miles Gerety, Lyn Romano, Nancy Wight and the Wilkins family — who shared with me not only their personal stories but also those of their relationships with the loved ones they lost. Nova Scotians involved in this tragedy also responded to my endless questions with the same instinctive grace and generosity they showed to the victims and their families in the aftermath of the crash. I thank them as well.

At Swissair, I would like to thank Urs Peter Naef, who, without hesitation or question, tracked down all sorts of information and graciously arranged more than a dozen interviews with airline officials for me. Urs von Schroeder, a writer formerly with Swissair, also offered invaluable insights into the airline and its operations.

There was much that Larry Vance, the Canadian Transportation Safety Board's deputy chief investigator in the Swissair crash, couldn't talk to me about. The board is rightly cautious about appearing to reach conclusions before it completes its investigation, but, within those constraints, he was generous in helping me understand the process investigators are using to figure out what caused the Swissair crash and explaining his own role in the investigation.

Stuart Allsop, who modestly describes himself as a "low-time private pilot" but who has an obvious passion for, and a rich knowledge of, the ins and outs of airplanes, helped explain to me how planes work — and sometimes don't. Alex Richman, an epidemiologist who now applies the diagnostic techniques he learned in medicine to determine the "health" of airplanes, offered invaluable insight on the state of airline safety. Allsop and Richman, it should be noted, both lost loved ones to aircraft tragedies.

I am also grateful to many of my journalist colleagues — particularly Richard Dooley of the Halifax *Daily News*, Stephen Thorne of Canadian Press, Kelly Toughill at the Toronto *Star* and Paul Koring of the *Globe and Mail* — who have all written extensively about the crash and whose reporting I often drew on while researching this book. I also want to thank my agent, Anne McDermid, and John Pearce, the editor-in-chief at Doubleday Canada, for their support for this project. Pamela Murray, my editor at Doubleday, was a godsend, helping keep the narrative on track and on time. I thank her for that. I also thank Shaun Oakey, my super-conscientious copy editor, who saved me from more than a few grammatical and factual slip-ups.

I won't presume to know how well I've succeeded in telling the human story of Swissair Flight 111 and its aftermath. I do know I've learned a lot about a lot of things, including the fragility of human life. As Lyn Romano explained it one day: "After going through something like this, you learn not to take things for granted. When my boys go off to school now, the last thing I tell them every morning is that I love them. Because you never know."

Stephen Kimber

Prologue

The crash of Swissair Flight 111 stopped being an abstraction for me — one of those horrific, isn't-that-awful-and-what-else-is-there? news items that, this time, just happened to have happened in my backyard — shortly after six o'clock on September 3, 1998, the night after the plane plunged into the waters off Peggys Cove, killing all 229 people aboard. I was preparing dinner at home in Halifax, half-listening to the latest news about the accident on the radio. The announcer said that the victims — a list of their names had just been officially released — included many prominent figures: Jonathan Mann, the internationally renowned AIDS researcher, and his wife, Mary-Lou Clements-Mann, also well known as a public health specialist, and several United Nations officials, most notably the director of operations for the United Nations High Commissioner for Refugees in the Great Lakes Region of Africa, Pierce Gerety —

Pierce Gerety?

The name sent an icy shiver of recognition through my body. I knew him. I didn't *know* him, of course, but I did know someone who knew him very well. I had met him only once, in an office for just a few minutes, in the summer of 1975. I had gone to New York to meet the family of my new girlfriend, Jeanie Steinbock. Her brother Dan was the associate director of Prisoners' Legal Services, an advocacy group that acted on behalf of convicts in New York state prisons. Since Dan worked near Chinatown, we agreed to meet at his office and go to lunch from there.

Jeanie introduced me to Dan, Dan introduced me to his boss, a strikingly handsome man named Pierce Gerety. Gerety and I made small talk before Jeanie and I left with Dan. I never saw Pierce Gerety again.

But I followed his career after that through Dan, who became my brother-in-law when I married Jeanie in 1976. When Gerety left Prisoners' Legal Services a few years later to go to Thailand to set up refugee camps for Cambodians on the run from the brutal Pol Pot regime, Dan joined him as education coordinator in several of the camps.

Dan eventually moved back to the U.S., where he married an American woman he'd worked with in the camps. The couple began to raise a family as Dan settled into the more tranquil life of a law professor at the University of Toledo. But Dan stayed in touch with Pierce and would occasionally, almost in passing, make reference to things his friend was up to.

Pierce Gerety dead?

In spite of the hard truth that I didn't really know this man at all, had no more profound connection with Pierce Gerety or his life than that I had once talked to him for no more than five minutes more than twenty years before, hearing his name on the radio suddenly made me realize that the 229 people who died in the crash that night — from "Abady, George, dual citizen of Curaçao and Canada" to "Zuber, Florence, Switzerland" — were something more than names on a too-long passenger list.

That connection is one reason I decided to write this book. I wanted to know more about at least a few of the people behind the names on that list. And I wanted to know too about some of the people whose lives they had touched, and whose lives had been profoundly changed by their passing. Not just their families and friends but the strangers who had tried to save them or console those they'd left behind — strangers who were also changed by the experience.

For the first few days and weeks after the crash, I was awestruck and humbled by the almost instinctive eagerness of my Nova Scotia neighbours to offer aid and comfort to perfect strangers. First of all, there were the fishermen who risked their own lives that first night in the roiling seas in a desperate, fruitless search for survivors. Later, there were shopkeepers who opened their stores in the middle of the night so bereaved strangers could get the toothpaste and shampoo and sundries they'd been too upset to remember to bring from home. These retailers agreed to develop the poignant pictures of Peggys Cove that the families had taken and just couldn't wait for morning to see. What's more, these same shopkeepers often refused to accept payment for their goods or services, let alone for their kindness.

Dozens of businesses and hundreds of individuals, often without even being asked, filled the local Legion hall to overflowing with tractor-trailer loads of barley soups and chicken casseroles and fresh apple pies and homemade brownies, even chewing gum and dental floss, all to keep searchers fed and fortified for their depressing but necessary duties. Office workers, teachers, bus drivers and other ordinary folk abandoned their day jobs, often for weeks at a time, to act as searchers, drivers, caregivers, gofers — whatever was required.

The newspapers were full of touching stories.

"When the full scope of the tragedy hit [Arlen Crocker], he did what came best to him," the Halifax *Chronicle-Herald* reported. " 'I just went into my work-shed and I didn't come out until I was done,' he said … He placed the turquoise sign [To All The Families, Relatives And Friends Of The Casualties Of Flight 111, Our Thoughts And Prayers Go Out To You One And All] with hand-painted red flowers at the foot of his driveway for the families to see as they passed."

"When [St. Margarets Bay Branch 116 Royal Canadian Legion Branch President Burton] Morash heard that volunteer ground search and rescue members were sleeping in their trucks and cars, he said, 'No, no, we can't have that,' and some Legion members started opening their homes to them."

"Twelve-year-old Danielle Thibodeau of Elmsdale sent a package of chocolate chip cookies that she baked, along with a letter to thank the searchers for their efforts."

"Dawn Upshaw said her original idea was to take a carload [of friends] to Peggys Cove to sing spirituals and provide comfort to the families, local residents, searchers and everyone else affected by the plane crash. 'I contacted the African Nova Scotian community. Originally I had hoped to get about six people to go down and sing some spirituals on the rocks. Then I realized I needed a bus. In the end, I needed four buses and three vans.' "

Gary Kerr, a provincial government worker who volunteered to act as a driver for grieving family members, told the Halifax *Daily News* that he didn't find the long hours — drivers worked 156 hours in 10 days — that difficult. " 'We considered it an honour,' he said. 'I just keep thinking if I was in a strange place during a terrible time like this, it would be nice to have someone look after me and take care of me. That's what we tried to do. Look after them like they were our neighbours.' "

They did. And those "neighbours" responded in kind. "From the very first night, the people of Nova Scotia have been generous, thoughtful and brave in helping our family and many others," Pierce Gerety's brother Tom, the president of Amherst College in Massachusetts, wrote in an open letter to Nova Scotia premier Russell MacLellan. "All of us join in thanking you as a nation and a province."

"My heartfelt thanks to all the wonderful people of Nova Scotia and Canada," Nancy Wight, a New York woman who lost her 18-year-old daughter in the crash, wrote in a letter to the editor published in a number of Canadian newspapers shortly after the crash. She enclosed two pictures of her daughter. "All my love to the Canadians and the starkly beautiful landscape of Peggys Cove," she concluded. "My heart lies there forevermore."

A few months after the crash, Wight quietly moved up to Halifax for a month to volunteer at a local church. Earlier, in Nova Scotia immediately after the crash, she'd met Robert Conrad, a St. Margarets Bay fisherman who'd taken part in the initial rescue effort. Wight became friends with Robert and his wife, Peggy, and they would occasionally have dinner together when Wight was in town. Wight later asked the Conrads to help her find a cottage so she could return the next summer to spend time near where her daughter died.

She wasn't the only family member to find comfort in the place, or in the people. Any number of unlikely friendships forged in those first few days as strangers — people who would probably never have met otherwise and, even if they had met, almost certainly never would have found common ground if not for the tragedy of Swissair Flight 111 — became members of the same exclusive club, a community of sorrow to which no one else could ever belong. Even more unlikely, some of those flash friendships survived the immediate aftermath of the tragedy. And endured.

I became curious about that sense of community. What is it about an airplane crash that not only seems to make it different but also makes people respond differently to it than to, say, a stranger's heart attack on the street, or a car crash, or even a natural disaster?

My curiosity eventually led me to Hans Ephraimson-

Abt, a frail but energetic 76-year-old American whose 23-year-old daughter was killed when Soviet jets shot down Korean Airlines Flight 007 in 1983, and who has since become one of the world's leading lobbyists on behalf of those who lose their loved ones in plane crashes.

"What makes an air crash so different?" Ephraimson-Abt repeats my question, lets it hang briefly in the air. He has thought about this question, of course. "An airplane crash is a major event, involving the sudden deaths of hundreds of people at the same moment. It often happens far from where those people, or their families, live, sometimes in places so remote they are all but inaccessible. Because it is such a major event, it generates massive, intrusive, gory publicity that can go on and on. There is the long process of recovering the bodies or belongings. But in many cases, there are no bodies, or the bodies are not intact. That creates its own psychological trauma for the families. There can be no finality, no closure. And then, as people are trying to come to terms with their own personal grief, they must also deal with the inevitable speculation about what caused the plane to crash in the first place. The investigative process to determine what really happened is almost always lengthy. So is the process of litigation. It never seems to end, the glaring light of publicity always shining on them, reminding them."

He pauses. "What image do you remember most from Pan Am 103?" he asks about the plane that a terrorist bomb blew out of the sky over Lockerbie, Scotland, in 1988. "The cockpit," he answers his own question. "Whenever there's a story about the crash, the television news always shows the same pictures of the plane's cockpit in a field. If you look closely at the bottom of the cockpit, you'll see there's a briefcase in the picture. That briefcase belonged to John Cummock. Every time that image appears on the television screen for years and years to come, that briefcase will be there too, to remind his widow and three children, a visual symbol of what happened to their husband and father. There is no escape for them. Ever."

KAL 007, Pan Am 103, TWA 800, Swissair 111 …

Airplane crashes are not only different from other kinds of accidents but they are, I discovered as I spoke with more people about more crashes, often eerily similar to one another in the ways in which people respond to them: the arc of shock and sorrow and coming together and splitting apart and anger and bitterness and vengeance and sadness and — perhaps eventually — accommodation and understanding that almost everyone touched by these circumstances goes through.

Over the course of this book, you'll meet a cast of characters whose lives were changed forever by what happened the night of September 2. Plane crashes don't transform people into something they're not, Hans Ephraimson-Abt once explained to me, but they can — and often do — accentuate and intensify the traits that make them what they are.

Housewife Lyn Romano, for example, has always been a feisty, larger-than-life character. That's why she is such a dominant force in her Goldens Bridge, New York, neighbourhood. That's also why, when her husband was killed in the crash of Flight 111, it only made sense that she would play out her me-against-them moral certainties on a larger stage, quickly becoming what she liked to refer to as Swissair's "worst nightmare."

Miles Gerety, Pierce's younger brother, is a small-town Connecticut lawyer who'd spent most of his life in the long shadow of a brother he both admired and desperately needed to compete with. Flight 111 offered him the chance to assume a role his brother might have taken on had he survived: prime protector of those who lost loved ones in the crash.

It was probably inevitable that Lyn and Miles, both

strong-willed and self-possessed, would eventually clash. And that others — like Peggy Coburn and Mark and Barbara Fetherolf, who also lost family members in the crash — would be forced to pick sides in their conflict.

Disputes among family members have become commonplace in the aftermath of airline disasters. The 1996 TWA 800 disaster off Long Island, New York, for example, has spawned four different, often bitterly divided groups, each claiming to represent the real interests of the families of the victims. The difference in the Swissair crash is the speed with which groups were formed, as the Internet made it much easier for families to communicate — and miscommunicate — with each other instantaneously.

Air crashes affect more than just those who die and those they leave behind, of course. In these pages, you'll also meet John Butt, Nova Scotia's chief pathologist, who considered himself a hardened professional until Flight 111 reminded him, and everyone else, just how human — and humane — he could be.

Veteran television news reporter Rob Gordon thought he'd seen it all too, until the night he spent on the water in the middle of what was left of Swissair Flight 111 convinced him there are some things no one should ever have to see. Fishermen Robert Conrad and Harris Backman were out in the middle of the "debris field" that night too. They had responded, as fishermen do, to the first word of people in danger on the water. But even they weren't prepared for what they encountered, or for how it would affect them.

That, in the end, is what this book is all about. It's an attempt to see the crash and its aftermath through the eyes of just a few of those who lived it, to tell you a little about the people affected by this tragedy and what happened to them as a result.

Wednesday, August 19, 1998

Goldens Bridge, New York
7:30 p.m. EDT

"Don't go."

"It's only for two days."

"If it's only for two days, why not do it by phone?"

"Because they want the personal touch, that's why. Don't you worry, Little Girl, I'll be back on Friday."

"But—"

They'd had this conversation before. Perhaps a hundred times. Lyn admitted to a horrific fear of flying. She had what she liked to call "an insightful gift"; she just knew something terrible was going to happen sooner or later, whereas her husband, Ray, didn't put much stock in insightful gifts. That's just the kind of couple they were. "He's pure logic," she would tell her friends, "I'm pure emotion."

As if she really had to tell anyone that. It was obvious. Whenever they'd have to attend some company black-tie function together, Ray would inevitably give her "the speech."

"Little Girl, be good," he'd say.

"Sure I will," she'd answer. "Until someone pisses me off."

And, of course, someone would. And Lyn would let them know just how they'd pissed her off. As only Lyn could.

One night at a party at their place, a woman whose husband was one of Ray's most important clients "imposed herself" on Lyn. "She touched me on the shoulder, started offering me her opinion, which was not in line with my opinion, and I hadn't asked her to butt in. So I said to her loud enough so everyone could hear: 'Did I ask for your opinion?' " She laughs. "Ray was across the room making coffee. I could see him looking at me with these pleading eyes. He stayed beside me the rest of the night." Afterwards, Ray asked her why she felt compelled to do such things. "Because it's crap," she'd say. As if there could be any other answer.

She let Ray know too when he did something she didn't like. When Ray decided they should join the exclusive Mount Kisco Country Club, he got Lyn to type up the application letter. Over and over. It had to be perfect, he told her. He wanted to make sure they were accepted.

"Why?" she replied. "Because I'm never going to go there with you. You won't catch me sitting on that porch at that club house with all those ladies. You go if you want. Fill your quota with clients. But don't expect me to go with you. That's not my scene."

It was sometimes hard to believe they'd grown up just a few miles from one another in tiny Valhalla, a community of 6,000 just 40 minutes north of New York City. Their families were both Italian Catholic. Italian-Irish and Italian-English. Ray's father owned the local cab company. Lyn's dad ran a restaurant. Lyn and Ray graduated from the same high school, but they didn't date. They just knew one another in the way kids from small towns who go to the same school know each other.

That all changed on the night of Wednesday, January 31, 1973, when they were both 19. Lyn can tell you it was a Wednesday because Wednesdays have always been significant days in her life. Lyn and a few girlfriends had gone to G.G.'s North, a popular hangout in nearby Armonk, to drink and dance, to see and be seen. Lyn saw Ray Romano lazily leaning against a post by the bar. He was wearing sneakers, sloppy jeans and a brown corduroy waist-length jacket over a T-shirt. His hair, she remembers, was "long and funny. But he didn't have a moustache then; I made him grow that later."

Lyn admits she can't explain why — it was just another of her "insights" — but she knew then and there, on that Wednesday night in the middle of the bar at G.G.'s, that there could never be anyone else but Ray for her and her for Ray.

Ray took a little longer to convince. Just like he took a little longer to figure out what he wanted to do with his professional life. While Lyn got her degree in psychology and settled into a job as an administrator for a judge in their local ninth district, Ray played academic hopscotch, getting an associate degree in engineering and a bachelor of arts before finally finding his true path in the MBA and CPA programs at Pace University in nearby White Plains. During his final year at Pace, the international accounting firm KPMG recruited him for its Stanford, Connecticut, office. He was already 26 years old.

"What took you so long?" asked the recruiter.

"It just takes me a while to make up my mind," Ray told him.

Though they continued to date, it took Ray nearly seven and a half years after that night in the bar to finally propose to Lyn. Ray, who was as obsessively Republican as Lyn was vocally a-pox-on-all-their-houses, chose his moment carefully. He popped the question in the car on the day of the 1980 presidential election.

"I want to go shopping," he'd said.

"For what?" she said.

"For a ring."

"What sort of ring?"

"An engagement ring," he said.

"Thank God Reagan won," Lyn says now. "Otherwise my engagement night would have been ruined."

That night they went out to Madera's in Thornwood for dinner. They ordered a bottle of Dom Perignon to celebrate their love for one another. And then they went home to his parents' house to tell them the good news — and to watch the rest of the good news of the election returns.

"Of course," Lyn says, "it took him a year after that to set the date for the wedding. My girlfriends told me to dump him. They said he's never going to marry you. But I knew. I just knew."

She was right about that. She was right too about how rock-solid their union of opposites would turn out to be. Even though they grew up in the seventies, their relationship had a kind of fifties quality to it. On fall Sundays, Ray would wash the cars, "whether they needed it or not," and then he and the boys — Raymond Jr. and Randy — might play some football in the yard. Ray was always competitive, never the kind of father to let his kids win out of some misplaced kindness. The boys loved it, loved it even better when they did win. Afterwards, they'd all go into the living room, where Lyn had laid out a tempting spread of homemade food on the coffee table. They'd light a fire and, together, watch the football game on TV.

They lived in a sprawling ranch house on a hill in Goldens Bridge, a rural-suburban community of a few hundred less than an hour's drive from New York City. And they were still only a few miles from the families and friends they'd grown up with in Valhalla. In fact, their house had once belonged to Ray's parents. Ray found it for them back in 1968 while it was still being built. He'd been driving along back roads on his way to a drag race when his clunker du jour broke down in front of the construction site.

Ray, who was always a big "toy person," loved to race cars and motorcycles when he was younger. He sold his last motorcycle when Randy came along in 1987. Now that he was a family man, he told Lyn, he figured he'd never get the chance to indulge his fantasies again.

But that was before he bought the GTO. It was a 1968 hunter green model, one of only 6,900 of the muscle sports cars Pontiac made that year. When Ray found it advertised for sale — the owner, the *original* owner, was a "little old lady who only drove it on Sundays" — Lyn pushed him to buy it. "Better he gets a car than a girlfriend," she joked to her friends. He was doing well in his job, she pointed out to him, so they could afford it. "For a lousy $8,000, Ray," she said, "you can have your dream car. Go for it."

The day he brought the GTO home, Ray sat in it in the driveway and just revved the engine. Neighbours came to admire the car and to revel in Ray's boyish delight at his new toy.

"He was always working on it," Matt Devey says. In fact, one of Matt's first memories of the man who would quickly become one of his best friends was seeing the GTO in pieces in the driveway and Ray hovering over it lovingly. It was 1990 and Matt had just moved into the house above Ray and Lyn on the hill. He was still a bachelor then, and the Romanos took him under their wing. There was always a beer in the fridge for him, an open invitation to stop by for a drink or a meal or just to have a chat. Matt was a lapsed accountant. He'd gotten a degree but never practised. "I was really stressed when I found out Ray was a partner in a big accounting firm," Matt says. "Whenever I'd say I hated it, Ray would say I must have just been in the wrong area. He loved accounting, he loved the organization of it."

Later, after Matt married Moira, and Tony and

Darlene Goncalves moved into a third house on the hill at the top of their shared lane in 1992, their little enclave was complete. The neighbours became best friends.

Although reality is always more complicated than the view from the outside, the Romanos' marriage, like their family life, did seem like something from a different, less complicated era. Lyn happily gave up her job to raise their boys and be there for Ray when he got home from the office. "My life revolved around him and the house," she says without the least trace of post-feminist regret. "My only other passion was the kids."

During the summers, she'd spend her days around the pool with her kids and the neighbours and their kids. Partly because of the pool, the Romanos' backyard was a favourite gathering place. Lyn liked that too, liked being at the centre of things. But each day at four o'clock, she'd get out of the pool, shower, change and be there to greet her Ray at the door. It was the way they both liked it.

The pool was the setting for more than just neighbourly gatherings, as Matt and Moira and Tony and Darlene found out the evening they got together for a night of parlour games. Ray loved to play games. On this night, it was the newlywed game, in which players ask each member of a couple the same questions and compare their responses. When they asked Ray and Lyn how often they made love, it was Ray's answer they all remembered later: If it was up to Lyn, he told them, it would be seven nights a week. When they asked Ray and Lyn their favourite spot to make love, their answer — the same from both — surprised their friends: the pool, they said, without hesitation. "After that," remembers Darlene, "it was hard to walk past the pool without thinking, 'Ah, the pool' … "

Like Lyn and Ray's life together, Ray could be more complicated than he appeared. He was part the high school class clown all grown up, part the protective big brother, part the obsessively ambitious, upwardly mobile professional. If Lyn's life revolved around Ray and the kids, Ray's revolved around Lyn and the kids and the house and the neighbours — and, of course, his career. It may have taken him a while to find himself professionally, but Ray very quickly made up for lost time.

In 1993, he became a partner at KPMG. His clients included such corporate giants as Xerox, GE, Pittston Oil and Union Carbide. He was proud of his accomplishments, and he was keen to take on the trappings that came with his business success. But Lyn had a way of zeroing in on what was really important to him. When he began to worry that other partners were making more than he was, Lyn demanded: "Are you happy with how much you make?"

"Yeah."

"So why do you give a shit what they make?"

"Because," he would say, "I work hard. I think I deserve to make as much as they do."

Ray would never admit it to her, of course, but he knew Lyn was right. Once, after he told his mother how much he earned and she told him how proud she was of him, Ray's seemingly disconnected reply was simple: "Lyn keeps me grounded," he told his mother.

He could tell his mother, Lyn would complain later, but he couldn't tell me.

Ray was hardly a conventional romantic, but that made the odd moments when he would make some tender, out-of-character gesture all the more meaningful. One day, for example, when he was in New Orleans on business, a large bouquet of flowers was delivered to their door in Goldens Bridge.

At first, Lyn couldn't figure out who they could be from. In all of their 14 years of marriage, Ray had never once sent her flowers for no reason. But the card confirmed they were from Ray. The card elliptically praised the benefits of one-stop shopping. Everything I need, the card said, is right there.

When Ray arrived home from his trip that night, Lyn, as usual, was waiting at the door.

"So," she began without preamble, "who is she?"

Ray looked puzzled. Then he laughed. "I did good, didn't I," he said. He had, she conceded.

"Just don't expect me to do it again," he said.

And he didn't. But he could be full of surprises. Earlier that summer, he'd called her from a partners' meeting he was attending in Florida. It had been a lousy summer for Lyn. Her father had suffered a heart attack and she was emotionally and physically exhausted from helping to care for him. When Ray called her from Florida, it was to announce that he'd booked a villa for her and the kids.

"I can't," she protested. "I don't have the time."

"It's already booked," he said.

"But I hate flying."

"It'll be fine," he said.

And it was. "The place was unbelievable," Lyn remembers, "the most beautiful place I ever stayed."

Not all of Ray's surprises were as welcome. Even though he loved their home and their life in Goldens Bridge almost as much as Lyn did, Ray was still eager to move to a bigger house that better reflected his status in the firm. All the other partners have bigger houses, he would say. They would occasionally spend a Sunday afternoon driving around looking at larger and more luxurious homes in the area, but Lyn would always find some reason why whatever house he found just wouldn't do. The truth was it was because none of those bigger, more luxurious homes were located next door to Matt and Moira and Tony and Darlene.

But then one weekend afternoon in January 1998, Ray got a telephone call at home from one of the firm's senior partners. Lyn and his mother were sitting in the kitchen when Ray came in after taking the call in his home office. "His face was grey," Lyn remembers.

"You're not going to believe this," he said, "but I've been offered a real great opportunity. They want to transfer me to Pennsylvania. It'll be a major step —"

Lyn began to cry.

Ray knew better than to push. "I suppose we should talk about this some other time," he said.

Ray's mother was less reticent. "How could you be crying?" she demanded. "It's his career. It's the same with flying," she added. "You may not like it but he's got to do that too. He has to. For his job."

Lyn understood that. But it didn't make it any easier.

Ray tried to find a way to make it all sound like an adventure. He knew how much Lyn liked to garden. "I'll get you a great house," he said, "and it'll have a greenhouse out back —"

Lyn had heard enough. "The two of you don't get it, do you? You don't have a damn clue. I waited three years to get a porch built on this house. I don't care about any of that stuff. I like living here. I like living with our friends."

Later, after Ray had left for the office, Lyn softened. She sent him an email. She addressed it to Maym. She couldn't remember why she'd started calling him that in their emails, but the reason didn't matter. It was a pet name, like Little Girl, which is what he always called her.

"You know that I don't want to move," she says she wrote, "but I will follow you to the ends of the earth if that's what you need me to do. I love you."

In the end, the transfer fell through. Lyn was relieved,

but she knew the relief was probably only temporary. Ray was moving up in the company, as she knew he deserved to. There would be another transfer offer, another promotion. She would just have to learn to live with it.

As she had learned to live with Ray flying.

Ray's latest business trip, to Switzerland on behalf of a Union Carbide spinoff, had already been postponed twice this summer. Now the date had finally been set again. Ray would leave in two weeks' time: on Wednesday, September 2, 1998.

Still, as they sat on the deck on that warm August night drinking a beer with Steve, their helicopter pilot neighbour from down the road, Lyn couldn't resist one more why-do-you-have-to-fly? conversation.

Steve, like all of their friends, knew all about Lyn's flying phobia, knew that before she'd relent this time — as every time — she'd make Ray promise to call the minute his plane landed, make him leave her a detailed itinerary with phone numbers for every stop "including the nearest pay phone outside the hotel." It wasn't quite that bad, of course, but Steve knew enough to sit back and drink his beer while Lyn and Ray played out their routine.

Finally, Ray turned to Steve for help. Ray, as he often did, had quoted statistics to Lyn, told her how much more likely it was to die in a car accident than in a plane.

"Isn't that right?" he asked Steve.

"That's right," said Steve.

"See," he said to Lyn, "everything will be okay." He took a swallow of his drink. "Hey," he said suddenly. "I just had an idea. Why don't you come with me, Little Girl?"

Lyn laughed. "Yeah, right," she said.

Sunday, August 30, 1998

St. Margarets Bay, Nova Scotia
12:30 p.m. ADT

Rob Gordon cut the boat's engine, felt the freshly stirred sun-warmed summer breeze on his face. Finally. The Bay had been so flat calm when he and Alan Jeffers were preparing to set sail from Mahone Bay an hour before that he'd decided they had better stop and buy some extra gasoline in case the wind didn't pick up and they were forced to run the engine for the entire 40-mile, 10-hour journey to Halifax. In fact, they'd motored all the way out of Mahone Bay, past Little Tancook and Pearl Islands. "You won't run into another piece of land between here and France," Gordon told Jeffers as they were passing between the tip of the Aspotogan Peninsula and Ironbound Island around Seal Ledge. That's when he finally felt the wind come up.

Time to raise the sail.

August was still the best month in Nova Scotia, Gordon thought to himself, the only month when you could really depend on the weather. This year, he had spent his August wisely. On vacation. Gordon and his two sons from his first marriage, Angus, 14, and Mathijs, 12, had camped out on the 20-foot Nordica for the past two weeks. They'd hung out for a while among the dozens of wooden and non-wooden sailing ships at Mahone Bay's annual wooden boat festival, puttered around along the province's South Shore, exploring some of the dozens of uninhabited islands and beaches that dotted St. Margarets Bay, and just generally had a good father-sons time.

Now the boys had gone back home to Halifax, with their mother, Corinne, Gordon's former wife, with whom he shared custody. Gordon and Jeffers would sail the Nordica back up across the mouth of St. Margarets Bay and then, hugging the coastline, sail past Peggys Cove and Prospect and Pennant Point and Chebucto Head and then into Halifax's Northwest Arm, where they would tie the small boat up at its mooring at the Armdale Yacht Club.

Tomorrow, Gordon knew, he would have to go back to work. He tried to remember what was going on in the world of local news, what stories he might end up covering this week. But he gave it only a moment's consideration. There would be plenty of time to worry about all of that tomorrow.

Today, there was just sunshine, sweet sea breezes, good friends and better plans. He and Alan had been friends since they met more than a dozen years ago as young reporters at the Halifax *Chronicle-Herald*. They'd remained close through marriages, kids, divorces and various job changes.

These days, Jeffers was Mobil Canada's chief spokesperson in Atlantic Canada. Gordon was now a general assignment reporter at the local CBC-TV supper-hour news show, *First Edition*.

Despite their different, occasionally conflicting career paths, Gordon and Jeffers still got together at least once a week for a beer after work, occasionally more than once a week — and often for more than one beer.

It was during one of those nights last winter, in fact, that they'd come up with the idea for a book on the *Titanic*'s connections to Halifax. James Cameron's

Hollywood movie about the 1912 sinking — partly filmed in Halifax — had just been released, and it seemed everyone was trying to think of inventive ways to cash in on the public's new-found fascination with anything to do with the famous marine disaster.

Why shouldn't he and Jeffers cash in a little too? Halifax, after all, was where many of the victims had been buried. The local media was already reporting the first movie-inspired pilgrimages to visit the *Titanic* gravesite in Halifax. And it was still the dead of winter, for God's sake. Think how many tourists might make the trip to Nova Scotia in the summer to look for real *Titanic* lore.

Gordon and Jeffers decided to write a quickie guidebook, an everything-you-ever-wanted-to-know-about-Halifax-and-the-*Titanic* kind of book designed specifically to fill in the gaps for all those *Titanic*-hungry visitors. Why not? They were both Nova Scotians, both steeped in the province's history and both excellent reporters and writers.

In a few inspired weeks of research and writing, they put together *Titanic Halifax*, a slim 108-page collection of eclectic Halifax-related *Titanic* trivia. Nimbus, a local publisher, agreed to publish it. Even though the book hadn't made it to the bookstores and tourist shops until that July — halfway through the lucrative summer season — sales were already living up to their expectations. They'd heard rumours it had already sold out most of its first 4,000-copy print run.

And that could be just the beginning. Even after the movie-inspired *Titanic* hype died down, there would almost certainly still be a steady stream of people coming to the province every year to find out more about the real story of Halifax and the *Titanic*.

Perhaps they might even be able to come up with other ways to make use of their knowledge. Gordon had begun working on an idea for a screenplay, a docudrama built around the city's connections to the disaster. That was the other reason they were sailing back to Halifax together on this sunny Sunday afternoon — to discuss Gordon's screenplay and any other ideas that might come up.

Gordon took out a beer, passed one to Jeffers and stared out at a sea that seemed to stretch to forever. Gordon loved the smell and taste and feel of the ocean. There was a time when he had planned to make his career on the sea. In truth, he had initially become a journalist more by process of elimination than desire.

The oldest of three children of a prominent Halifax doctor and his wife, Rob Gordon had surprised and shocked his family by dropping out of school at 16, then spending the next five years just bumming around. "It was a time when there was a whole lot going on," he remembers. "You could stay in a youth hostel for 50 cents a night." He did stints as a seaman in the coast guard and a cook on offshore oil rigs before returning to school, largely to escape the ghetto of unskilled labour.

After earning an honours degree in strategic studies from Dalhousie University, he enrolled at the Nova Scotia Nautical Institute with plans to get his navigation officer's ticket and begin his career as a ship's officer. But after only a few months he realized that, if he did get his ticket, he would probably have to spend much of the rest of his life at sea. As much as he loved the idea, he couldn't really imagine spending his life that way. So he dropped out and enrolled instead in a new public relations program at Mount Saint Vincent University in Halifax, largely because "it seemed like a way out of going to sea."

After his first year there, he traded on a family connection to land a summer job as a reporter at the Halifax *Chronicle-Herald*. After a few months of writing up obituaries and Lions Club luncheons, he got his first taste of journalism's intoxicating joys. A friend told him that the owners of a trawler tied up at a Halifax pier had skipped town and the Mounties were using dogs to search the vessel. Gordon wrote a dry factual news story about it. A fellow reporter took a look at his copy on the terminal.

"Good story," he said.

"Yeah?" replied Gordon.

"Yes," the reporter dryly informed him, "but not the way you wrote it."

"He helped me rewrite the piece … perhaps he did rewrite it," Gordon concedes with a laugh. "It was a good story. And I got to follow it up — I found out the boat had been involved in a drug bust in Lebanon. I was calling up FBI guys in Virginia … It was a crossroad. I realized you could have fun — and do interesting stuff." He never went back to PR.

He had no regrets — about any of it. He was 43 years old and he couldn't imagine being anything but a reporter. Still, on that late summer day, he wished he had one more week of vacation. He wasn't ready for it to end.

Noank, Connecticut
4 p.m. EDT

"Nice." Pierce Gerety examined his kid brother Miles's Ericson 35 sailboat with the keenly appraising eye of an expert sailor. "Mom buy this for you?" Pierce asked finally, still staring at the boat bobbing at the dock in Noank, a slight smile playing at the edge of his mouth.

"No," Miles replied too quickly, almost defensively. "I got a second mortgage for it." Even though he'd had the boat for three years, Miles realized Pierce had never seen it before. He realized too that, even after all these years, Pierce still knew how to push his buttons — even though Pierce, the much older brother at 56, and Miles, 48, were both successful adults with careers and wives and grown-up children of their own.

Sibling rivalry, it sometimes seemed, came with the turf of being born a Gerety. That didn't make it any easier to compete with a living saint. Pierce was the saint. Miles was ... well, Miles was not Pierce. But they were both Geretys, Fairfield, Connecticut's version of the Kennedys, a large and larger than life Irish-American clan full of boisterously competitive overachievers.

Their father, Pierce Sr., had himself been one of nine brothers, the sons of a Depression-era "turnaround artist" who, Miles says, eventually "got some disease and couldn't work." So the boys had to grow up fast. Their uncle Edward, for example, became a contractor when he was still too young to sign bank loans, helped pay the family bills by building houses and then put himself through medical school with the proceeds of his contracting business. Today he was a successful heart surgeon. The brothers — except for the youngest, who died in World War I — had all gone on to achievement: among them were two lawyers, one of whom became a judge, two priests, one of whom became an archbishop, and two doctors.

Pierce Sr. had been one of the lawyers. Miles, who would grow up to be a public defender, says his father was a "great trial lawyer" but eventually switched to tending to the legal needs of corporations to support his growing family. Pierce Jr. was the oldest, Miles the youngest by close to a decade. In between came Peter and Tom. "When Pierce and Peter were little, our family didn't have much money," Miles says now, "but when I was 15 and Pierce was long gone, my parents installed a swimming pool in the backyard. So it was almost as if we grew up in different worlds."

By then, Pierce Sr. had become a prominent and

highly successful corporate lawyer with practices in both Bridgeport and New York. He had once wanted to run for Congress but declared his candidacy too late. Miles had also dabbled in politics, losing his own lone bid for the State Assembly by 11 votes.

If Miles inherited his father's interest in law and politics, Pierce Jr. — under pressure from birth, says his mother, Helen, to be the good one in the family — was much more influenced by the elder Gerety's role as a public servant during the Eisenhower administration as well as by the example of his two uncles, Peter and John, who had both become priests.

During the fifties, President Eisenhower appointed Pierce Sr. to head the U.S. refugee relief program overseeing the admission of refugees to the United States after World War II. Later he became chair of the International Rescue Committee's Far East Refugee Program. "As a little kid," Miles says, "I remember Dad getting dropped off at the White House on Saturdays."

By then Pierce Jr. was already an overachieving teenager. After he'd won the gold medal for academic achievement at his Georgetown prep school, his father took him up to Yale, ostensibly to show him the school he'd be attending a year from then. But Pierce had top scores on his College Board exams so Yale admitted him immediately. He was 16.

"He was too young," his mother says now. "He wasn't ready socially and he was very lonely that first year. But he adapted."

By contrast, Miles concedes he was "never very successful in school. They even kept me back in the eighth grade." Sports became his saving grace: he played ice hockey for an undefeated school team and he learned to sail competitively. He was good at that, but, of course, Pierce, the junior commodore at the local yacht club, had taught him to sail the summer before he went off to Yale. Seven-year-old Miles was then still the butt of schoolyard jokes. Other kids would sometimes even hold up Olympic-style score cards with zeros written on them in big red letters to mock him as "retarded."

By the time Miles was diagnosed as dyslexic and finally began to live up to his academic potential, Pierce was out of the picture. But his older brother's reputation remained, a continuing source of pride, admiration, envy and jealousy for his kid brother. Even now, when Miles talks about his brother, it is often to compare himself. "I talk all the time, he didn't. He read all the time; when I was a kid, I couldn't read a goddamned word."

During his years at Yale, Pierce often went sailing with his uncle Peter, then an inner-city parish priest in New Haven, and discussed what he should do with his life. After he graduated in 1962, he announced to the family that he had decided to become a priest like his uncles.

That fall, he left for Europe to study theology and philosophy at the Institut Catholique in Paris. In his spare time, he set up a soup kitchen for the city's poor, cadging food from local hotels. When the family came to visit him at Christmas that year, Pierce's only request was for a coat — for a priest at the institute. Miles, who was 12, remembers the visit for two reasons: watching his big brother break up a knife fight between two beggars in the street ("He ended up with blood all over his clothes") and meeting "this sexy French girl wearing white boots with fringe on them."

The sexy French girl was Marie de la Soudière, the daughter of French nobility who had become Pierce's girlfriend. When Marie visited the U.S. the next summer and stayed with the Geretys, Pierce's father would often accompany them to church, introducing them to other parishioners as "my son the seminarian and his girlfriend." By then, Pierce had already decided he could not become a priest. "I remember he came home from his aunt's funeral," Helen says, "and he was crying. He told me he was sad because he didn't want to be a priest anymore. I told him he was wrong to feel that way. He shouldn't be sad. I thought he'd be lonely as a priest."

He would not be lonely. He had decided to marry Marie instead. At first, Helen recalls, Pierce Sr. objected, believing his son was still too mixed up to know what he really wanted. He even took Marie with him to New York one day in the train's club car to try to talk her out of the marriage. "He has no job, he has no prospects," he told her. "This is crazy." But I don't care, she replied. I love him and I want to marry him. Finally, says Helen, one of her husband's older brothers took him aside. "Pierce," he said to him, "what have you got against Marie? She's a good Catholic, she's a bright girl and they're very happy together."

In the end, Pierce Sr. served as his son's best man at the wedding at Marie's family's estate near Bordeaux. Uncle Peter performed the ceremony. After a honeymoon in Majorca, the couple returned to the Gerety family home in Fairfield, where, Helen recalls, they were initially at loose ends. "They wanted to help people but they didn't quite know how." They finally joined Catholic Relief Services and were assigned to India. Their first son, also Pierce, was born in Delhi in 1966.

In 1968, they returned to the U.S. so Pierce could go back to university. He enrolled in economics at Harvard but quickly switched to law. When he graduated in 1971, a number of big New York law firms came courting. "But they didn't interview him," Helen remembers with a laugh. "He interviewed them. 'Who do you represent? Who are your clients?' "

In the end, he passed up all their offers, choosing instead a job with Federal Defender Services of the New

York Legal Aid Society. Three years later, he joined the society's special litigation unit, where he used the law to take on such controversial issues as police brutality. A year after that, he became the executive director of Prisoners' Legal Services, a program for prisoners he'd help create to tackle everything from conditions in state jails to the legitimacy of individual convictions. Using what his associate director, Daniel Steinbock, would later describe as his "unique combination of passion and diplomacy," Pierce secured the cooperation of state legislators, the bar, the courts and even some prison administrators, creating a six-office statewide program in a matter of months. As director, he could be, Steinbock recalls, a demanding taskmaster. "He was probably the most elegant legal writer I have ever known," he notes, "and he expected no less of his staff." They would often find their legal drafts returned to them heavily edited and with the notation: "PG (picayune grammarian)." Prisoners' Legal Services would eventually end up handling tens of thousands of cases over the next two decades, but by then Pierce himself would again be long gone, this time into international refugee relief.

Though he and Marie had bought a house in Brooklyn, they rarely spent much time there. In 1979, Pierce joined the International Rescue Committee as its country director in Thailand, helping set up refugee camps for fleeing victims of Cambodia's oppressive Pol Pot regime. It was dangerous work. When Helen and Pierce Sr. came to visit them once, Helen remembers being frightened by a mortar exploding nearby. "Don't worry," Marie told them, "they're not very good shots."

Four years later, Pierce joined the United Nations High Commission for Refugees and began a series of postings to what could pass for the answers to a quiz on the names of the world's most dangerous places: Indochina, Afghanistan, Sudan, Somalia, Rwanda,

Burundi and the Congo. Eventually, he became the director of operations for the United Nations High Commissioner for Refugees in the Great Lakes Region of Africa. Marie became director of the International Rescue Committee's program for uprooted children.

Neither was content to do a job from the comfort of an office. Over the years, they'd been shot at more than once, risked their lives landing in small aircraft on narrow dirt roads in remote areas of Africa and luckily missed at least one flight that was blown out of the sky by a bomb planted by one side or the other in a conflict. And Pierce once faced down Somali warlord General Mohammed Adid, walking unarmed into his heavily armed camp and persuading him to release a group of humanitarian aid workers he'd taken as hostages.

"I worried all the time about them being killed," Miles says today. "Wherever they were, all hell always seemed to be breaking loose." He did most of that worrying at a distance. The brothers would see each other for only a few days each summer, when Pierce and Marie visited Fairfield to see Helen, but the gulf in their ages and experiences had separated them.

Miles believed that gulf was finally beginning to narrow as they both settled into successful, more comfortable middle age.

Though Miles had always shared his oldest brother's passion for helping the weak and the oppressed, he painted his own good works on a smaller-scale canvas than Pierce. He got his undergraduate degree from Wesleyan University in Connecticut and then earned his law degree from the smaller, less prestigious Antioch in Washington, D.C., and happily took up a post as a public defender in Bridgeport, where his father had once practised. He and his wife, Silvia, now lived in Redding, just a 20-minute drive from his mother's home in Fairfield and a few more minutes from his office, with their two children, Miles Jr., 20, and Patrick, 13.

Miles is good at what he does — a flamboyant and theatrical courtroom performer who prides himself on his expertise in forensics, he claims he hasn't lost a trial in two years — but he is the first to admit he has been dogged much of his adult life by the self-doubt that is the baggage of having been branded retarded as a youngster. "I spent most of my life trying to get over it," he says simply.

This deep-seated insecurity may explain why he likes to point out to anyone who will listen that he's been included — along with a number of Nobel laureates — in a Harvard University study of successful dyslexics. He has recently become an outspoken lobbyist for the cause, championing a variety of state and national legal and educational reforms on behalf of dyslexics as well as once single-handedly frightening the giant Mitsubishi corporation into withdrawing a television ad campaign he thought demeaned dyslexics.

Of course, Miles's dedication to the cause wasn't a way of directly competing with his older brother, but he would be quick to point to his efforts on behalf of dyslexics whenever anyone dared to suggest his other interests or accomplishments might somehow be more parochial or less significant than Pierce's.

Still, Miles says, there was less rivalry between the two brothers in their middle age and more acceptance of each other's strengths and weaknesses. Miles, in fact, could sense "a kind of sweetness" growing in Pierce that he hadn't seen before: "He seemed to be mellowing." For all his public reputation as a global do-gooder, Miles says, Pierce "was always more complicated than his image. He could be sullen and distant sometimes in the family. But I think we all get wiser as we get older."

Miles was hoping he could eventually achieve a

degree of peace with Pierce that he'd finally developed with their father in the last few years before he died of colon cancer in 1983. "When I was growing up, Dad was always too busy," Miles says, "but we had come to a real accommodation before he died."

Pierce Jr. had always been too busy too, but now there was talk amongst family members that he and Marie might finally settle full time in New York so they could spend more time with their grown children.

Miles thought it was a good idea. "Pierce was so busy saving the world I think he sometimes didn't always have enough time for his own kids," he suggests gently. During one conflict, Pierce and Marie had had to send their youngest daughter, Maeve, back to the U.S. for a number of years to live with Helen in Fairfield and attend high school there because it was too dangerous for her to stay where they were. And Sebastian and Little Pierce, as their oldest son became known, often spent their summers in Fairfield when they were younger.

"Little Pierce was the link to all of us," Miles says now. "I was only 15 when he was born, so he became more of a brother to me than a nephew. And he was only 12 years older than my own son, Miles, so they're close too. He's the connecting point for the generations."

In fact, Little Pierce, now 32 and a field worker for the Irish relief group Concern, had also been the link that last glorious sunny Sunday of the summer. He and some friends had spent the weekend visiting in Fairfield and had even gone sailing with Miles the day before. "It was the first time Little Pierce had brought friends to sail," Miles says. They'd motored out to Fishers Island — "a beautiful, peaceful spot" — swum, shared a bottle of wine and enjoyed a pleasant afternoon of conversation.

Miles had invited his mother to join them for another

sail. Now 79, she'd broken her hip that winter, and Miles had had his doubts she'd ever be able to manage clambering on and off the sailboat again. But she'd decided to give it a try, largely because Tommy, one of Miles's older brothers, was visiting from Amherst for the weekend and would be going out with them too. Tom, four years older than Miles and the president of Amherst College in western Massachusetts, was recovering from recent treatment for prostate cancer.

"We had a wonderful time," Miles says of the leisurely afternoon they all spent anchored near Fishers Island, soaking up the sun and telling family stories while the younger ones swam in the clear waters off the northern tip of Long Island Sound.

They'd just docked at Noank when Pierce and Marie showed up unannounced. They'd spent the past few weeks vacationing with friends in Maine and were on their way back to Brooklyn for a few days together before Pierce returned to UN headquarters in Geneva.

While Pierce talked with Tommy, Miles showed a suitably impressed Marie — still wearing high heels — around his sailboat. He'd bought the boat used three years before for $25,500 and spent much of his spare time fixing it up. He'd put in a new cabin floor with mahogany strips he'd had cut especially. He showed her that, as well as the chart table he'd made with a little railing around it. "It wasn't perfect, but she noticed," he remembers happily. "She said she thought it would be nice to do that in their kitchen in Brooklyn."

With Pierce and Marie on hand, the afternoon turned into an impromptu family reunion, which they capped off by driving to nearby Mystic for pizza and beer. "It was the best time we ever had as a family," Miles says. "I thought that Pierce and I were really coming to an understanding. I thought things would only get better."

Bayswater, Nova Scotia
6:30 p.m. ADT

From the picture window of his Bayswater bungalow on this sunny late-summer afternoon, Harris Backman had a commanding view of the path from Tancook Island to Peggys Cove that Rob Gordon and Alan Jeffers had sailed across a few hours earlier on their way from Mahone Bay to Halifax.

Backman would have liked to be out on the ocean too. Not to sail for pleasure, of course, but to fish for his livelihood, to fish for his life. These days, however, he could only wish. Doctor's orders. "You may know everything there is to know about fishing," the doctor had told him last year, "but I know your heart. And I know that if you go back out there fishing again, you're going to die and there won't be one whole hell of a lot we can do about it."

The last time Harris Backman had been fishing — "The nineteenth day of January, nineteen hundred and ninety-six," he recalls painfully — he'd collapsed at the wheel of the *ABS Enterprise*, the 35-foot fishing boat he'd named for his wife, Audrey, and sons, Bryce and Steven. They'd been out setting lobster traps when he suffered the angina attack. It should have come as no surprise. His father died of a heart attack in 1977. And Harris himself had spent most of the previous year sick with what seemed like one thing after another. Nine days before the attack, his doctor had sent him to the hospital for a dye test. They'd put him on a waiting list for bypass surgery. The day before his attack, the hospital had called to tell him he was scheduled for his operation on January 24. But the next day — boom. Harris had a quadruple bypass. And that was the end of fishing.

Harris Backman would tell you he came from a long line of fishermen. But they all had had to do other things too, simply to survive in Nova Scotia's harsh, unforgiving coastal environment. Harris's father, Ivan, for example, supplemented his fishing income by working as a carpenter and boat-builder. On their rocky, windswept family property overlooking the Atlantic Ocean, Ivan had also kept a few head of cattle and some hens and geese, and even grew sauerkraut cabbages — "hard-headed ones you'd take out with the roots" — to help make ends meet. But for all that, Ivan Backman still would have described himself as a fisherman. So would Harris. Fishing wasn't simply what you did. It was who you were. And that made not fishing anymore even harder.

Harris started fishing with his father and grandfather the summer he turned 10. School held no interest for him — "I got my education at the University of Downtown Bayswater," he jokes today — and he confesses he wasn't disappointed when he had to drop out of school for good after his father's first heart attack, in 1958. He was 18 and he was a fisherman.

It wasn't nearly as easy to remain one. By the early sixties, the fishery "got so bad you couldn't make five cents," and he eventually lost his boat. So, when the provincial government decided to pave the highway around the Aspotogan Peninsula from Hubbards to East River, Harris applied for a job on the road-building crew. That's how he met Audrey, a fisherman's daughter from nearby Northwest Cove. She was still in high school. They married in 1966 and now had two grown kids, Bryce, 26, a factory worker, and Steven, 24, a fisherman like his father.

Harris didn't get back to fishing full time until 1977, the year Ivan died and his mother took ill, and he and Audrey came home to take over the family business for good. During the preceding 15 years, he'd worked all over the province, first for the highways department and later for private contractors. He'd worked his way up to the position of general superintendent — his last job was managing a million-dollar water and sewer project in Halifax — but "the construction industry was going downhill then so it seemed like time for a change," he explains simply. He also missed fishing.

In 1979, two years after Canada declared a 200-mile coastal limit and made clear its determination to claim all the fish within its vast new territory, Harris borrowed $225,000 from the provincial Fisheries Loan Board to buy a 48-foot dragger so he and a crew of four could cash in on the booming offshore fishery off Georges Bank. The work was hard, the fishing physically exhausting. He would often have to work 24 hours at a stretch, sometimes longer — once, he says, he fished "70-some hours" without a break — in order to fill the ship's gaping 57,000-pound hold before racing back to port so he could sell his catch to the buyer before the first fish he caught began to go bad.

But the emotional toll was even greater than the physical. Harris had to pay $22,000 a month on his loan, "and then there's gear." The financing was so delicate it only worked if nothing went wrong. In 1983, something went very wrong: his vessel's engine broke down at sea and he had to be towed into port by the coast guard. He tried to get the engine fixed at a local shipyard, but the initial repairs didn't solve the problem and the boat ended up in the yard for six weeks at the height of the summer fishing season. "By the time I got it off the slip, it had cost me $62,000," he says. Not to forget those other, non-monetary costs: the five occasions during the five years he owned the dragger when he ended up in hospital suffering from high blood pressure and other ailments.

In 1984, just as the bottom was falling out of the offshore fishery anyway, Harris decided to sell the dragger and get a 35-foot gillnetter instead. That not only reduced the economic pressures but also meant he could fish closer to shore, make shorter trips and often fish with his teenaged sons in the bargain. When they went lobster fishing, Audrey joined them as crew too.

"The first time I went out," she remembers with a laugh, "Harris ran her up on a rock."

"I was only tormenting her," he says. "The rock was back under water as soon as the tide came in. I just wanted to see what she'd say."

She said plenty. "I wasn't laughing," she says now. "I said, 'Can I walk to shore?' "

But they got past that, and Audrey remembers the times she and Harris fished together as among the best moments of her life. "I found fishing calming," she explains. "I'd do it today if I could." But, like Harris, she can't. In 1991, she developed arthritis. To help the family make ends meet, she signed on as a seamstress at Suttles and Seawinds, a nearby manufacturer of fashionable clothing and accessories for the American carriage trade. She worked in the company's New Germany factory for five years until an environmental sensitivity to the fabrics forced her to quit, in August 1997, shortly after Harris's bypass operation had ended his fishing career. They sold the boat to their son Steven.

"He's a good fisherman," Harris says proudly.

"He had a good teacher," adds Audrey.

These days, Harris and Audrey work as organizers for the Canadian Coast Guard Auxiliary, a volunteer flotilla of fishing and pleasure boaters who help out in marine search and rescue missions. Harris is the Maritime region's operations officer, one of the few paid positions in the CCGA. Audrey isn't officially an employee but she happily shares the workload with her husband.

The coast guard, which has only a few vessels and

aircraft of its own on call for rescue work, set up the CCGA in 1978 to help it cope with what was becoming an overwhelming number of marine distress calls. Traditionally the coast guard has depended on everyone from the crews of just-passing cargo ships and navy vessels to pleasure boaters and fishers to pitch in whenever the need arises. Although mariners are almost invariably willing to help out in an emergency — it is part of the code of the sea — few of them were trained in search and rescue, or even in basic survival techniques. And finding volunteers when and where they were needed often ate up valuable organizing time the coast guard should have been able to devote to the actual search and rescue effort.

The auxiliary provides the coast guard with an on-call navy of more than 450 trained members in Nova Scotia, New Brunswick and P.E.I. (Newfoundland has a separate organization), most of them fishers, who collectively crew 350 vessels. The coast guard in turn provides its auxiliary members with valuable training as well as money for gas and incidentals when they're on assignment.

Harris and Audrey had been among the first in their area to join the auxiliary — "I was number 19, Audrey was 20" — and the whole family has been involved in more than their share of rescue missions.

In the fall of 1995, Harris and Steven won a Directors' award from the coast guard for their part in rescuing three yachtsmen. They'd been sailing their 28-foot pleasure boat, the *Seabreeze*, from Lunenburg to Boutiliers Point when they got caught in a sudden storm — 15-foot seas and 30-mile-an-hour winds — near East Ironbound Island. The winds knocked over the vessel's mast, smashing it through the cabin. To make their situation more precarious, the engine then failed. With its anchor powerless to resist the winds and the waves, the *Seabreeze* began drifting toward the rocky shores of the island, where almost certainly it would be smashed to bits. With no other communication equipment aboard the vessel, the skipper, Joe Allan of Halifax, fired off a red distress flare.

"We got the call at 2:08 a.m.," Harris remembers. The Rescue Coordination Centre in Halifax told him someone had seen a flare. "I said to 'em, 'You must be out of your mind.' This is no night to be out foolin' around. But they told me exactly who had sighted the flare and I knew they were reliable, so Steven and I decided we'd better go out and see what we could find." After an hour in the choppy seas, Harris and Steven found the *Seabreeze* drifting dangerously close to Ironbound Island and stayed with the vessel and its crew until the coast guard cutter *Sambro* could arrive and tow it to safety.

These days, because of his health, Harris didn't take part in the search and rescue missions himself. But he and Audrey kept busy nonetheless. Just the week before, he'd been in Halifax picking up $80,000 worth of pumps and floater suits for auxiliary members. The pumps are for use when vessels are taking on water; the floater suits are designed to keep people afloat in the cold ocean long enough for someone to rescue them.

Harris had stored all the gear in his basement and back building. He'd spent the week organizing it into trip-sized loads, which he and Audrey would spend the next few weeks delivering all over the Maritimes, distributing the bundles to auxiliary members from Yarmouth to the Magdalen Islands.

It was important work. And it kept Harris and Audrey from thinking about how much they missed fishing.

Tuesday, September 1, 1998

East Brunswick, New Jersey
9:30 p.m. EDT

She was being silly. She knew that. But she couldn't help herself. Peggy Coburn sat all alone in her living room, the kids' toys scattered around, the television playing absently on the top of the shelving unit across the room. She wasn't crying because of what was on the screen; she wasn't even paying attention to the program. And she wasn't feeling any more overwhelmed than usual by the pressures of looking after three kids under six, one of them a breastfeeding seven-month-old, in a tiny two-bedroom apartment in East Brunswick, New Jersey, either — though, Lord knows, there were days when she did question the wisdom of their decision to forgo pleasure in the present to build the better tomorrow they both wanted. No, she was simply thinking about Richard, and about how much she loved him and how much she was going to miss him when he left for that trade show the next day.

Rich was in the next room, she knew, busy at the computer. It sometimes seemed he was always working on the computer. He'd arrive home from the office around nine o'clock, spend a few minutes with her — and the kids, of course, if any of them happened to be awake — and then head straight for the bedroom and the computer. Working, working, working. This was his busy season, she knew, trade show season. His firm's clients, manufacturers of medical equipment, not only needed Rich's technical computer graphics wizardry to create razzle-dazzle displays that could draw customers to their trade show booths but they also depended on Rich's visual flair and quirky sense of humour to turn dull, dry presentations into I-can't-wait-to-tell-them-back-at-the-office events.

Rich didn't intend to spend the rest of his life creating trade show presentations for corporate clients, of course. Someday, he was going to open his own computer animation business. "He wanted to make a splash," Peggy says.

Richard Coburn was 37 years old, an age when many men are settling not only into their careers but also for something less than they'd once dreamed of for themselves. But Rich had been a late bloomer, and he was still trying to make up for lost time. The lost time had begun, Peggy says now, when he was 12. He'd been singled out to participate in a special educational program for artistically gifted youngsters in San Diego, but his mother decided to move the family to Hawaii instead. She never even told Richard until he was an adult about the opportunity he'd missed or — perhaps more important — that others had considered his talent worth nurturing.

So Rich had followed both his father — an American serviceman who met, married and divorced his Japanese mother while on assignment in Japan — and his stepfather, who married his mother when he was five, into a career in the U.S. navy. He spent most of his six years in the navy on a nuclear submarine. Afterwards, he went to work at a nuclear power plant. Later, he became fascinated with computers and taught himself how to use them. He talked himself into a job creating visual aids for the New York Power Authority, then landed a job with a smaller company creating computer graphics. Today, he worked for MJW Corporation, a company that specialized in developing software and creating multimedia presentations for companies in the health industry.

He and Peggy met January 31, 1987, at a singles weekend in the Catskills. Peggy was a 27-year-old orthodontist's daughter from Freeport, Long Island, who worked in PR in New York. She had been dragged along to the meet-your-mate weekend by a friend. "I didn't really want to go," Peggy says now. "I knew I wasn't going to meet anyone." She was standing in the lineup waiting for a turn on the snowmobile rides when she did meet someone. Rich Coburn, who was living in Boston at the time, had also been talked into going by a friend. He didn't think he would meet anyone either.

"He just seemed nice," Peggy remembers. "I liked his vibe." They talked. And talked some more. She ticks off his attributes: "He was nice, affectionate, considerate, fun, smart, a gentleman." By the end of the weekend she told her girlfriend, "I think I could marry this guy."

And she was right about something else she knew instinctively from the start: that he'd make a great father. "Before we got married and we'd visit friends who had kids, Rich would be almost embarrassing. He'd give those kids more attention than their own fathers would."

After their own children had come along — Dylan, Kira and now baby Alea — Rich was like a "playful puppy" in the way he behaved with them. "I didn't have the energy to play around with them, but Rich just loved to get down on the floor and play with them."

He could be a good father — and a good husband — in other ways too. The previous week they'd joined the local synagogue so Dylan could attend religious school. That was important to Peggy, whose family is Jewish. "Rich didn't necessarily commit to the idea of God," she says, "so we'd often have arguments about religion. Rich was a very spiritual person but he didn't think you needed organized religion to commune with … not necessarily a deity, but with nature, I guess." Despite his misgivings about God and organized religion, he'd been quick to agree when she suggested they join the synagogue. "That was him being supportive of me," Peggy says. "That, and I think he saw merit in us being part of a community."

Perhaps because his own father had left home when he was just two, "Rich wanted his own kids to have the best upbringing they could," Peggy explains. They'd agreed that part of that best upbringing included Peggy staying at home to look after the kids instead of getting a job to supplement Rich's modest salary. "That was our priority."

Rich was supportive around the house. He was very much a participating dad, and he encouraged Peggy to take time for herself. "He'd scold me, tell me, you know, you have to take a break once in a while too," she says. "Last month, the mothers' club I belong to was having a moms' night out. I didn't want to go, I didn't want to spend the $25, but Rich insisted. He said he'd take care of the kids. 'You go out and have some fun.' "

On the weekends, he'd take the kids with him on errands. He'd also arrange to spend special time with each of the older ones individually. He and Kira, for example, would go to Taco Bell or Dunkin' Donuts and just hang out together for a while. He and Dylan might take in a movie together. "Dylan really bonded with Rich," Peggy says. "When he'd come into our bedroom in the morning, Dylan would always go around to Rich's side and crawl in beside him. 'Dad, Dad,' he'd say. 'It's 6:23.' And then, 'Dad, Dad, it's 6:24.' I'd be cracking up just listening."

There was still a bit of the kid in Rich too. He loved to read *Mad* magazine or see animated films, especially the newer ones with computer animation. Of course, that was different. "He'd make us sit through all the credits," Peggy remembers. "It was like he needed to see everyone's name." And perhaps imagine his own up there someday.

If his dreams were big, Rich was a very practical guy. He wanted to own his own business one day, so he and Peggy had decided several years before that he wouldn't go to work for some big corporation where he'd be just another little cog in a big corporate wheel. "He didn't want to take the safe route," says Peggy. Instead, he worked mostly for small companies so he could have a bigger role in the operations and learn the business side. "He wanted to be ready when the time came to start his own firm." Occasionally, as was often the case in the computer animation business, the small companies he worked for didn't survive, but that was okay too. He was laying the groundwork for their future.

Someday, he said, they'd move back to San Diego. Even though he'd been born at a military hospital in Japan, Peggy says, he thought of himself as being from San Diego. The weather's nice there, he would say, and there are lots of museums to take the kids to.

Peggy Coburn had no doubt at all that it would all work out just the way Rich said it would. She understood too that in order to achieve all of that — for them — Rich had no choice but to travel as part of his job. She understood it — but she missed him so.

Was that why she was crying now?

This certainly wasn't the first business trip he'd had to take. But it would be his first trip to Europe. It was so far away! He was leaving the next day for Geneva, to set up a multimedia display for a client at an international rheumatology convention. She knew he was excited about going. He'd even taken *Fodor's Guide to*

Switzerland out of the library. He was hoping to get some time away from the convention to visit a few museums.

She hoped he'd have the opportunity. He'd earned it.

She felt silly crying. Rich used to be the one who would be embarrassed to let his emotions show. She could still remember the night, soon after they were married, when they went to some tear-jerker movie. Rich was the stoic, holding her hand, comforting her. But when the lights came up, she saw that he'd been crying too. But only from his left eye. "How do you do that?" she'd demanded. It had upset him to realize she'd "caught him in the act of not containing his emotions," she says. But Rich had changed. The last movie they'd seen together was *Saving Private Ryan,* which had jerked some tears from both of them. From both eyes. When it was over Peggy whispered to him: "This is the part you hate — when people can see that you've been crying." But he wasn't embarrassed in the least anymore. "I don't care," he told her.

Well, neither did she. She couldn't help it if she loved him, couldn't help it if she would miss him. She got up, turned off the television and headed for the bedroom.

"Myhoneymylove," she said as she came up behind him at the computer. She didn't say it as four words, but as one. It was their special name, the one they used only with each other.

"Myhoneymylove," she said again.

Wednesday, September 2, 1998

St. Margarets Bay
10 a.m. ADT

Over the years, Robert Conrad had become immune to the often mysterious ways of Canada's fishing bureaucracy. But even he had to admit that the tuna regulatory system was more Byzantine than most. It was now ten o'clock in the morning — he had been on the water since four-thirty — and he would be stuck here off Dover for God only knew how much longer, waiting for all of the necessary parties to arrive so his crew could finally legally land and kill the five giant tuna swimming around in their trap net.

He'd already called both his buyer and the monitoring company's rep on his cell phone. Under the rules, he and they both had to be on hand to witness the landing, killing and transfer of the fish. It was all part of a three-year-old fish-monitoring program the federal fisheries department had designed to make sure fishermen didn't exceed their tuna quota. But government budget cutbacks had reduced the ability of the private contractors to supply enough monitors for what was turning out to be a very good season this year, perhaps the best in the past decade. So Conrad would sometimes have to wait for hours for all the right officials to arrive at the same time. That problem was compounded by the fact that he held six tuna licences and worked with several joint venture crews around the Bay — like the one that morning from Dover — who all caught tuna on his behalf. Since the rules stated that the licence holder had to be present when the fish were landed, he sometimes had to be in two places at once. "If one fish is caught in Dover and another in Northwest Cove, neither of them can be landed unless I'm there." He shakes his head in frustration.

It's not that Conrad doesn't understand the importance of fishery regulations. But all this officialese could be wearing. Perhaps more important, he worried that, while he idled near his catch that morning, the currents that sometimes sweep through the Bay could play havoc with his trap net, and one or more of those tuna — his income — might escape.

While he waited, Conrad filled the downtime as he usually did, talking to the other fishermen, recatching the last fish. How deep was it? How many were close by? They were doing what fishermen everywhere do — trying to think like a fish, in order to become better at what they do.

Tuna visit the area around St. Margarets Bay twice a year, once in early July and then again in late August and early September. The second run is usually the best, with more and healthier fish to catch, but even that short season is not nearly as good as it used to be. When Conrad was growing up, it wasn't unusual for local fishermen to land 500 fish each year. These days he says, 50 fish is a good year.

Robert Conrad was very good at what he did. In fact, he'd almost single-handedly revived what had been a moribund St. Margarets Bay tuna industry. He'd been part of the first tuna boom back in the late 1970s after Jay Ettman, an eccentric New York writer of men's true-adventure magazine stories, came up with the idea not only of ranching tuna like cattle — catching them when they first swam into the Bay in the spring and then fattening them up in huge pens over the summer — but also of using increasingly efficient air freight to ship the freshly slaughtered fish quickly to markets in Japan, where raw tuna was a prized, and pricey, delicacy. Conrad had been one of the early tuna ranchers.

But by the early nineties, Ettman was dead, and a combination of too much success and subtly changing tuna migration patterns had combined to virtually wipe out the tuna fishery in St. Margarets Bay. That's when Conrad discovered — in a conversation with a fisherman from Tancook Island, just beyond the sheltered confines of the Bay — where the tuna had migrated to. The Tancook fisherman knew just where the fish could be found but he didn't have one of the limited-issue licences required to catch them. Conrad had six tuna licences but they were all stationary licences — good only for catching fish inside the Bay. The solution seemed simple enough: get federal fishery bureaucrats to allow them to team up, transferring Conrad's licences to his new partner's location. Easier said than done. "One fellow was so insensitive," Conrad recalls, shaking his head, "that he kept this sign face down on his desk. After we finished talking to him about our plan, he just turned up his sign to face us. It said NO." They finally did end up in the office of "a man whose job it was to make things happen. I call it providence," Conrad says. "He listened and then he said, 'I think we can do this.' "

That first season, the pair managed to land only one fish before the tuna moved on for the year. But it was a start. Today, Conrad, who is the president of the St. Margarets Bay Bluefin Tuna Fishermen's Association, says there are 110 fishermen inside the Bay who make at least part of their living catching tuna. And 1998, he adds, was looking to be their best year in a decade. By the beginning of September, they'd landed more than 210 tuna (which sell for as much as $20,000 each on the Japanese market), and projected a catch of 300 before the season ended.

Conrad himself had five more that morning, sitting in his trap, waiting to be landed. He hoped the buyer and the monitor would arrive soon.

New Jersey Turnpike
3 p.m. EDT

Watching his daughters watching the silly, happy Spice Girls movie *Spice World* on the small television set in the back of the limousine as it sped along the New Jersey Turnpike on the way to JFK International Airport, Mark Fetherolf dared to dream that life might finally begin to offer some joy again. To an outsider, it might have appeared that the Fetherolfs — Mark and Barbara and their two daughters, Tara, 16, and Amy, 12 — were already living the American Dream. And, in a sense, they were.

Mark and Barbara were children of the sixties. She was born in 1953, the daughter of upwardly mobile parents who'd made the move from Manhattan's Lexington Avenue to Wantagh on Long Island. Barbara's childhood passion was figure skating, and she was good enough to win several competitions. But not confident enough to strut her stuff in front of large audiences. Abandoning competitive skating, she decided to study philosophy at Susquehanna, a residential liberal arts college in Pennsylvania, primarily because it was a small school and, she says, "I wasn't very outgoing at that point in my life."

Mark Fetherolf was. He was the illegitimate son of a Florida Lutheran minister's daughter and a jazz drummer whose whereabouts, as he put it lightly, were "generally unknown." In high school, his dream was to be a rock musician, but his real talents turned out to be in the fledgling field of computing science. At Susquehanna, Mark studied math and computer science.

He and Barbara married in 1975, the year after Barbara graduated. They moved to Philadelphia so Mark could take his MBA in math and computer statistics at Temple University. Their daughter Tara was born November 27, 1981, two days before Mark took his final exam in advanced statistics. Amy came along almost four years later.

By then Mark was already making a name for himself in the software business. In 1987, he co-founded the consulting company Aston Brooke Software, where he worked with corporate clients to develop Oracle-based applications. In 1994, the much larger Platinum Technology bought the software division, and he became vice-president of Platinum's Aston Brooke Development Lab, resulting in what he calls a "great lifestyle improvement."

But while the family's lifestyle may have been looking up, life had other plans. The next year Barbara was diagnosed with invasive breast cancer. Within a year, doctors discovered she had cancer in both breasts. The couple went from hospital to treatment centre to institute, as far away as the UCLA Medical Center in California, in search of a cure, or at least a way to cope. There were lumpectomies and mastectomies and reconstructive surgeries — at least eight operations in all — not to mention all those massive courses of chemotherapy and radiation.

Even as they were trying to cope with Barbara's treatment, Mark's own familiar world began to crumble. In 1997, his stepfather, a late-stage heart patient who'd lost hope he would ever get better, shot and killed himself. Two weeks after that, Mark's mother was killed in a car accident. The Fetherolfs attended the funeral in

Pennsylvania, then flew back to L.A. so Barbara could have more reconstructive surgery.

It wasn't an easy time for their elder daughter Tara either. She was in eighth grade in a new school, Episcopal Academy in Merion, Pennsylvania, the smart kid who didn't quite fit in. She'd tested at eighth grade reading level back in Grade 1; last year, she'd had the same score in math on her SATs as Mark had the year he entered university. For most of her school years, in fact, she'd preferred the company of her teachers to her fellow students; they seemed to have more in common. But now, she was a teenager and social life and popularity with the other kids were becoming more important to her. Socially, Barbara recalls, Tara didn't feel accepted at Episcopal that first year, "hiding out in the bathroom at lunchtime so nobody would see that she had no friends." To make matters worse, the school put her in some advanced high school courses even though she was technically only in eighth grade, further isolating and alienating her from her peers.

By that first spring at Episcopal, however, things were starting to look up. Tara had not only won a great number of academic awards but she had also landed the lead in the school play and was finally beginning to make friends. "I sat at the graduation ceremony thinking and crying, 'Oh my God, will I be here to see her graduate from high school?'" Barbara recalls. "I was so proud of her."

But Barbara did survive — "It was the thought of seeing both my precious girls grow up that got me through those difficult times," she says now — and, by this year when Tara was 16 and in tenth grade, Barbara was already beginning to see her older daughter blossoming as a young adult.

Like her father, Tara was gifted in mathematics.

She'd attended the Johns Hopkins University Center for Talented Youth summer program, taken accelerated math courses and managed to complete all the requirements for her high school math credits by the time she finished Grade 10.

This summer, she'd had to choose between the Outward Bound Hurricane Island sailing adventure program or taking calculus II at St. Joseph's University in Philadelphia. Since she'd already gone on one Outward Bound adventure, she chose calculus.

It fit better into her plans, which included attending a top-ranked university. And soon — she was impatient. She was considering Harvard, Yale or Princeton, but had begun to lean to the idea of applying for early admission to the Massachusetts Institute of Technology instead. Then she began to expand her academic horizons even farther afield. Why not Cambridge? What about Oxford?

She knew she'd achieved almost everything she could in high school, but was she really ready for the leap to university, especially one that was half a world away from her family and friends? Perhaps, she suggested to her parents, she should spend a transitional year at an English boarding school to improve her chances of getting admission to Oxford or Cambridge next year. It would be a wonderful opportunity for her to spend some time in a new culture, she told them.

Barbara and Mark — Barbara reluctantly, Mark with more adventurous enthusiasm — eventually took Tara to an academic counsellor, who suggested they consider Aiglon College, which describes itself as "the Multicultural British International Boarding School in the Swiss Alps, providing a world-class English-style residential education for 300 boys and girls aged 9–18 from 53 nations." Not only did Aiglon offer the academic education Tara was looking for but it also — tempting for a teenager — promised excitement and adventure. Mountain biking, orienteering, canoeing and rock climbing were integral parts of the curriculum. So were weekend hikes into the surrounding mountains and daily skiing trips.

That was all very well, but Barbara wasn't convinced. Aiglon in the Swiss Alps was a long way from Haverford in Pennsylvania, and Tara, after all, was still only 16. Besides, Barbara wasn't sure all the family's emotional scars from her illness had healed yet. "I had sensed Tara was feeling some anger toward me." That's one reason why Barbara had deliberately spent most of this past summer with her daughter. "We were really beginning to be very close to each other again."

Switzerland seemed so far away.

Still, Barbara did finally agree to fly with Tara to visit the school in mid-August. Since Mark had business meetings in Dublin, Barbara and Tara had flown from there to Geneva and then travelled on by car to nearby Chesières-Villars, where the school was. "It looked like something out of a storybook," Barbara recalls. They toured the facilities and met with Mary Sidebottom, the director of admissions. "Tara completely took over the interview," Barbara says. "I was very proud of the way she handled herself, and was really beginning to see that she was no longer a child but growing into an adult."

By the time they reunited with Mark in Ireland, Barbara had agreed to allow Tara to spend the next year at Aiglon. But there wasn't much time to get ready. After a few days of post-business-meeting touring in Ireland — they were 20 miles from Omagh when a terrorist bomb exploded in the village, but they didn't know anything about what had become a major international news story until they got back to their hotel in Belfast that night — they flew home by way of San

Francisco, where Mark had still more business meetings, and Barbara and Tara shopped frantically for school clothes.

Barbara tried to be upbeat about it all, but a part of her wished she'd never given in. "For selfish reasons," she admits. "I was *not* ready to let her go." Mark thought she was being too protective. But the decision had been made, and now there was little left to do but get on with it.

By the time they were home in Pennsylvania, Tara had less than a week left to complete her packing and preparations. More clothes to buy. Friends from school to say goodbye to — plenty of friends now. One of the teachers at Episcopal, in fact, would later tell Barbara that she saw Tara so often with so many different groups of students and in so many places around the school in those last few days that they almost imagined she'd become an angel, magically appearing wherever and whenever she wanted.

The night before, Barbara's mother and sister had come all the way down from Maine to see her one more time before she left for Europe. Tara insisted they all go back to the neighbourhood where she'd grown up for pizza and ice cream cake.

There was also a special boy to say goodbye to. She'd met him in the eighth grade. When his family had moved to Boston at the end of Grade 9, it was very hard on her, Barbara says. "Tara didn't take things lightly." They'd kept in touch by phone and visited each other as often as they could. Once, when he'd visited their place, Barbara watched discreetly from the house as the two of them tangoed together in the backyard. "They looked so beautiful," she recalls. Tara insisted they were just friends, but her mother was beginning to think she perhaps liked him more than she let on. That day, she'd been taking pictures of Tara as she got ready to go; the last one was of her on the phone talking to the boy in Boston.

Her little girl was growing up. She could see it too in the way she'd begun to become more supportive and protective of her younger sister. Tara had always been the more boisterous and outgoing of the two girls, and she tended, as big sisters can, to dominate her younger sibling. But when Tara and Barbara had gone up to Lake George to visit Amy, a promising violinist who was spending that summer at the Luzerne Music Camp in upstate New York, Tara insisted on sitting through all her sister's concerts. "Why isn't Amy first seat when she's obviously better than anyone else?" she would demand of her mother. Barbara liked to hear those expressions of sisterly loyalty, liked too the sense she felt of her family coming together again. Several times that summer, Mark and Barbara and Tara and, occasionally, Barbara's mother had flown to Albany, rented a car and driven to the camp, where they picked up Amy and spent the weekend together, playing race car games and skiball at the video arcade in Lake George, just enjoying one another's company, talking about everything and anything.

Those summer weekends had helped rekindle Mark's hope that the worst — the cancer and family deaths — was now behind them and that they could all begin to enjoy the life, and the lifestyle, that should have come with selling his software business when he was 40. Was it in Lake George when they'd first begun talking about Tara going to school in Europe? Mark couldn't remember. But now, suddenly, here they were in a limousine on their way to JFK, on their way to see their oldest daughter off on the adventure of a lifetime.

They wouldn't usually have taken a limo to the airport, Barbara says, but Tara had so much luggage — "The last thing I packed was a stuffed animal that she loved" — it wouldn't all fit in their car.

Barbara had given up hoping to persuade Tara not to go away to school, but she still wasn't quite ready to let her go off on her own. What if the whole family accompanied her on the flight to her new school and then helped her settle in, she suggested at one point. But Tara wouldn't hear of it. It was her adventure and she wanted to do it on her own.

Why not? thought Mark. You're only young once. He turned back to the video in the limousine. The scene was changing. A jet crossed the screen from left to right. One of the Spice Girls — Baby? — asked in a plaintive voice-over: "Are we there yet?"

On Highway 104, near Pictou, Nova Scotia
6:15 p.m. ADT

There were days when John Butt couldn't remember why he had ever decided to uproot himself from Alberta — where he'd been born, where he'd been his province's well-respected chief medical officer for more than 20 years, where he'd made a comfortably pleasant life for himself as well as a more than adequate living — to move lock, stock and two dogs across the continent to Nova Scotia to take over a woebegone, underfunded, under-respected forensic pathology office in a social backwater where you had to have lived at least three generations before anyone would even think to invite you over to their place for dinner on a Saturday night.

This was one of those days. He'd spent most of it cooling his heels in a little courthouse in New Glasgow waiting to testify at a committal hearing for one of two teenagers charged with the brutal murder of a local taxi driver. The 53-year-old man had been robbed of less than

$100, strangled and stuffed in the trunk of his cab. One of the youths had already pleaded guilty to the murder and was awaiting sentencing. The hearing this day was simply to consider a Crown application to have the second — a 17-year-old boy — tried as an adult. Butt's job was to explain to the court how the man had died.

But the hearing had dragged on and now it was after six and John Butt still had more than an hour-and-a-half drive back to his house in Glen Haven, a little village on St. Margarets Bay.

That would give him more than enough time to ponder, as he was wont to do more and more these days, the twisted path that had led him, at age 63, to be living alone in the country, spending his evenings at home with just his two golden retrievers, and his days in town beating his head against the frustrating wall of bureaucracy that passed for political and social power in Nova Scotia.

John Butt hadn't set out with the ambition of ending his career in Nova Scotia. He hadn't set out to be a pathologist or — perish the thought — everyone's favourite family doctor. Becoming a doctor had been his mother's ambition for him. For her, as for a lot of parents who came of age during the Depression, education was the path to a better life, and being a doctor represented the best of that better life. "You're going to be a doctor, *aren't you?*" she would say to him.

Butt himself was more intrigued with the notion of joining the merchant navy as his salesman father had done. As a teenager, Butt had served a stint in the Naval Reserves, even spent some time training in Halifax. He became a lieutenant and led the reserve unit at the University of Alberta while he was attending medical school …

Medical school?

It was an afterthought. His commitment to his medical studies was so casual that the dean wanted to kick him out in his final year. He had to "lick the boots" of the university president, he jokes now, just to be allowed to finish his degree.

By his own account, he wasn't much better suited to the practice of medicine itself, which he abandoned after two unhappy years. He admits he didn't have the hands for surgical work, "and I had difficulty with spatial relationships, so I knew I should stay out of situations requiring that sort of skill." Not to mention poor people skills. He had never thought of himself as having much of a bedside manner.

Knowing more what he didn't want to do as a doctor than what he did, Butt, who had just gotten married, headed to England to combine his honeymoon with six months of post-graduate medical studies.

During a stint in neurology there, he discovered by accident his interest in pathology. He saw a notice advertising a pathology lecture, and thought, What the hell. "It was amazing. I got a glimpse of something that really interested me. I thought, 'God, this is incredible. This is what I want.' "

He didn't immediately like everything about his new-found passion. Early on, he would frequently vomit before autopsies, and would have to cover the head of the body with a cloth to keep from thinking too much about the life of the person whose death he had to explain. Occasionally, he'd inexplicably start crying about the death of someone he knew only as a cadaver.

What fascinated him was the detective aspect of the job, figuring out the answer to the puzzle of how a person had died. The clues, he says, "are all there before you get started." That's why he learned to examine each body on his examining table in minute detail before he even picked up his scalpel. "There must be something on the outside of this body that's going to tell me what's inside," he would explain.

Much as he had discovered that he liked being a pathologist, however, he also came to realize he hated living in England. It was an insular, stultifying place where outsiders found it almost impossible to fit in. He'd morosely concluded that he'd never be accepted by the locals, never be a real Englishman. And that, of course, meant that his career — the one he was just now beginning at the age of 40 — was going nowhere either. In 1974, he decided to go home.

Back home in Alberta, everything changed. He landed an appointment as his province's first chief medical examiner. Over the course of the next 20 years, he not only earned an international reputation as a practitioner of the death science but also made the Alberta office a model for plenty of other jurisdictions to emulate. He brought all the province's autopsy, investigative and toxicology facilities under the same roof to make it easier for investigators to do their jobs. He helped design the new state-of-the-art forensic facility so family members coming to identify their next of kin would walk into a plant-filled solarium instead of a sterile morgue. He also pioneered the use of nurse-investigators in the medical examiner's office, developed a detailed disaster response manual and oversaw the identification of victims of several disasters, including the 1986 Hinton train wreck and the 1987 Edmonton tornado. He even served a stint as the president of the U.S.-based Association of Medical Examiners.

Butt's reputation may help explain why the Nova Scotia government came looking for him to become its chief medical examiner in 1995. The province didn't have a qualified pathologist at the time and the man who'd held the post for the previous 10 years — a medical doctor — had been accused of everything from lack of administrative skills to screwing up autopsies.

So the province was more than eager to hire Butt as its $120,000-a-year chief pathologist, and Butt had his own reasons for taking the post: he was 61, old enough to want to slow down but not yet ready for retirement. He was looking for what he thought would be an interesting last challenge in a city a little more laid-back than a hectic, booming oil town.

But Halifax turned out to be far more laid-back than he'd expected. Despite Nova Scotia's reputation as a friendly, welcoming place for tourists, Butt found people — shades of England — insular and inhospitable to what were locally referred to as CFAs, those come-from-aways who chose to settle here. You could spend your days in the seemingly friendly company of colleagues and co-workers but, at the end of the workday, no one would ever invite you home for dinner, or even out for a beer and gossip. Just as the neighbours would be cheerful enough when you saw them on the street, but that was it.

In his more sanguine moments, John Butt could rationalize all of this. Nova Scotia was simply a very traditional society where people often traced their roots back four and more generations. They already had their own friends, their own network of supports based on family and growing up together. They didn't need to make new friends.

But he did. He'd come to Nova Scotia by himself. Though he'd lived alone since 1978, when what he jokingly describes as a "close encounter with a flying pot" ended his marriage, he remained close to his two daughters, now adults. In Calgary, he had circles of friends from his childhood and university days as well as from his professional life. That was the key difference between Halifax and Calgary, he thought. Because Calgary was still a frontier town where virtually everyone was a come-from-away, people tended to be more open to making friends.

He had been thinking a lot about the differences

between the two societies lately, thinking now about whether he should retire to Calgary after his contract ended.

Professionally as well there had been some miscalculations in his decision to move to Nova Scotia. Butt was not the kind to get along by going along; he could be as combative as he was skilled. In Calgary in 1989, for example, he and his deputy had gone so far as to quit their posts in a bitter wrangle with the provincial government over wages and benefits. The government had given in and re-hired them. But Nova Scotia was not Alberta. The government in Nova Scotia wanted to improve the quality of the medical examiner's office but it wasn't keen to pay a lot more than the $625,000 annual budget already allotted to accomplish that. Although Butt had conceded to one newspaper reporter shortly after he arrived in January 1996 that he knew he would be working under "very, very serious constraints," he was also privately expecting the government to find the extra funds to bring the operation at least up to modestly professional standards.

His hope was in vain. Butt still worked out of the cramped two-room office he had inherited in a far-from-central corner of the old Victoria General Hospital complex. He even had to share his "private" office with a secretary. Worse, there was still no other trained pathologist to help him perform the 150 or so local autopsies that had to be handled in Halifax each year or supervise the 175 others done around the rest of the province, or ease the burden of providing expert testimony about cause of death in court cases.

John Butt had spent the day doing the usual legal hurry-up-and-wait in the New Glasgow courthouse — time he should have been spending fighting the good fight for better office space and a bigger budget back in Halifax.

Or freshening up his lecture notes for the course he was teaching in two weeks' time at the Canadian Police Academy in Ottawa. He'd been lecturing officers there on the finer points of crime scene investigation for more than 20 years. Or, closer to home, he could have spent the day preparing for the two more days of workshops on forensic policing he'd scheduled the following week in communities along Nova Scotia's South Shore. Since few small-town police forces could afford to send their officers to courses in Ottawa, Butt had set aside whatever time he could to conduct roadshows on the basics of dealing with the deceased.

During these three-hour workshops, he and Sgt. Pat McCloskey, a Halifax RCMP officer, would show 30 to 50 local cops photos and graphs from murder investigations and discuss what they should do when they encountered a suspicious death. They offered advice on everything from moving the body (don't) to whether the fact that the victim is dressed up in Sunday-go-to-meeting clothes should be considered a sign the person may have committed suicide (it should).

Butt would use these trips as an opportunity to meet with local doctors and funeral directors too, encouraging them to become more aware of how to deal with suspicious death. "Dr. Butt was like a new toy," McCloskey recalls. "Everyone wanted to try him out."

Perhaps that night, when he got home to Glen Haven, after he had dinner and fed and walked the dogs, he would spend some time going over his notes to get ready for the workshops next week in Bridgewater and Liverpool.

Or perhaps he would just eat and go to bed. He was beginning to feel awfully tired.

JFK Airport, Terminal 3
6:15 p.m. EDT

"This is a special announcement," declared the voice on the terminal's public address system as the Fetherolf family located the Swissair check-in counter. Mark had booked Tara's flight through Delta Airlines, but Delta and Swissair had what was known as a code-share agreement, meaning Delta could market the flight to its customers as its own.

"For security reasons," continued the pre-recorded message that would be repeated several more times before Tara's flight took off, "please keep your luggage with you at all times. Unattended luggage will be removed for inspection and may be destroyed."

At that moment, Barbara Fetherolf wasn't worrying about terrorist bombs or exploding luggage. Or even airline safety. She simply didn't want her 16-year-old daughter travelling halfway around the world by herself. Truthfully? She didn't want her to go away to school at all.

"Are you sure you won't let me fly over with you?" Barbara asked her one more time as they stood in the line to get her ticket.

"No." Tara laughed. "You'd only ruin it for me." She was joking, of course. She and Barbara had enjoyed their time travelling together in Ireland and over to Switzerland, but this was different. This was Tara's chance to show her parents and herself she was ready to fly on her own, figuratively and literally.

If Tara wouldn't allow her mother to accompany her on the flight, Barbara decided, they should at least upgrade Tara's ticket. "I wanted her in first class," Barbara says now, "so she would be taken care of properly because she was travelling alone and was still pretty young to be on her own." Mark agreed. She would be in seat 2A, the woman at the ticket counter explained cheerfully. There was no one in seat 2B, so Tara would be able to stretch out, maybe get some sleep.

Ticket in hand, Tara, Amy, Barbara and Mark made their way down a long corridor toward the gates for international departures. From Terminal 3, you could fly almost anywhere — from Albany to Zurich — aboard 10 airlines that all shared space with Delta at the terminal. They passed the usual array of airport shops — the duty-free shop, a fragrance outlet, a Tie Rack, a Press Relay newsstand. They stopped at the newsstand for a few minutes so Tara could choose some magazines for the long flight ahead.

Despite its polished tile floors and mirrored pillars, the dully lit terminal building was showing its age. Signs along the hallway announced that the airport was in the midst of a $7.4-billion, 12-year renovation project to celebrate its fiftieth anniversary. But there were few signs the renovators had made it to Terminal 3.

The brightest spots in the hallway were reserved for advertising messages, including a backlit white sign near the entrance to Swissair Flight 111's departure gate. The ad touted Delta's Skymiles Club, a promotional program that rewards frequent flyers with bonus airmiles. Though no one realized it at the time, Tara's name and address, thanks to the first-class ticket in her name, had already been automatically added to a database of those who would be targeted for future Skymiles Club mailings.

Taking advantage of Tara's ticket, the Fetherolfs went upstairs to the first-class lounge to wait until her flight was called.

Below, in the main waiting room, the rest of the flight's more than 200 passengers were also gathering. They were travelling for all the usual reasons — business, pleasure, dream vacations, family reunions, anniversaries, education — but, perhaps because this was a flight between two of the world's most sophisticated, cosmopolitan cities, these passengers were an especially impressive and eclectic lot. They carried passports from 18 countries, from Afghanistan to Yugoslavia. An overwhelming majority of them — 131 — were from the United States, but there were 30 French, 26 Swiss and half a dozen British citizens preparing to board too. The number and diversity of the other countries represented aboard Flight 111 — Iran, Italy, Germany, Greece, India, Lebanon, Mexico, Saudi Arabia, Spain, St. Kitts and Nevis, Sweden, Russia — almost made the gathering seem like a mini United Nations.

In truth, the United Nations itself was well represented. Since Flight 111 flew directly from New York, the UN's headquarters, to Geneva, its main European base, it had become known among many of its frequent flyers as the UN Shuttle. World Radio Geneva, an English-language station, even announced the flight's arrival time as part of its regular daily programming. Those planning to pick up passengers knew enough to listen for the announcements; if the tailwinds were favourable, Flight 111 often arrived half an hour early.

Tonight, the UN-related contingent of staff members and associates aboard the plane totalled seven. The most prominent among them was Dr. Jonathan Mann, the former director of the UN anti-AIDS program at the World Health Organization in Geneva. Mann, a pioneer in the battle against AIDS, quit the WHO in 1990 after a clash with the organization's director general. Mann was currently dean of the Allegheny University School of Public Health in Pennsylvania, but he continued to be a regular participant in WHO conferences and consultations. In fact, he and his wife, Mary-Lou Clements-Mann, also an AIDS researcher, were flying to Switzerland to attend a series of AIDS-related meetings. Since their marriage a year ago, they'd made a pact to fly together whenever they could. Given that they worked in cities a hundred miles apart, it was often the only time they could carve out of their separate hectic schedules to spend time together.

Other United Nations staffers on the flight included Joachim Bilger, 49, and Ludwig Beaumer, 61, senior officials with the World Intellectual Property Organization; Yves de Roussan, 41, a Canadian who was the central and eastern Europe regional adviser for the UN Children's Fund; Kathryn Calvert-Mazy, 37, a counsellor in the refugee unit who had just transferred to Geneva to be near her husband and baby; Ingrid Acevedo, 32, the New York–based director of public relations for the United States Committee for UNICEF; and, of course, Pierce Gerety. Gerety wasn't actually supposed to be on this flight. He'd been scheduled to fly out earlier in the day on a KLM flight to Geneva by way of Amsterdam, but that plane had been overbooked, so he'd been bumped to a Swissair flight to Geneva via Zurich. When that one had been cancelled, he'd finally been added to Flight 111's passenger list.

Swissair Flight 111's passenger manifest could also easily have been mistaken for the roster of speakers at an important scientific conference. In addition to Mann and his wife, there were at least a dozen scientists and researchers on the flight. Some, like Dr. Roger Williams, a cardiovascular geneticist at the University of Utah, were travelling directly to Geneva. Williams, 54, was chairing a meeting at the WHO on one of his projects. Others were using Geneva as a gateway to Europe. Klaus Kinder-Geiger, a dashing 36-year-old German physicist who played electric guitar and was well known among his colleagues for his skills as a caricaturist, was going to Trento, Italy, to speak at a physics workshop. Per Spanne, a 53-year-old Swedish scientist, was on his way to

Grenoble, France, where he was on the staff at the Synchrotron Light Source. His specialty: experimenting with ways to use radiation to treat brain cancer. Don Scheer, a 49-year-old biochemist from Norfolk, Massachusetts was heading first for the European Molecular Biology Lab in Heidelberg and then on to Greece to present a technical paper. But his real goal was to promote another new product he'd designed, this one to separate DNA strands. He'd spent most of his professional career travelling the world promoting his scientific developments, but he was tiring of it. After this one last trip, according to his brother Jerry, he was "going to sink into his couch, flick on his 35-inch television and cheer for the Cleveland Indians."

Jay Jasan, 40, a Basking Ridge, New Jersey, virologist who worked for Merck & Co. testing the effects of its pharmaceuticals on people, was flying to Europe for business meetings. Although his business was pharmaceuticals, Jasan's passion was animals. His colleagues at Merck, in fact, called him "the animal doctor" and often brought him their sick pets. Five years earlier, he'd even earned a second degree in veterinary medicine. Though he kept his day job, the bachelor scientist devoted most of his free time to his passion, giving talks to schoolchildren about animals and their habitats and volunteering at the Staten Island Zoo and Raptor Trust, a sanctuary for injured birds in Morristown, New Jersey.

Tom Hausman, the 33-year-old head of Continental Grain's Latin American division, was on his way to company meetings in Geneva. He was flying with another Continental official. There were supposed to be three of them on this flight but their colleague had discovered — after he arrived at Kennedy — that he'd forgotten his passport. He'd have to go back home to get it, then catch a flight to Geneva the next day.

Joe Lamotta was travelling on business too. The 49-year-old son of boxing legend Jake "Raging Bull" Lamotta had grown up on the mean streets of the Bronx. His turbulent early life had been the backdrop to the movie *Raging Bull*, which starred Robert DeNiro as his father. The film chronicled Jake's climb to the middleweight championship and his short reign at boxing's pinnacle. To this day, Jake still described Joe — who'd entered golden gloves boxing competitions as a kid and once dreamed of following his father into the ring — as "a lot like me." Over the years, they'd even grown to look alike. These days Joe sported a salt-and-pepper beard, but his flat, full face, laughing eyes and receding hairline still reminded many people of his father. The father and son had recently become business partners. Their company, Lamotta Food Products, had developed a marinara sauce they described as the "sauce of champions." According to company promotional materials, Jake used to cook up pasta and his own specially prepared marinara after each pre-fight weigh-in in order to prepare for the match to come. The father and son had later perfected the sauce — "thick and spicy, with lots of fresh garlic and onion, fresh basil, extra virgin olive oil and ripe tomatoes" — and marketed it as a kosher product in New York. Tonight, Joe was heading to Europe to try to expand their market.

Not everyone was travelling for business, of course. For many of those waiting to board Flight 111, this trip was to mark a special, personal occasion. Lori Moran, 34, a New Jersey figure skating coach who'd once been a U.S. figure skating team gold-level skater, and her New York architect husband, Michael Ditchkus, also 34, were going to celebrate their third wedding anniversary in Europe. Lori had spent most evenings for the past year poring over travel guides and planning the details of their dream trip. They were to stop in Geneva to visit

Michael's sister, then head to Paris and Grenoble. The trip, they'd told friends, was also intended to mark the beginning of a new phase in their relationship. They had just moved into a house in Teaneck, New Jersey, which Ditchkus was obsessed with fixing up. Now that they felt settled, Moran and Ditchkus had confided, they planned to start a family when they came back from Europe.

Dr. Eugenia Spanopoulou, a cancer researcher, and her husband, Andrew Hodtsev, an immunologist, who both worked at Manhattan's Mount Sinai Medical Center, were taking their son, Plato, to be christened in Athens. Denis and Karen Maillet of Baton Rouge, Louisiana — who didn't even speak each other's languages when they'd met several years ago as engineers — were on their way to Lyon, France, to introduce their 14-month-old son, Robert, to his French grandparents.

Tara Nelson, 35, a naturopath, was going to meet her boyfriend in Geneva and then travel on to Grenoble, where she planned to help her sister, Judy, give birth. Tara had another reason to be in high spirits — she was expecting a marriage proposal from her boyfriend.

Ralph and Gilda Mallin of Boca Raton, Florida, had attended their daughter Cindy's wedding last weekend in the Hamptons. They were travelling to France to meet their new in-laws and attend a second wedding reception there. In her luggage, Gilda had packed a special quilt she'd made as a gift for her new son-in-law's parents. The Mallins, in fact, were flying over to Geneva a few days ahead of other members of the wedding party because this was also the beginning of their seven-week European vacation.

Albert Tahmoush, 77, a retired chief executive officer of Frank B. Hall, an insurance brokerage in Briarcliff Manor, New York, had planned his vacation around a visit to the 63-year-old son of the Belgian couple who had nursed him back to health when he was an injured army officer during World War II. He hadn't seen the man in 40 years.

For Paul Hammond, 75, and his wife Joan, 10 years his junior, who were planning to visit his brother in Switzerland, airport waiting rooms almost certainly held special memories. They'd first met in one in Minnesota 27 years ago, when Joan was a young widow with three children and Paul was a medical researcher. While they waited for their flight to be called, she'd asked to borrow his *New York Times*. By the time the plane took off, they were seated together. Within the year, they were married. After he retired from the faculty at the University of Cincinnati Medical School, he and Joan had moved to Washington State, where Joan was now the deputy auditor for Snohomish County. Ironically, given how they'd met, Joan Hammond had recently become fearful of flying. She'd especially begun to fret about terrorist threats on international flights like the one they were about to take. Before they'd flown out of Seattle-Tacoma International Airport that morning she'd confided to friends that she was happy they were booked on Swissair, an airline she considered among the safest in the world.

If few of those passengers would have intrigued Tara Fetherolf, she might have found some common ground with Rowenna White or a few of the other young Americans who were heading off to Europe, on their own for the first time in their lives, to study too.

Rowenna was also planning to attend school in Switzerland. And, like Tara, the pretty 18-year-old New Yorker with lively blue eyes had a neatly planned out life and career ahead of her. She was going to study at Switzerland's Hotel Institute Montreux, one of Europe's best-known hotel management schools, for the next three years, interning each summer at ever more sophisticated and demanding hotels throughout Europe. Then she'd return to the United States to take her final year at Cornell University and get her degree in hotel management. An American degree from a good school was important, she would explain, because her goal was to become the special events coordinator at the White House.

Few — perhaps least of all her mother, Nancy — doubted Rowenna would achieve whatever she set her mind to. She was just that kind of teenager. She'd spent the past summer preparing herself for that future, working at the trendy northern Italian restaurant Nello Ristoranti in Manhattan, which was described by one reviewer as a " 'chichi' Madison Avenue scene where Ivana and crowd come to see and be seen; even though the food is very good, it's less important than watching what car people pull up in." When she wasn't at the restaurant, Rowenna was polishing her language skills at Alliance Française and, of course, spending time with Adrian, her boyfriend.

That may explain why there just hadn't been time for the graduation party her mother wanted to throw for her, or the official pictures her mother wanted taken. In fact, Nancy Wight thought wistfully, it sometimes seemed there wasn't time anymore for any of the things she suggested to her daughter — going to one of the Mostly Mozart concerts they used to enjoy together, or to the beach, or visiting a lake upstate, or going to the movies together. "She really had her own life, work, interests and friends she did things with," her mother explains.

Like Barbara Fetherolf, Nancy Wight (Rowenna used her father's name, White) had been keen to accompany her only daughter to Switzerland. Earlier in the summer, in fact, she'd suggested they fly over in late August, tour around together for a few days and then arrive at her school in time for its September 3 start. Nancy could then fly home in plenty of time to prepare to start her own job as a university lecturer the day after Labor Day. Like Tara, Rowenna was having none of it. She intended to work at the restaurant up until the last possible moment, she told her mother, then fly to Geneva on September 2. In July, they'd even had what Nancy would later call a "heated argument" over Rowenna's departure date. In the end, Rowenna quit her job early to take some vacation time and then urged her mother to fly to Switzerland with her on September 2. This time, it was Nancy's turn to refuse. "I had to work right after Labor Day. I did not want to go over and come right back for a weekend." So Rowenna, like Tara, was heading off to school in Switzerland on her own.

So too was Monte Wilkins, a 19-year-old sophomore from Walla Walla, a liberal arts college operated by the Seventh-day Adventist Church in Washington State. Monte, the son of an ophthalmologist and his wife, was about to become the fifth member of his family to study at a small language school in the foothills of the Alps. His older brother Darren had even met his wife there in 1991.

Monte was a sparkplug of a young man who had spent the past month in a whirlwind of goodbye activities. One day, he and Darren had taken a 16-mile hike up an 11,000-foot mountain. Then as soon as they got home, Darren recalls, "he dragged me out to play tennis." But Monte's real sports love was golf. The weekend before leaving for Switzerland, he'd spent the day enjoying a goodbye golf game with his family. He called his driver his "big dog." "Sometimes," says Darren, "he would let me borrow it when we played together. I would hit my ball and he would say, 'No, no, no. You have to let the big dog eat.' Then he would take the club and hit his ball 30 yards past mine."

When the voice on the public address system finally

announced that first-class passengers, as well as those needing assistance, could begin boarding the plane, Mark and Barbara Fetherolf walked Tara to the last walkway to the plane. She was about to hand her ticket to the agent when she dropped it.

As she bent down to pick it up, Barbara couldn't resist the impulse. "I begged her one more time to let me go with her," she says.

"What would you do when you get to Geneva?" Tara demanded.

"Turn around and come home."

Tara lightly mocked her mother's protectiveness. "Just because you aren't going," she joked, "the plane is going to crash."

Barbara looked at her in shock. She knew Tara was kidding, but she didn't like to hear the words. "Please don't even say a thing like that," she told her daughter.

Tara shook her head. "What are you going to do when I go away to college if you can't handle this?"

She kissed her parents and her sister goodbye.

And then she was gone.

Halifax, Nova Scotia
8:00 p.m. ADT

Rob Gordon was still working his way through his post-vacation funk. By the time he got to the trendy downtown Halifax bar the Economy Shoe Shop, for a beer and some more discussion with Alan Jeffers about their *Titanic* projects, he'd long forgotten whatever it was he'd been doing at work that day. For the best, he thought.

Sometimes, Gordon was hard to figure, even for himself. He would be the first to tell you he couldn't imagine ever being anything other than a local general assignment reporter. He harboured no ambition to be a high-profile network correspondent. Or a producer. Or, God forbid, a PR type like Alan. He wasn't even interested in a slightly higher-on-the-pecking-order local job as his station's legislative beat reporter. "I would hate the legislature," he says, "absolutely hate it. All you do is sit down, you're indoors all day, you're covering the same stuff day after day."

Rob Gordon preferred to be moving, to be out of doors, to be doing something different every day. A murder one day, a strike the next, a drug bust the third. Now, that was his idea of a good week.

From his earliest days at the Halifax *Herald*, Gordon had developed an enviable reputation as a natural street reporter whose mental Rolodex of contacts was as extensive and as varied as a politician's on polling day, and who could be incredibly dogged in pursuit of anything he considered a big story.

During his nine years at CBC, he'd done more than his share of those big stories. In 1991, just before the Gulf War, he'd reported from Halifax-based Canadian naval ships on patrol overseas. In 1992, he was the first television reporter to suggest that the Westray mine disaster that killed 26 miners may have been something other than an unfortunate act of God. In 1993, he'd broken the story that the RCMP were investigating the province's former premier for allegedly sexually assaulting a number of young women during his years in power. In 1996, acting on a tip, Gordon pieced together the first report that police were investigating the Taiwanese officers of the container ship *Maersk Dubai* for allegedly tossing three Romanian stowaways overboard in the middle of the Atlantic.

If he had a natural instinct for ferreting out information, he was, as he would be the first to admit, far less gifted as an on-camera performer. In the beginning, in fact, his singsong delivery so irritated producers at CBC-TV's *The National* that they refused to air his reports, even on major exclusive stories from the Atlantic region. Even after he managed to get his cadences under control, he still sometimes appeared to be smirking on air — an unfortunate tendency that irritated plenty of viewers, as well as more than a few news sources.

But Gordon is fascinated enough with the power of television that he had worked hard at improving his delivery. Geoff D'Eon, then the executive producer of the *First Edition* supper-hour news show, spent countless hours teaching him what Gordon calls the "voodoo of television. Unless you know it, you don't know it." Gordon also became a student of the nuances of the craft, learning the fine and difficult art of telling stories with pictures.

Though he had earned his journalistic reputation for his reporting of major stories, Gordon sometimes seemed more proud of his ability to craft even a fairly inconsequential story into "good television. I can do the little stuff and do it well too," he insists. He recalls covering one minor traffic accident in which no one was killed but one of the passengers was trapped in the van. "No big deal, but it was awesome TV," he boasts. "They were trying to get this person out and you could do the TV thing with it, shooting it from every angle, then using the pictures to maximum advantage."

He pauses. "I love everything about being a reporter," he says simply.

"Rob coasts sometimes," concedes a producer who has worked with him. It is the less enviable part of his reputation. "When there's nothing major happening, he can be frustrating to get motivated. He's like a hyperactive kid. He can't seem to sit still long enough to finish anything. He's constantly on the prowl, wandering up and down the halls, bothering other people. No one can find him. I can't tell you how many times he gets paged to go back to the newsroom. He drives his bosses nuts sometimes."

He could be lazy too. If he wasn't interested in a story, it would show. "You'd be vetting a script and you'd have to say to him, 'C'mon, Rob, there's not much here. You're going to have to go get more.' And Rob, to his credit, would laugh and agree with you. It was like he was just checking to see if you'd notice. The thing of it is that you tend to forgive Rob his foibles because he really is such a nice guy." And a good reporter. "When a big story comes along," the producer is quick to add, "there's nobody I'd rather have out there than Rob."

The problem, Gordon thought as he savoured his beer and waited for Jeffers to arrive, was that there were too few big stories these days to get his reporter's juices flowing. Stories like Westray. Now, there was a story. Westray had been the last really big story in Nova Scotia. "It was this big, live, totally fucking uncontrolled event that went on for days and days and you just rode with it the best way you could," he says. Covering that disaster, doing continuing live reports for *Newsworld*, CBC-TV's national 24-hour news channel, had made Gordon acutely aware of the power of live television to bring big events into people's homes in real time. He was keen to do more of that sort of broadcasting. "I felt like I was stagnating," he was to say later. "I'd gotten into TV and I'd spent a lot of time learning how to do it. It was very slow at first, then fast, then you get it, then you're on this plateau. I always figured there needed to be another learning curve, and I figured live TV would be that second curve for me."

The problem, of course, was that stories like Westray that cry out for continuing live coverage don't happen all that often. Certainly not in Nova Scotia.

Gordon's morose musings ended as suddenly as they had

begun. Jeffers arrived, and they began to talk again about the many and various ways they might cash in on what had been one of the world's most famous disasters, the *Titanic*. Now, that would have made interesting live television.

Soon, it was eight o'clock, and time to go home. Gordon's younger son was spending the night at his ex-wife's, but Angus would be home. School had just started and Gordon wanted to be home to make sure Angus got his things ready for classes the next day, not to mention being in bed by 10 p.m. Gordon didn't plan to stay up much later than that himself. He was tired. Funny how sometimes not working could tire you out more than working.

Dover, Nova Scotia
8:15 p.m. ADT

It was hard to square the brutal, brutish-appearing slaughter of tuna taking place at the dock in front of him now — roaring chainsaws biting angrily into fish flesh as sleekly magnificent 800-pound fish were inelegantly headed, tailed and reduced to giant chunks to be packed for shipment to Japan — with the almost rhapsodic way Robert Conrad could talk about that majestic fish and what it's like to be a fisherman.

Fishing, he says, is a spiritual experience. "When you leave the wharf, you enter a new dimension with none of the hustle and bustle you get on land. It's an experience you just participate in. You feel the closeness of the tie to nature. The tide. The beauty of the sky. The particular fish or whale you encounter. Out there, there's always the potentional for something new."

Conrad's main spiritual grounding comes from the Seventh-day-Adventist Church, which he joined 30 years ago at the age of 21. He says the church, "as a community of the faithful," helped him get through the trauma when his first marriage broke up. He and his second wife, Peggy — also a Seventh-day Adventist with a previous failed marriage and a child — raised the two daughters of their first marriages together. Both girls are now attending university in Halifax.

Robert and Peggy are pillars of their local church — together they run the church's food bank, and Peggy operates a puppet ministry for children — who take stock of their lives at the end of each week. How did we do with what the Lord put in our path last week? How does He want us to help in the next week? But Robert describes himself as a "Christian first, a Seventh-day Adventist secondary."

By the time he was 39, his love of talking and thinking about the meaning of the Bible had become almost overwhelming. One summer day in 1986, Conrad remembers, he and his family were picking strawberries in a field near Chester when "God said, 'I've got something for you.' "

Conrad applied to the Atlantic Union College, a small Seventh-day Adventist liberal arts college in Massachusetts, to study theology. He expected he'd end up as a preacher but it turned out "it was not for me." Four years and a bachelor's degree later, he returned home to Nova Scotia to see "what the Lord has for me now."

At first, the answer seemed to be not very much. The year he graduated from Atlantic, 1991, was the worst year ever for tuna. But then, that same year, he met that fisherman from Tancook who knew where the tuna were hiding and, well, the Lord certainly knew what he was doing.

Better yet, the 1998 season seemed destined to be the best in 10 years. Five more fish today! On the Japanese market, each fish could be worth as much as $20,000. Tomorrow ... who knew?

At this moment, however, Robert Conrad knew only that he was very tired. He'd be happy when he and his crew finished cutting up these fish for the buyer. It had been a long day.

Aboard Swissair Flight 111, JFK International Airport 8:00 pm EDT

Inside Flight 111's cockpit, Capt. Urs Zimmermann and co-pilot First Officer Stephan Loëw completed their final pre-flight checks as the airport's ground crew loaded the cargo hold. In addition to the passengers' personal luggage, the plane would be carrying more than 15 tons of freight — from textiles to spare parts for automobiles — close to a ton of mail and hundreds of pounds (and millions of dollars' worth) of diamonds, watches, jewels, gold, currency and artworks. Surprisingly, a version of Picasso's *Le Peintre*, valued at $2.2 million (Canadian), wasn't specially packaged for shipping; it had simply been packed inside a wooden frame and stowed with the rest of the general cargo. Most of the other valuables, however, were being handled with greater care. The manifest showed that the plane's valuables case — a special four-foot high aluminum container with reinforced walls, a locked door and a metal seal — contained a diamond from the recently completed "Nature of Diamonds" exhibition at the American Museum of Natural History, which was being shipped back to its owner in Europe, along with 110 pounds of banknotes destined for a U.S. bank in Geneva, another 2 pounds of diamonds and about 10 pounds of assorted jewellery.

If Flight 111 had become well known as a shuttle bus for United Nations staff, it was equally popular, if publicly less well known, as a courier service for jewellers who had to transport valuables back and forth between gem centres in the United States and Europe. Sometimes, the valuables on board were worth more than the $160 million plane itself.

Even less well publicized but no less well known among those for whom it mattered was that Flight 111 was also regarded as an ideal carrier to transport undeclared — perhaps ill-gotten — cash from the U.S. to Geneva for deposit in numbered Swiss bank accounts. There was probably some undeclared cash discreetly stowed within personal luggage in the plane's cargo hold tonight too, though no one could be sure in which pieces of luggage, or how much, or even whether the gain was ill gotten.

Flight 111 had come to serve so many purposes to so many people because it was now Swissair's only direct flight between New York and Geneva. Nearly a year ago, the airline, which had reported significant losses in 1995 and 1996, had hired Jeffrey Katz, a hard-driving American, to bring Swissair back to its previous levels of profitability. Katz, formerly with American Airlines, had helped retool Swissair's entire schedule, hubbing virtually all its long-haul flights out of Switzerland's main business city, Zurich, instead of Geneva, in order to increase passenger loads. The only exception was this daily Geneva–New York flight; it was kept on because it alone continued to be profitable. And profit seemed to be the chief motivator at Swissair.

Urs Zimmermann had been a Swissair pilot for 27 years and a captain for 11, certainly long enough to have observed Swissair's transformation from an insular, proudly Swiss national icon into a lean-and-maybe-even-mean competitor in the increasingly competitive international airline business. Back in 1990, at what one journalist called "the price-is-no-object Swissair of old," management had happily spent more than $1.3 million to give each of its 2,500 flight attendants $530 canary-yellow designer trench coats to wear to work. Now it was time for the Katz-run airline to replace them all — but with conservative blue models, costing less than $200 each. And there were far fewer coats to buy. In the past two years, Swissair had cut more than 2,000 employees from its payroll. There were rumours, Zimmermann knew, that the airline would soon be seeking wage and other concessions from its pilots too.

Zimmermann, a father of three whose family was planning a big party Friday to celebrate his fiftieth birthday, was one of Swissair's most experienced pilots. Although he'd been flying MD-11s only since June 1997, he'd flown more than 9,300 hours in total, 900 of them in MD-11s. He'd even been selected to star in a corporate video about the "dream job" of a Swissair pilot. His co-pilot tonight, Stephan Loëw, was 13 years Zimmermann's junior, but he boasted plenty of experience in the cockpit as well — 2,800 hours flying time, 220 of them in the MD-11 since being appointed a first officer on the aircraft in May. Like Zimmermann, Loëw, also the father of three and in the midst of moving his growing family into a new house, was considered experienced enough on the MD-11 to be rated as an instructor for other pilots.

Swissair had been among the first airlines in the world to order MD-11s. During the seventies, its predecessor, the DC-10, which had been designed to carry large numbers of passengers on long-haul flights, had helped transform the airline industry, finally making flying an affordable transcontinental option for ordinary people. The MD-11 was bigger than the DC-10, could travel even farther and offered more sophisticated options. In the early 1990s, Swissair had begun replacing its aging DC-10s with MD-11s. The airline now had a fleet of 16, nearly 10 per cent of the total number in service around the world, and several more on order.

Despite Swissair's loyalty to the MD-11 as a passenger carrier, however, it had not sold well elsewhere. After Boeing bought out McDonnell Douglas in 1997, in fact, the company announced it would stop producing the triple-engined jet and two other models because of declining sales. In the end, the MD-11 had found its real niche as a cargo plane. Federal Express, the American courier service, with 23 MD-11s in service, now operates the largest fleet of MD-11s in the world.

A Federal Express plane, by chance, was one of only two MD-11s to have ever been involved in what the airline industry likes to call a "major incident." On July 31, 1997, FedEx Flight 14 from Anchorage, Alaska, crashed and burned while landing at Newark, New Jersey. The MD-11 bounced as it hit the runway, losing its right main landing gear and right wing as it smacked down on the ground for the second time. The two pilots and three FedEx employees all escaped, but the plane had been destroyed. Although investigators suspected human error, more than a year later they were still trying to ascertain the exact cause of that crash.

But it had long since been determined that poorly designed controls on a China Eastern Airlines MD-11 had been responsible for a 1993 incident — the only other major one involving an MD-11 — in which the pilot overreacted after the slats on the plane's wings inadvertently deployed at 33,000 feet, causing the aircraft to shake so violently that two people were killed and dozens seriously injured. Following the China Eastern deaths, Swissair, like other MD-11 operators, modified the lever so it couldn't accidentally switch on in flight.

Swissair was proud of the MD-11's — and its own — safety record. The last time a Swissair plane had crashed was in 1979, when one of its DC-8s overran a runway in Athens, smashing into a fence and killing 14 of the 142 people aboard. Swissair's worldwide reputation for safe operations had certainly been well earned. Back in the late seventies, for example, the airline had pioneered a program of evaluating every one of its flights, compiling incidents reported by its pilots as well as information from flight data recorders, to create a database on the performance of each of its aircraft and crews. While the airline was careful to keep the human details confidential — there was only one highly classified file in which the data about incidents identified which crew members had been involved; Swissair refused to share that even with Delta, its American partner airline — the company used all the information it gathered to fine-tune its maintenance and safety programs as well as to make sure its pilots and aircraft were performing up to expectations.

The MD-11 aircraft Zimmermann and Loëw would be piloting, tail number HB-IWF, was known within the fleet as the Vaud. Named after a Swiss canton, it had logged more than 36,000 hours of flying time and nearly 6,600 takeoffs and landings since Swissair took delivery of it as one of the first MD-11s manufactured by McDonnell Douglas back in August 1991.

In the past 72 hours alone it had crisscrossed the world: from Los Angeles to Zurich and then back to San Francisco on Sunday, August 30; back to Zurich and on to Singapore the next day; from Singapore to Jakarta, Indonesia, and return to Singapore on September 1; and then, finally, from Singapore to Zurich to JFK as Flight 102 on September 2.

A year before, the plane had successfully undergone its "D Check," a detailed routine heavy-maintenance examination performed every six years or 30,000 flight hours. During such an examination, the aircraft essentially is dismantled, inspected and re-assembled. In August of 1998, just a month before, it had passed another one-day exam. And, of course, the pilots and ground crew had given the aircraft the once-over again that night before clearing Flight 111 for takeoff.

Flying an MD-11 was both simpler and far more demanding than flying the old DC-10. The aircraft's design philosophy was to automate not only routine tasks but also even emergency procedures. The designers proudly pointed out that in one DC-10 engine failure they had analyzed, the plane's flight engineer had been forced to perform 110 separate steps to complete his emergency checklist. On the MD-11, by contrast, computerized system controllers would perform all but five of those steps.

Those five steps, however, would now have to be performed by the pilots instead of the flight engineer, since the MD-11's design had eliminated the need for the traditional third member of the flight crew. Everything the flight engineer used to do was now performed by a bank of automatic controllers that had, according to Capt. John Miller, McDonnell Douglas's chief of flight operations for the MD-11, captured "the guile and cunning of a flight engineer" in a software program.

In fact, computerized controllers now operated all of the aircraft's hydraulic, electrical and fuel systems. With a glance at a diagram on the configuration page display on a screen in front of him, the pilot could see the position of the aircraft's flaps, slats, ailerons, elevator, rudder, spoilers and landing gear — not to mention find out the temperature of each brake and even the air pressure in each tire. On the progress page, he could see his aircraft's position, altitude, time in the air and time to the destination, as well as the outside air temperature, the wind speed, the amount of fuel in his tanks, the distance to his destination, the fuel that would be remaining when it got there, even the distances and fuel needed to get to an alternative airport in case of a problem. The flight management system could check the conditions and inform the pilot of the optimum speed and altitude to get to his destination fastest or, alternatively, in order to use the least fuel. Not only did all these sophisticated systems run in parallel, meaning they operated independently of one another, but each system was also run by two separate computers, one of which could take over for the other in case of a malfunction.

Every automatic system in the cockpit, which had been designed with input from pilots from 37 airlines, could still be overridden by the pilot, if need be. By simply pressing a button, the pilot could switch operations from automatic to manual and then back again.

The pilots were ready tonight, as was the rest of the 15-member flight crew. Collectively, the cabin crew boasted more than 65,000 hours of flying time. They had all arrived in New York the previous day on the Geneva–New York leg of their assignment and spent the night at the Hotel Marriott in Brooklyn. Regula Reutemann was probably still nervous. The 23-year-old daughter of a retired Swissair captain was in the midst of her first assignment since completing her flight attendant training a few days earlier. A university student taking the year off from her studies in geography, Reutemann was one of Swissair's new young hires, part of a recent mini-expansion that had followed the airline's return to profitability under Katz. At the other end of the experience spectrum was Patricia Eberhart, 50, Delta's representative on the Swissair flight. She had begun her career nearly three decades earlier as a flight attendant for Pan Am. She called the inside of the plane her living room. Like Eberhart, Jeannine Pompili, 42, was enthusiastic about her job. In fact, as a hobby, she collected old Swissair flight attendants' uniforms. Two weeks before, during the 50th anniversary celebrations for the Zurich airport, Pompili had staged a fashion show of old uniforms. She'd once told her mother, "If anything ever happens to me on a flight, you can tell people that I died very happily." She liked to travel for pleasure as well as business. The year before, she'd gone to Nova Scotia, visiting Peggys Cove, and came back bubbling with enthusiasm about the province's rocky coast. On Flight 111, she was a late replacement for an attendant who'd called in sick. Irene Betrisey-Sidler, 34, was not feeling well either; but, even though she had the flu, she had decided not to call in sick because she'd just returned to work after a month of vacation.

As usual, the flight crew had arrived an hour before departure for a pre-flight briefing — going over the latest weather forecasts for the flight path, discussing any passengers with special needs, and so on — and plane check. Thirty minutes before takeoff, as the first passengers began to board, the attendants began passing out newspapers — in deference to the diversity of its passengers, Flight 111 carried not only the major Swiss and American newspapers but also *Le Monde*, *Frankfurter Algemeine Zeitung* and the London *Times*, among others — "refreshing" towels, welcome drinks and menus to first- and business-class passengers.

Fifteen minutes before takeoff, 25-year Swissair veteran René Oberhänsli, the maître de cabin, or chief flight attendant, welcomed the passengers aboard Flight 111 in English, French and Swiss-German and then introduced the safety video.

At 8:13 p.m., five minutes before departure, the crew members each began their own final preparations, just as they did before every flight: securing the galleys, which were filled with two complete meals — a dinner that would be served shortly after takeoff and a breakfast for before they landed in Geneva — and checking to make sure that all the passengers were wearing their seat belts, that their chair tables and backs were in their full upright position and that all cabin baggage was safely stowed in the overhead bins or in the space beneath the seats in front of them.

As Flight 111 waited in position at one end of Runway 13-Right for clearance to depart, the cabin crew finally strapped themselves into their jump seats and began what Swissair describes as "one minute of silent review" of their own duties in any emergency. No one expected they would need to know those procedures that night.

Finally, the control tower cleared the flight for takeoff. The jet picked up speed as it rumbled down the runway and then Swissair Flight 111 was airborne, flying into the night sky past Long Island Sound, then east across Nantucket Island and out over the Atlantic Ocean. In business and first class, passengers sampled hors d'oeuvres while they pondered which movies — *Titanic*, *Night Watch*, *City of Angels*, *As Good as It Gets* or any of 17 other mostly Hollywood films — they wanted to watch on their individual inflight entertainment system.

Swissair was proud to be one of the few airlines in the world offering such a sophisticated, multi-faceted movie system. Designed by Interactive Flight Technologies of Phoenix, Arizona, it featured a personal pop-up video screen recessed into the armrest of every first-class and business-section seat. Those passengers could select video and music selections on demand, play popular video games or — on flights other than ones, like this one, that originated or ended in the U.S., where there were rules against inflight gambling — use their credit cards to play the slots, keno, poker, blackjack, even bingo on their individual computerized screens.

The problem was that these entertainment systems, which cost as much as $4.5 million per plane, were notoriously unreliable. The first systems, installed during the late eighties and early nineties, had been plagued with problems with their reliability that led to lawsuits between the airlines and the system suppliers. Many of these lawsuits were still working their way through the courts. The problems probably shouldn't have been unexpected. Hooking up such a system involves putting the equivalent of a personal computer under each seat and then connecting all of them to a central computer over a complex network of wires — a technological feat even on the ground. But the vibration, heat and dry air in an airplane at 35,000 feet make it next to impossible to operate all those sensitive electronics at peak efficiency all the time. According to a report in the *New York Times*, one airline claimed that its maintenance crews spent an extra 35 hours a week servicing each plane that had an entertainment system. According to one estimate, 80 per cent of the electronics on a wide-body jet are now located in the passenger cabin rather than the cockpit, and "there are more lines of code in the entertainment software than in the programs flying the plane."

But that hadn't dampened the demand from passengers for high-tech gizmos, and airlines claimed they had no choice but to give passengers what they wanted. "Why are the airlines crazy enough to invest in technology that is never 100 per cent reliable and extremely expensive?" Karl Laasner, Swissair's head of inflight entertainment, had asked rhetorically in the article in the *New York Times* published just two weeks earlier. "If you want the image of being the world's best," he explained simply, "you have to keep up."

Swissair had installed its new system just 18 months before. Because of the airline's reputation for quality control, other airlines — which had been burned by the earlier problem-plagued experiments with video and gambling systems — were watching carefully to see how well this new generation of entertainment systems worked. "Once those fastidious Swiss engineers have checked out our system," Steve Fieldman, Interactive Flight Technologies vice-president for business development, had bragged shortly after Swissair bought his company's system in 1996, "you don't need any more due diligence." Perhaps. Or perhaps not. In June of 1998, Interactive announced it was abandoning the inflight entertainment business to build a chain of drycleaners instead.

Forty minutes after it took off from Kennedy and 25 minutes after the cabin crews began serving dinner, Swissair Flight 111 entered Canadian airspace at a point about 160 miles east of Kennebunkport, Maine. Although the ground time changed at this point from Eastern Daylight Time to Atlantic Daylight Time — meaning it was now 9:58 p.m. ADT — the aircraft itself, like all international flights, operated on Greenwich Mean Time, which was three hours ahead of Atlantic time.

For most of the last 15 minutes of its flight through American air space, investigators would later report, Swissair 111 had failed to respond to calls from Boston air traffic controllers. Whatever the reason for that, no one apparently thought it important enough to ask the pilots about it when the plane resumed communication.

Responsibility for shepherding the plane through Canadian air space was now the job of Moncton, New Brunswick, air traffic controllers. Flight 111 was one of about 500 planes they would guide eastward over the course of the night. To the controllers, who worked in a windowless room filled with terminals, Swissair Flight 111 appeared as a bright green hexagon on a large round screen showing the coast of Nova Scotia. The official name of the plane — SWR111 — appeared as text near the icon.

Nothing was amiss.

Fox Point, Nova Scotia
9:30 p.m. ADT

Robert Conrad was too tired to spend even a few minutes sitting on the massive granite plate rock that had heaved itself up out of the ground before he was born, and which now rose up into the sky behind his house overlooking St. Margarets Bay. On nights when the moon was full and the sky was clear, he liked to come outside, sit down quietly on the rock, let his feet dangle over the edge and lose himself staring out at the great beautiful expanse of ocean stretched before him. He usually found it a peaceful, almost spiritual experience. But not that night. The weather was closing fast. The last remnants of Hurricane Danielle were passing near the coast. There was fog and low cloud and high wind and "miserable" rain, as Conrad described it.

Besides, having just gotten home from another 16-hour day struggling with the tuna bureaucracy, Robert Conrad felt too exhausted to contemplate the beauties of nature. Not to forget that, in less than seven hours, he'd have to get up and start all over again. He went inside the house instead. His wife, Peggy, was already in bed. He turned on the television set and just lay down on the couch, just for a few minutes, he told himself, to ease the transition from work to sleep.

Suddenly, he was asleep. Perhaps it was a reflection of just how tired he was — or of the traumas to come — but when he talked about this night a few days later, Robert Conrad would not be able to remember what show had been on the television screen when he fell asleep. But when he woke up some time later, the news was on.

Aboard Swissair 111
10:12 p.m. ADT

In the MD-11 cockpit, the two pilots were just finishing their dinners. They were, in fact, talking about food when Stephan Loëw told Zimmermann he smelled something. Was it smoke? He wasn't sure. He asked Zimmermann to take over the controls for a moment while he looked around for the source of the odour. He opened the trap door in the floor of the cockpit and looked into the avionics compartment, where much of the aircraft's sophisticated radio, navigation, computer and other electronics systems are located, but he found nothing unusual there.

One of the flight attendants came into the cockpit. Loëw asked her whether she had smelled smoke in the passenger cabin.

No, she said, but she could certainly smell something here.

Now Zimmermann could see it as well as smell it. There was definitely smoke in the cockpit. It could be nothing serious, but then again—

Pilots are trained to initiate standard operating procedures as soon as they discover smoke in the cockpit. The captain and co-pilot are immediately supposed to don full-face oxygen masks, covering their eyes, nose and mouth, so they can — with luck — continue to operate the plane in spite of smoke or fumes. They're also instructed to notify controllers on the ground that they have a problem and request an immediate diversion to the nearest airport capable of handling their aircraft, and then alert the cabin crew — usually using a chime similar to the fasten-seat-belts signal — that there's an emergency situation. Finally, they're supposed to begin a careful step-by-step process of trying to figure out where the smoke is coming from and what to do about it.

Zimmermann and Loëw tried to decide whether they should turn the plane around and head back to New York, or try Boston, where Swissair had a landing base, or perhaps Bangor, Maine, which would certainly be closer to their current position. But could the airport there handle an MD-11?

"Swissair one-eleven heavy is declaring Pan Pan Pan," Loëw told Moncton Air Traffic Control. "Heavy" is the jargon for a wide-bodied jet. Pan is a corruption of the French and German word *panne*, which means breakdown. Pilots use this code when they have a problem they believe is serious but not yet an emergency. "We have, uh, smoke in the cockpit," Zimmermann explained. "Uh, request immediate return, uh, to a convenient place, I guess, uh, Boston."

While Zimmermann and Loëw adjusted their oxygen masks to help them breathe, the flight attendants probably continued to serve dinner to the passengers, who remained oblivious to the tense drama unfolding in the cockpit just beyond their view.

After initially accepting Zimmermann's plan to head back to Boston, 345 miles to the south, the ground controller had second thoughts. "Would you prefer to go to Halifax?" he asked.

"Uh, standby." The pilots quickly checked their charts. Halifax was just 80 miles away. "Affirmative for Swissair one-eleven heavy. We prefer Halifax from our position."

The controller, who had already cleared the pilots to begin an immediate descent from their cruising altitude of 33,000 feet to 31,000 feet, added: "Descend now to flight level two-niner-zero" — 29,000 feet.

The crew of a passing British Airways flight, listening in on the conversation, offered the Swissair crew the latest weather report for Halifax. "One-zero-zero at niner knots, one-five miles, scattered at one-two-zero, broken at two-five-zero, plus 17, plus 12, two-niner-eight-zero. Over." Translated, that meant the winds were blowing out of the east at nine knots with a visibility of 15 miles. There were scattered clouds at 12,000 feet, broken clouds at 25,000 feet. The temperature was 17 degrees Celsius with a dew point of 12 degrees Celsius, and the barometric pressure 29.80 inches of mercury. In short: reasonably clear.

"Roger, Swissair one-eleven heavy, we copy the, ah, altimeter is two niner-eight-zero."

The pilots didn't have handy their landing charts for Halifax, so they had to ask a flight attendant to get them from the rear of the cockpit. They also asked René Oberhänsli, the chief flight attendant, to notify the passengers that they would be diverting the plane to Halifax and would be landing there in 20 to 25 minutes. He, in turn — as calmly as possible — announced in three languages that the plane would be making an unscheduled landing in Halifax and asked the other flight attendants, who were still completing the dinner service, to begin collecting meal trays instead.

"Swissair one-eleven, you're cleared to 10,000 feet," the air traffic controller said.

Loëw, who was piloting the aircraft while Zimmermann began to work his way through his emergency checklist, made the turn toward Halifax as he passed on to Zimmermann the controller's clearance to reduce altitude.

Not so fast, Zimmermann replied quickly. He was breathing heavily now, his respiration rate — picked up by the microphone in his mask — registering 25 breaths per minute, which may have been an indication either of high stress or perhaps simply that he was having difficulties with the oxygen mask.

Loëw, whose own respiration rate remained a more normal 11 breaths per minute, followed Zimmermann's admonition, slowing the big plane's rate of descent from 4,000 feet per minute to 3,100. But he wasn't happy about it. He told the captain he thought they should bring the plane down as fast as possible so they'd be in a position to land quickly if the smoke got too thick.

Still, he followed the captain's instructions, explaining to the ground controllers that they only wanted to descend to 8,000 feet "until the cabin is ready for landing." There was still a lot of preparation to do. The crew not only had to collect and stow all the cabin service items from the interrupted meal but they would also probably want to take the time to re-brief the passengers on emergency landing procedures, such as the use of life jackets and assuming the brace position. They might even want to rearrange the seating plan to make sure that those seated in the exit-row seats would be physically able to get out of the plane quickly so there'd be no logjam for other passengers trying to get out the emergency exits.

By this point, air traffic control had passed from Moncton to Halifax International Airport. After introducing himself, the new controller told them again that they were cleared to descend to 3,000 feet but they could "level off at an intermediate altitude if you wish. Just advise."

They were now at 19,800 feet. It was 10:20 p.m., 12 minutes since Loëw first smelled smoke. "You've got 30 miles to fly to the threshold," the controller informed them, referring to the end of the active runway at Halifax. He had already guided the plane a little to the north to bring them in on a flight path slightly to the left of the airport so they would make a direct approach and land on Runway 06, the airport's longest at 8,800 feet.

The controller asked for "the number of souls on board and your fuel on board please for emergency services."

Loëw checked his instruments. The plane's gross weight, including fuel, was 233 tons — 22 tons more than the manufacturer's maximum permitted landing weight. Although it's possible to land the plane above that maximum weight, doing so could put severe strain on the airframe. That added weight, coupled with the rapid descent, would also make it almost impossible to bring the plane to a complete stop before it reached the end of the runway. Though he probably wouldn't have had the time or inclination at exactly that moment to calculate the finer points of what might happen, other experts with more time would later estimate that the plane not only would probably have overshot the end of the runway by as much as a mile and a half but would also have been travelling as fast as 100 miles an hour into whatever was beyond the end of the asphalt — including populated areas.

"We must, uh, dump some fuel," Loëw urgently informed the controller. "May we do that in this area during descent?"

They could have. Under Canadian law, the pilots couldn't dump fuel over land once the plane descended below 10,000 feet, but the aircraft was still well above that ceiling and still over water. Despite that, the controller didn't answer them directly. "Uh, okay," he began, "I am going to take you ... are you able to take a turn back to the south or do you want to stay closer to the airport?"

"Uh, standby short, standby short," Loëw replied, using pilots' shorthand for "I'm too busy to answer you right now." And they were. Their plane was too high and too heavy for a routine approach to Halifax. Could they bring it down safely? They would have known that other pilots had managed to make successful emergency landings flying overweight planes. But they had never flown into Halifax before, it was night, and the weather conditions were unfavourable. Not to forget, of course, that there was smoke in the cockpit. What should they do? Dump fuel immediately over land — possibly spattering people and houses on the ground — in order to reduce the weight even as they brought the plane down rapidly for the descent into the airport? Or did they have time to double back out to sea, jettison as much excess fuel as they could while reducing altitude and then turn back toward Halifax for a lighter, lower, safer landing?

There was no time left to think.

"Okay," Loëw replied 19 seconds after the controller's question, "we are able for a left or right turn towards the south to dump." They were 10 miles from the coast, 25 miles from the airport. The plane was at 11,900 feet.

The dimensions of the emergency would probably still not have been clear to the passengers, but there were certainly indications that things were not right. As part of his emergency checklist, for example, Zimmermann had already turned off all non-essential power to the passenger cabins. That meant the flight attendants had to use flashlights to see to collect the meal trays and a bullhorn to tell the passengers about the plane's emergency landing procedures. No one knows for certain what the atmosphere in the passenger cabins would have been like at this point, but most survivors of plane crashes and near misses report that an eerie silence often descends on an aircraft as passengers, trapped by the reality that they truly have no control of their destiny, retreat into their own thoughts and emotions. At this point — given that they'd been told they wouldn't be landing in Halifax for nearly 20 more minutes — it's unlikely many would have panicked.

The tension inside the cockpit, however, may have been reaching near-panic conditions as the captain and co-pilot tried to cope with the increasing smoke and heat. As Loëw followed the controller's instructions to make a

sharp 120-degree turn to the left in preparation for dump-
ing fuel over the ocean, he worried that the jet might stray
too far from the airport. Should he reduce air speed to
keep the plane close to land? he asked the captain.

But Zimmermann was too busy working his way
through his emergency checklist to think about the question.

Do what you think you should, he told his co-pilot.

"Du bisch in der emergency checklist für air conditioning smoke?"

"Uh, Swissair one-eleven," the controller radioed
back. "Say again, please."

"Ah, sorry," Loëw responded quickly. "It was not for
you. Swissair was asking internally. It was my fault.
Sorry about ..." He'd been trying to find out from
Zimmermann if he was using the emergency checklist for
air conditioning smoke but he'd accidentally broadcast
the question, in a mix of Swiss-German and English, over
the air control frequency.

Zimmermann probably continued to follow procedures. One of them called for him to check for the source
of the smoke by turning parts of the plane's electrical
systems off and then back on. Using a smoke switch,
Zimmermann would have been able to turn off one-third
of the plane's electric components and one of its air conditioning packs. If that didn't isolate the problem, he
could move the switch to a second position, turning off
another third of the electrics and another air conditioning
system while simultaneously restoring power to the first
systems. If that didn't work, he could move the switch to
a third and final position that would repeat the process.

It may never be known whether Zimmermann got this
far in his checklist, but some experts say that if he did, he
may have inadvertently sealed the plane's fate simply by
doing what he had been told to do. The argument is that if
damaged insulation in the wiring of the electrical system

above the cockpit had been responsible for the initial smoke in the cockpit, turning one of the electrical systems on again just after it had been shut down could have created a power surge and led to arcing — lightning-like leaks from wire to wire — resulting in a massive electrical failure.

Whatever caused it, there is no question the giant plane did suffer a sudden and massive domino-like breakdown of all its electrical systems. Within about a minute and a half, the flight data recorder would register "anomalies," or errors, in 40 of the 250 systems it measures.

First, the autopilot stopped working. Loëw tried to remain calm. "Ah, Swissair one-eleven," he said over the sound of an intercom ringing in the background. "At the time we must fly manually. Are we cleared to fly between ah, ten thou — 11,000 and 9,000 feet?"

On the ground, the controller — who could hear the signal as the autopilot turned off, though he might not have known for certain what the signal meant — replied in the affirmative, but Zimmermann and Loëw had probably stopped listening by then. The plane's electrical systems had begun to stop working, one after another, in increasingly rapid sequence. Loëw was already having trouble controlling the plane when the bright video displays showing his instrument readings may have suddenly gone blank and dark.

The two pilots began speaking simultaneously.

"Swissair one-eleven heavy is declaring emergency—"

"We are between, uh, twelve and five thousand feet. We are declaring emergency now at, uh, time, uh, zero-one-two-four—"

"Roger."

"Eleven heavy, we starting dump now. We have to land immediate—"

"Swissair one-eleven," the air traffic controller responded. "Just a couple more miles. I'll be right with you."

"Roger ... And we are declaring emergency now," one of the pilots said again. "Swissair one-eleven."

"Copy that," the controller said. Just over 10 seconds later, he said: "Swissair one-eleven, you are cleared to, uh, commence your fuel dump on that track and advise me, uh, when the dump is complete."

There was no answer from the plane.

"Swissair one-eleven, check you're cleared to start the fuel dump."

Still, there was no answer.

It was shortly before 10:26 p.m. Atlantic Daylight Time.

Rescue Coordination Centre, Halifax
10:30 p.m. ADT

"We've lost 'em," Capt. Mike Atkins heard the voice of the air traffic controller on the phone declare, a new urgency now in his voice. "We don't have them on radar anymore." In his command centre at the Rescue Coordination Centre in Halifax, Atkins listened intently to the Halifax air traffic controller for a moment, then picked up another phone and called Canadian Forces Base Greenwood.

It was time to scramble some planes.

For the past 12 minutes — ever since air traffic controllers had called to tell him a plane bound for Europe had reported smoke in the cockpit and was being diverted to Halifax — Atkins had been on tense standby alert. It wasn't so much the fact that the plane would be making an emergency landing. Such landings were more routine than most people believed. But this was only Atkins's third shift in charge of operations in the control centre. That was making him understandably nervous. At RCC, you could never tell when something routine might turn instantly and without warning into a full-blown emergency.

Housed in a small war room full of maps and monitors on the ground floor of an unassuming red-brick building in the bowels of Canadian Forces Base Halifax Dockyard, the RCC is a kind of 911 service for ships and aircraft in Atlantic Canada. Actually, Atlantic Canada is a misnomer. The centre, one of five search and rescue operations centres in Canada, is responsible for a vast expanse of territory, from Quebec in the west to Baffin Island in the north to just past Sable Island in the south to the mid-Atlantic in the east — 1.8 million square miles in all, three-quarters of it water.

The centre is regularly staffed 24 hours a day, seven days a week by a team of three: a search and rescue pilot or navigator like Atkins, a coast guard officer and a radio operator. As soon as someone calls in an air or sea emergency, the RCC swings into operations mode, dispatching ships and aircraft to the scene, coordinating the efforts of military and civilian personnel to carry out searches and rescues and making sure nearby facilities such as hospitals are notified and ready to care for any survivors. In an emergency, the officer in charge can call in whatever help he needs.

As soon as Atkins heard that the plane had disappeared from radar, he instructed the duty military officer at Greenwood to dispatch one of its Hercules aircraft as well as a Labrador helicopter to head for the plane's last reported location.

It could be nothing, of course. The next call could be the air traffic control centre telling him that the plane had landed safely. But he couldn't wait for that to happen; he couldn't take the chance. He noted the time and other information in his log book. This was case number 1,707. That was how many emergencies the RCC had handled in 1998 alone.

Then he picked up the telephone to call his boss, Maj. Michel Brisebois. He had a feeling he was going to need some help tonight.

Aboard Swissair 111
10:31 ADT

No one knows for certain yet exactly what happened aboard Flight 111 after the plane lost communication with ground controllers. But it is possible, based on the plane's radar-monitored flight path as well as on what investigators would later piece together, to make some informed conjecture about what happened, if not why.

The passengers, who were already in darkness as a result of the pilots' earlier decision to turn off cabin power, may not have noticed much significant difference in their situation even in the first minutes after the plane lost all its electrical systems. There is some dispute over whether those in first class would have known more than other passengers about what was going on in the cockpit. Because the cockpit was separated from even the forward first-class passenger cabin by a galley and washrooms as well as the closed cockpit door, it's unlikely they would have been able to see the pilots struggling for control of the aircraft. But there have been reports that there was heavy sooting and other fire damage in the front of the ceiling of the first-class cabin, suggesting that the fire may have spread there too.

Inside the cockpit, that massive electrical failure changed everything. The pilots were now almost literally flying blind. Until the loss of electrical systems, and despite the smoke and likely increasing heat, they had been able to continue to control the aircraft using a vast array of sophisticated electronic wizardry that told them everything they needed to know, from how fast the plane was travelling to how much fuel remained in the tanks to how far they were from the ground. Because all that information is critical to safe flight, modern passenger planes are designed so that virtually every component has its own built-in backup — and sometimes more than one — in case the primary systems fail. The critical systems even monitor each other and notify the pilots if anything seems amiss. But no one contemplated, or designed for, such a total, massive, near-simultaneous failure of all of the systems powering all of the airplane's electronics.

The pilots' task now was more than daunting. They probably had no "artificial horizon" indicators on the blank flight director display screens in front of them to show where the horizon was. And the manual backup artificial horizon indicators were too small and too far away from the main console to be seen easily by the pilots, especially if the smoke was thick. The artificial horizon indicator is a simple device that shows a line on the screen that tells the pilot where the horizon would be if he could actually see it. Knowing where the horizon is is critical: it allows a pilot to keep his plane's wings level, preventing the aircraft from slipping into a potentially fatal spiral.

A spiral usually begins with a slight, almost imperceptible bank to the left or right. It may be caused by something as simple as the pilot putting a little too much sideways pressure on the plane's control column, or a slight imbalance in the weight of the fuel in the wings, or one engine producing a little more thrust than the other. Under normal circumstances, the pilot would first notice the problem on his artificial horizon and correct it. Without the artificial horizon indicator, or some other visual reference point, however, the pilot may not even realize that the plane has banked. The banking causes the plane's nose to drop slightly, increasing its airspeed a little. Again, under normal circumstances, the pilot would be able to use his airspeed indicators to tell him he's going too fast and make corrections. But without instrumentation to provide the necessary warnings, the unnoticed speed-up would cause the plane to bank even more, which causes the nose to drop even more, which causes the plane to go even faster. The plane eventually goes into a nearly vertical spiral from which the pilot cannot recover, and the plane crashes. In the early days of flying, before such instruments as artificial horizons were developed, spirals were the single biggest cause of crashes when planes were flying in bad weather.

Not only did Loëw and Zimmermann no longer have any instruments to help them figure out the horizon — or tell them that the plane's airspeed was increasing — but they also had no visual reference points either; the inky night sky into which they were flying had become so cloud-covered and overcast that they would not likely even have been able to see the moon above them, let alone the dark ocean beneath. And the few lights from land were off in the distance to either side of the plane.

Researchers at the University of Rochester once tested 20 student pilots in a simulator to see how long they could keep their planes in the air without instruments in bad weather. The answer: not long. Every one of the pilots lost control after anywhere from 20 seconds to eight minutes, and all of their aircraft ended up in what pilots call graveyard spirals. The average flying time before the test subjects crashed: just under three minutes.

Loëw and Zimmermann weren't student pilots, but they were facing far worse and more disorienting conditions inside the Swissair cockpit. Aluminum in the ceiling above and behind the pilots' seats had become so hot — at least 650 degrees Celsius — that it had melted, and drops of molten plastic fell onto the sheepskin fabric of the empty observer seat behind them. While the intense heat in the ceiling may have been localized, the smoke — whatever caused it, wherever its source — would probably have continued to fill their tiny instrument-filled, no-longer-functioning compartment even as they struggled to figure out what to do next. And, of course, there was a real urgency to figure out what to do next. This was not a test in a simulator.

Despite these grave conditions, the pilots somehow managed to keep their plane in the air for the next six minutes while descending to 1,000 feet as well as make the initial turns that should have enabled them to head back toward the airport. And they did it with only two functioning engines. The third engine — which was over the rear fuselage in the tail and needed the plane's electrics to pump fuel to it — had probably stopped working when the other systems went down.

Swissair Flight 111 circled out over St. Margarets Bay past East Ironbound Island and then back around over Big Tancook and Tancook Islands on a flight path that appeared to be leading them back toward Halifax International Airport. But then, instead of straightening out its flight path as it passed over Blandford, the big jet continued its circular clockwise path back out toward the open sea. Perhaps the pilots had become disoriented, or perhaps they realized they couldn't keep the plane aloft to land at the airport and decided to ditch in the ocean rather than crashing into a populated area. Whatever the reason,

Flight 111 was now in the final seconds of its doomed last approach.

The plane most likely began its fatal final plunge in an ever-faster, ever-tighter downward spiral, finally plummeting the last 800 to 1,000 feet into the ocean with its nose tipped down at an angle of at least 60 degrees and in a steep right-hand bank.

The passengers still may not even have realized what was about to happen to them. Like the pilots, they would have no visual reference points, and the increasing gravitational pressures on their body as the aircraft tightened into the spiral and picked up speed could have created the illusion that the plane was climbing rather than falling.

Those gravitational forces would have been intense. At the instant the plane hit the water, they would have been deadly. G-force, as it's called, measures speed changes over a given time. The simple force of gravity pulling down on your body, our everyday state, is calculated as 1 G. Zero gravity is the state of weightlessness astronauts experience. You've no doubt experienced the effect of G-force in a modest way if you've ever taken a high-speed elevator to the upper floor in a highrise building. As the elevator begins to speed up on its ascent, you feel yourself becoming heavier as the forces of gravity pull your body down even as the elevator floor moves upward under you, keeping you in place. The accelerating elevator would result in a force on your body of about 1.3 G. In other words you'd "weigh" one-third more than normal. When the elevator comes to a stop, you feel momentarily lighter, as if your body was still climbing. The effect of deceleration would be to momentarily reduce your weight to about nine-tenths of normal, a G-force of 0.9.

The human body, strapped face forward in an airline seat, can survive a force of about 30 Gs for three-tenths of a second without suffering any permanent damage. When Flight 111, probably travelling at about 600 feet per second, hit the water, the plane — and everyone and everything inside — would have experienced a force of 1,850 Gs during the milliseconds of the impact.

Nothing — and no one — could have survived it.

At 10:31.22 p.m. ADT, sensitive scientific instruments at the Bedford Institute of Oceanography near Halifax recorded a "peak" seismic event coming from the direction of the crash. Since it would have taken the shock wave about 11 seconds to travel from the impact point through the bedrock to the instrument, the most likely instant of impact is 10:31.11.

We tend to assume that crashing a plane into the more "forgiving" surface of the ocean is somehow smarter or safer than slamming it down on a concrete runway. That assumption is wrong. At the speed Flight 111 was travelling, water is just as "hard" as concrete. Even though the U.S. Federal Aviation Administration has determined, in theory, that the MD-11 is strong enough to survive a water landing, Harry Robertson, who runs the Crash Research Institute in Tempe, Arizona, and who has investigated airplane accidents for 40 years, says, "If I had a choice of where to make a crash landing, I would never pick water."

The problem is that when a plane hits the ocean — especially at the angle Flight 111 is believed to have come down — the action of the plane tearing into the surface of the water would cause the aircraft's fuselage to rip open. Because the aluminum alloys manufacturers use in modern passenger jets are stronger but more brittle than they used to be, the aluminum sheeting on the plane's exterior would also tend to shatter into thousands of pieces — "like an eggshell," as Roberston puts it — as it meets the ocean. To make matters worse, the large engines on newer planes like the MD-11 are slung beneath the wings. Those engines tend to catch as they smash into the surface, driving them backward into the wings and causing the body of the plane to disintegrate.

In the case of Swissair Flight 111, the violence of the impact would have been almost beyond human comprehension. The 200-foot-long plane travelling at about 400 miles per hour smashed nose first into the surface of the water with such force that it collapsed completely into itself, almost like a telescope being slammed closed against a brick wall. Only much faster. And much harder. It would have all happened within a few feet beneath the surface of the water. From the time the nose touched the water until the tail joined it would have been less than one-third of a second. Shards from the plane's tail section would later be discovered intermingled with pieces of cockpit instruments. The largest pieces of the cockpit that investigators could find measured no larger than a few square yards.

Inside the aircraft at the moment of impact, there would have been a deadly hailstorm of rocketing seats, baggage, cabin pieces, aircraft parts and people. Given the G-forces inside the aircraft, every person was driven forward with such velocity and stopped so suddenly that almost no one remained in one piece. The lone exception was a woman seated in the centre of the aircraft in the first row of the economy section, behind a bulkhead, or partition. Her body was likely trapped between her seat and the bulkhead, protecting it from the angry forces of physics that ripped the other passengers into pieces, many of them too small to ever identify.

And then, as awesome and awful and noisy as the crash itself had been, it was over.

There was now only the deadliest, deadest of silences.

Halifax
10:35 p.m. ADT

"Major, we've got a problem."

Maj. Michel Brisebois had barely settled in to watch a little TV before heading off to bed when Captain Atkins called. Brisebois, the head of the Halifax Rescue Coordination Centre, had arrived home less than half an hour earlier after a pleasant evening as the featured guest at the monthly meeting of a local scale-model-makers club. One of the club members had created a scale model of an oil rig that Brisebois had begun using for a demonstration in a search and rescue seminar he was conducting for offshore oil and gas workers. So that night he'd gone to the club's meeting to present a thank-you plaque to the man on behalf of the RCC. Presenting plaques was just one of his many duties. Handling late-night phone calls from his duty officer was another one.

"What is it, Captain?" he asked Atkins.

"We've just lost an MD-11 off the radar and I think we're going to need some help down here."

"Oh, shit."

Brisebois wasn't certain what kind of plane an MD-11 was, but he knew right away the news wasn't good.

Halifax
10:40 p.m. ADT

Rob Gordon had barely fallen asleep when his phone rang. Though he didn't know it, phones, cell phones and pagers were suddenly going off all over the city.

"Oh, fuck," he thought angrily. How many times had

he told Angus to tell his friends not to call after ten o'clock?

"Hello." It was less a question than a command.

"O'Connell here," the strained voice began without preamble. It was Dan O'Connell, Gordon's assignment editor. "O'Connell here" was the nervous, clipped, perfunctory way he introduced himself on the phone whenever he was excited. "There's been some sort of plane crash in St. Margarets Bay and we need people," he continued with barely a pause. "You in?"

Gordon was wary. It was late and he was tired. "How big?" he asked.

"Don't know. Could be eight. Could be a hundred. I just found out. I'm at home myself."

"On the Bay or on land?"

"Don't know."

"Okay. I'm on my way." He hung up. "There's been some sort of crash," he told his wife, Dawn. "I have to go in to work." As he dressed, he gathered up his cell phone, an extra battery and the handheld Global Positioning System, or GPS, indicator from his sailboat. Just in case.

Part of him hoped it would be something big. He didn't want to go to all this trouble for nothing.

Bayswater
10:45 p.m. ADT

Harris Backman was thirsty. He'd just gotten up to get a glass of water at his kitchen sink when he heard a thunder-like noise off in the distance. The whole house shook. He figured it must be Canadian navy ships conducting war games out beyond the Bay. They did that sometimes, though rarely this late at night. "The navy sure is pounding hell out of us tonight," he said to his wife as he slipped back into bed. The noise had woken Audrey too.

Before they could get back to sleep, however, someone from the local volunteer fire department telephoned the house. There was a plane down on the water, he said, and they needed volunteers with boats to conduct a search. Harris immediately contacted RCC headquarters in Halifax to notify them too, but they already knew. Harris told the dispatcher there that he and his son Steven would go immediately to their boat, which was docked three miles away at the government wharf in Aspotogan, to await further instructions. Harris, as was his habit when there was an emergency, immediately and conveniently forgot his doctor's admonition to take it easy.

But before he and Steven could leave the house, there was yet another telephone call. It was their neighbour Janet Irwin, a CBC radio producer. Nine years ago, she and her husband, Darryl Gray, a CBC cameraman, had bought Harris's late parents' place next door. Though they usually spent summers in Bayswater, Janet had been asked to go to Toronto that summer to sit in as the acting executive producer of the CBC Radio operation there. That's where she was now. Irwin told Harris that her husband had just telephoned her from Halifax to say there'd been a big plane crash near Bayswater and that he had been called back in to work. Janet was calling in part to make sure Harris and Audrey were all right but also in part — because she knew Harris and Audrey were involved in the auxiliary — to find out if they'd seen or heard anything or knew any details about the search operations. She was already on her way to the Toronto newsroom to act as a chase producer on the crash story, she explained, and just wanted to find out what they knew at this point.

It turned out she knew more than they did.

"Any idea how many people aboard?" Harris asked.

"A hundred and fifty, maybe more," she answered.

And all along, Harris had been thinking it was a small private plane that had gone down. How could there be survivors from a crash of a plane like that? he wondered. But perhaps there were. They could be alive. They would need his help.

Harris and Steven had barely pulled away in their pick-up when the phone rang again. Audrey answered it. This time it was a reporter from New York. How had he come up with their number? Audrey wondered.

"What can you tell me about what's happened there?" he began without preamble. Audrey tried to tell him what little she knew — what the weather was like, the sea conditions, that vessels were on their way to the scene. "If I was in a foreign country and something happened to me," Audrey would explain later, "I know that the people back home would want to know what people were doing for me." What she didn't realize at the time was just how many reporters would suddenly be calling to ask her questions. Or that she would eventually be fielding calls from as far away as Australia. "Once somebody gets your cell phone number," she says, "they don't stop."

Meanwhile, Steven and Harris drove as fast as they could to get to their vessel, the *ABS Enterprise*. At Bayswater Beach, about halfway to the wharf, they noticed that the first fire and emergency vehicles were already gathering to await instructions. The police had established a roadblock on the highway there. While Steven explained where they were headed, Harris called the RCC again to get instructions on where to go. The preliminary search area, they were told, was off Peggys Cove.

Glen Haven, Nova Scotia
10:50 p.m. ADT

Swissair? John Butt was incredulous. Perhaps she'd heard wrong, he suggested. Sharon Winters didn't think so. Winters, the on-call nurse-investigator this week for Nova Scotia's chief medical examiner's officer, had just received an emergency alert call from the Rescue Coordination Centre. The caller said they believed an aircraft may have crashed, probably at sea, probably in St. Margarets Bay off the Aspotogan Peninsula. It was a passenger plane, a Swissair —

Swissair? In St. Margarets Bay? None of it made any sense to John Butt. Butt lived only a few miles from where they were saying the plane had gone down. Wouldn't he have heard something? And Swissair? That made no sense to him at all. He knew commercial planes flew over his area all the time. He'd often watched the contrails as the jets made their way to Halifax International Airport. But he was almost certain Swissair had no service to Halifax.

"Could you call them back?" he asked Winters. "Get them to confirm it's Swissair and find out anything else they know." If it really was a Swissair flight, Butt knew, it would almost certainly be a big plane with hundreds of passengers aboard. God!

Even as he waited for her to call back, Butt began to prepare. He could feel the adrenalin. "If it really is a plane crash," he told himself, "I ain't gonna be home for a while." He got out his suitcase and began packing everything he thought he might need for the next three days. Then he called his neighbours up the road. Could someone look after his dogs while he was gone?

Winters called back. It was a Swissair flight. And it

was now confirmed. The plane had gone down.

Butt picked up the telephone to call his boss, Gordon Gillis, the province's recently appointed deputy minister of justice, to tell him what was going on, then realized with a start he didn't have his home phone number. He'd forgotten to get it when the province had recently shuffled its deputy ministers. He opened the phone book. Four Gordon Gillises, one G.A. He looked at the time. He couldn't worry about that. He began dialling. He had to be careful not to say too much. "Excuse me, is this the Gordon Gillis who ..." He finally reached Gillis's son, who gave him the right number.

Butt carefully explained to his boss what little he knew about what had happened and how bad it might be. And then he dropped the bombshell he had been trying not to admit, even to himself. During his tenure as president of the American Association of Pathologists, after all, he'd been a vocal proponent of the need for pathologists to develop their own disaster response manuals.

"Gordon," he said, almost wistfully, "we don't have a plan."

There was the slightest pause at the other end of the phone. "We don't?"

"We don't."

Rescue Coordination Centre
10:55 p.m. ADT

By the time Maj. Michel Brisebois arrived at the Rescue Coordination Centre just 20 minutes after the call from Captain Atkins, the operations centre was already "a tornado" of activity, he recalls. The usual complement of three duty officers had swelled to close to a dozen as emergency call-ins arrived, dividing and subdividing the workload as they came. There was still more than enough for everyone to do.

The first step was to figure out exactly where the plane had gone down. At sea? On land? Land would be better for the search and rescue operation, Brisebois knew. When what is known in the trade as a "sudden impact event" happens on land, you know the plane isn't going anywhere. It's simply a matter of figuring out where the plane is, then getting your rescue and recovery teams in and your casualties out. It isn't nearly as simple as that in reality, of course, but it's a piece of cake compared to coping with a crash at sea.

Pinpointing the location where a plane has gone down at sea is just the first step, Brisebois explains. You then have to drop indicators into the water and use computers to plot the speed and direction of the wind and currents to figure out where the drift might take any survivors. "In the water," he says, "the last known information we have about the location is only as good as the time it was received."

Brisebois looked around at the increasingly chaotic scene inside the coordination centre as his officers continued to try to determine where the plane had crashed, dispatch planes and boats to look for it, alert other emergency services and deal with the tidal wave of telephone calls. There were so many calls coming in that it was already impossible for his officers to find a free line to call out to get critical information or to direct searchers where to go. Most of the callers were journalists: from Australia, Africa, Asia, Europe, the U.S., everywhere. Somehow, they'd not only managed to get the centre's published numbers but had also tracked down all of its unlisted numbers as well. Even Brisebois's private cell phone was ringing with calls from reporters. While he understood immediately that this was a major international event and that part of his job was to release to the public whatever limited information he had, he also knew he had to find a way to section off all of the many jobs that needed to be done, including dealing with the media.

He hived off a corner just beyond the operations centre for the six military public affairs officers who'd been called in to handle the media inquiries. He rerouted those calls there. By morning, the demand for information would become so intense, he would have to assemble another 10 sailors just to answer phones and act as runners. Sean Kelly, a sailor who'd been watching sonar scans in a nearby building, was one of them. "When I got to the public relations area, the phone was ringing off the hook," he recalls. "I said, 'Do you want me to answer that?' They gave me a sheet of information and said, 'Sure.'" It was the first time Kelly had ever talked to a reporter. Over the course of the next sleepless 48 hours, he would do 86 interviews with media outlets from around the world.

Although the arrival of the public affairs officers helped ease the burden on his other officers, Brisebois had another problem to deal with. He realized he'd be hard pressed to manage a massive search of tiny St. Margarets Bay — likely involving military planes and helicopters, navy, coast guard and coast guard auxiliary, as well as volunteer fishing and other vessels — from the windowless depths of RCC headquarters in downtown Halifax.

Luckily, the captain of HMCS *Preserver*, a naval supply ship, radioed in at 11:40 p.m. His vessel just happened to be conducting exercises near the mouth of Halifax Harbour, so the ship was nearby and ready to join in the search — an unexpected bit of good news, for the *Preserver* boasted a large sick bay and a helicopter landing pad. If the RCC had had to call the vessel out from its dock at Canadian Forces Base Halifax, it would have taken at least two more hours for the ship to even be ready to leave the jetty. If the plane had indeed crashed into the ocean, the *Preserver*'s presence could be vital. Brisebois called the captain of the *Preserver*, delegating to him the role of on-site commander. "It was an unorthodox thing for us to do," he admitted later, "but it's in line with my philosophy, which is to section off duties wherever possible. Instead of having 40 people calling us to get their taskings, they'd be calling him." The captain of the *Preserver* agreed to report back to RCC once an hour.

Finally, Brisebois turned to the bookshelves in his office. The RCC had long ago developed thick binders of contingency plans and standard operating procedures for dealing with major marine and air disasters. "Usually, they gather dust, and then get hauled out every two or three years when we update them," Brisebois explains. "But because I'd only been assigned to the Maritimes in January" — he'd previously been based on the west coast — "I had read the air plan in March as part of my own familiarization process." And in June, RCC had conducted a marine disaster "paper" exercise — a ferry sinking between Sydney and Port aux Basques — to test its major marine disaster plan too.

The air plan included provisions for invoking what is known as MAJAID, or Major Air Disaster, a massive military response that included the army supplying a fully equipped field hospital that could be dropped into a remote location from the air. Given that he still couldn't be sure how big a disaster he was dealing with, Brisebois called his boss in Ottawa to ask him to invoke MAJAID, for the first time ever. Within minutes, soldiers at CFB Trenton in Ontario were being recalled to their base to get the field hospital ready to fly it to Halifax.

Meanwhile, the various ships and aircraft called out

by the RCC, as well as the fishermen who were volunteering to join them, made their way to Flight 111's last known position to begin scouring what still could be a huge swath of territory. Staff at RCC urgently continued to try to narrow the search field, plotting the coordinates of the 911 calls that were still coming in from local residents to see whether they could use their locations to get a fix on exactly where the plane might have gone down. But the coordinates didn't line up. An officer called the air traffic controller who'd handled the Swissair flight, taking him step by step through his conversation with the pilots, looking for clues to where the aircraft might have ended up. The pilots had talked about going back out to sea to dump fuel. Was there any indication they had actually done that?

While all this was going on, other officers began working their way through their list of emergency contacts with relentless efficiency. In any emergency, there is a pre-arranged notification tree to make sure everyone who needs to know about an accident finds out as quickly as possible.

Within minutes of getting their call, officials at Halifax's Queen Elizabeth II Health Sciences Centre, the region's largest hospital, began clearing emergency rooms of non-critical cases, preparing blood supplies, filling trolleys with hundreds of clean sheets and johnny shirts, and calling in all off-duty doctors and nurses to prepare for what everyone assumed would be incoming survivors.

Grant Lingley, the communications director for Nova Scotia's emergency health services dispatch centre, was near the top of the notification tree. He had just finished reading a bedtime story to his children when his pager went off. It simply said: "Airliner down with 100 souls on board please contact Comm. Centre ASAP." Within half an hour, the dispatch centre's own notification system had kicked into action too, sending 14 local ambulances hurtling toward some still ill-defined location along St. Margarets Bay and putting dozens more from as far away as Digby — nearly 200 miles from Halifax — on standby in case they were needed wherever the plane had gone down.

That uncertainty was still the problem. Ambulances, fire trucks, emergency vehicles and media vehicles began to cluster at strategic spots around the Bay — at SeaSpa, Northwest Cove, Bayswater Beach — waiting for someone to find the plane or figure out where it had gone down.

Finally, shortly after midnight, the Canadian Coast Guard vessel *Sambro* radioed from its location about five miles offshore from Peggys Cove. It had detected a strong smell of aircraft fuel.

Thursday, September 3, 1998

Owl's Head, Nova Scotia
12:30 a.m. ADT

Why was he doing this? To save lives? But what if there were no lives out there to save? It was a plane crash, for heaven's sake. People don't just walk away from plane crashes. Would he end up "another rubber-necker, a looker-on," one more ghoulish gawker at the scene of a tragedy? Perhaps he should turn around and go back to the dock.

Robert Conrad had just passed the sheer rock face at Owl's Head and turned the *Jubilee* toward the southwest, in the direction where his marine radio told him other fishing boats were already gathering. Over the VHF, he heard the voice of the captain of the *Preserver* calling for another flare, and then, he remembers, "the sky lit up. I could have turned off my instruments — it was like daylight out there." He could see the other vessels, perhaps a dozen or more, many of them his friends and fishing partners, off in the distance. He was about 45 minutes from them now.

Plenty of time to think. Time to turn back if he couldn't come up with a logical rationale for going out there. It had all seemed so simple, almost instinctive in the first few minutes after he'd woken up to the news on the TV. How long had he been sleeping? Steve Murphy, the anchor of the *ATV Evening News,* was on the screen.

Conrad wondered what he was doing on TV at this hour. Murphy seemed to be talking about some sort of disaster, an air disaster. "I remember I wasn't too together at that point and I was listening intently, trying to understand what he was saying, when I heard him say 'Blandford.' That raised the hair on the back of my neck, I tell you."

He woke Peggy, his wife, to tell her he was going to take the *Jubilee* and head out to the scene to see if he could help. He hadn't thought about what it was he could do, hadn't paused to consider the reality that there likely wouldn't be anyone to help. It was just what fishermen did for each other and anyone else at peril on the sea.

When he arrived at Seldon Miller's fish plant in Northwest Cove where his boat was tied up, several other fishing boats from the cove were already gone. Miller and a few other men were in the office listening to the marine radio. One of them called out to ask whether Conrad would be willing to take some newspeople out with him.

"No, thank you," Conrad said quickly. Perhaps too quickly. "It was one murky black night out there, the pitchest of old black nights," he recalls, and he certainly could have used an extra pair of eyes as he negotiated his way past the inner rock and through the northeast shoal. But he didn't need passengers, certainly not the kind who would be there just to take pictures of an accident. But what was his reason for going out there tonight? Was he really any better than the reporters and cameramen looking to hitch a ride?

He'd heard one report of survivors on his radio, but then that had quickly been changed to a request for a body bag. Everyone else was talking about bodies. On the radio now he heard the skipper of the *Island Venture*, a fishing boat out of Tancook, talking to the captain of the *Preserver*. The skipper had radioed in that he'd found a body and he wanted someone to come take it off his boat.

Immediately. "You could tell he was a wreck emotional-ly," Conrad recalls. "He gave his position and then he just lost it. I remember his expression. He said: 'I can't take this. I'm getting out of here.' Whatever it was he'd seen shook him so badly he was totally rendered useless for a while. It took him a good 15 minutes to get it together and get back to it. And I thought, 'What can I do?' I remember praying for a purpose for me being out there. And then my mind went back to this program I'd seen on TV a while back. There was this lady in Ontario, a retired woman with a deep sense of compassion for people who were dying in the hospital with no one around in their final moments. She'd made it her mission to make sure that no one would ever die alone. And I thought to myself, 'If I can find even a victim who has perished and be with them so that they're not alone in the darkness on the water, then that is something I can do that would make my going out there worthwhile.' "

And then suddenly, he was in the middle of the crash site. He turned on the *Jubilee*'s spotlight and cast it over the heaving waters. "The pieces were so small," he mar-vels. "Thousands of bits and pieces, nothing bigger than the size of a *Time* magazine as far as you could see." He was grateful he had at least ended up in a section of the debris field with fishermen he knew. He shone his light over at the *DCD Rocker*, 130 feet off to one side. "I could see that they had a body cradled to the side of the boat and they were having trouble lifting it aboard."

Conrad began doing circles of the area to see what he could find, to see who he could be with in their final moments.

Zurich
5:29 a.m. CET

"I'd like to speak to someone there who can tell me about the Swissair plane that's crashed off Nova Scotia." The telephone call, to Swissair's main switchboard in Zurich from a reporter at the Toronto *Star* 59 minutes after the plane crashed, was the first Swissair's European headquarters had heard there was a problem with one of their flights. The *Star*'s reporter didn't know the flight number, and the airline itself had received no notification of a problem with any of its planes.

Still, the telephone operator quickly called Martin Burri, Swissair's duty manager for operations, who immediately attempted to make contact with the company's three planes then in the air over North America — Flights 103, 107 and 111 — to make sure they were okay. But even before he could complete those checks, he switched on the television set in the control centre. At 5:48 a.m., as he noted in his log, CNN was reporting there had been an "SR (Swissair) accident."

Burri immediately called Beat Schär, the airline's chair of emergency organization. While Swissair had long had an in-house plan for coping with a crash involving one of its planes, that plan had recently been updated to comply with newly toughened American laws. Two years earlier, in the wake of the terrorist bombing of Pan Am 103 over Lockerbie, Scotland, the U.S. Congress passed the 1996 Aviation Disaster Family Assistance Act, whose goal was to force airlines to treat families more humanely and compassionately after an accident. Originally intended only to apply to domestic air carriers, the law had been extended in 1997 to cover any airline whose flights began or ended in the United States. Swissair had filed its official disaster response plane with U.S. authorities in June 1998.

Swissair Flight 111 would be the first major test of both the new law and also Swissair's own internal disaster response plan.

Redding, Connecticut
11:30 p.m. EDT, September 2

"Did you hear this shit about Swissair?" It was Miles Jr. calling from New York. He'd gone to the city for a few days to visit his uncle Pierce. Miles Gerety's 20-year-old son would be off to the University of Denver in less than a week to begin his freshman year, so this was a last pre-college chance for him to spend some time with his uncle and aunt as well as his cousin, Little Pierce, 32, who happened to be in New York for a while too.

As soon as he caught the urgent tone in his son's voice, Miles Gerety tried to clear away the sleep fog. He had gone to bed earlier than usual because he had a trial scheduled to begin the next morning and he planned to get up at dawn to psych himself for the courtroom. He'd only just fallen asleep.

"Pierce's plane may have crashed," Miles Jr. said again. "It's on the television."

Gerety knew his brother was flying back to Geneva this week, but he didn't know when. Were they certain? They weren't. At least not absolutely. Little Pierce had driven his father to the airport a few hours earlier; he'd been booked on two earlier flights and finally been bumped to Flight 111.

Maybe he'd been bumped again, Gerety suggested hopefully.

While his son and nephew hurried out to Kennedy to see what they could learn there, Gerety turned on the television, listened to the first sketchy, unhelpful reports, then decided to see what he could find out from the Internet. Nothing there either. Finally, he called his brother Tom, who had gone home to Amherst, to warn him about what his son had told him. And then his brother Peter too.

Shortly after midnight, Miles Jr. telephoned his father from the Crown Room Club, Delta's passenger lounge, in Terminal 3 at Kennedy. Though officials there were still scrambling to set up an emergency service centre for family members and the airline was refusing to release any information, Miles — "a schmoozer like his father" Gerety says proudly — had managed to talk a New York City cop into letting him take a look at the passenger manifest. Pierce's name was on it.

Gerety woke up his wife, Silvia, and their other son, Patrick, and they drove the 15 minutes to his mother's house. "I wanted to tell her in person," he explains. By the time they arrived, however, she already knew. She'd woken up shortly before midnight and turned on the television to see what was on.

By the time they got to her house, Helen Gerety had already telephoned Pierce's wife, Marie, in Brooklyn. Marie, Gerety recalls, was hysterical. He immediately decided they should all get in the car and drive to Pierce and Marie's house in Brooklyn.

He'd call his office from there in the morning to see about getting that trial postponed.

New Harbour, Nova Scotia
1:30 a.m. ADT

"Can you take us out there?" Rob Gordon could see right away that the two fishermen standing by the wharf at New Harbour were doubtful. "We'll pay," he added quickly.

"How much?" one of them asked just as quickly.

"A hundred and fifty," Gordon improvised.

"Ah—" The man glanced out at the choppy seas. It was rough out there. It would be a long night. He didn't say anything, but Gordon could see he was unimpressed by the offer.

"An hour," Gordon amended quickly. "We'll pay you a hundred and fifty dollars an hour."

"Let's go, then," the fisherman answered without missing a beat. "Let's go."

Gordon and his cameraman, Doug Carmichael, quickly gathered up the camera gear and loaded it onto the 28-foot fishing vessel. Gordon only hoped none of the other reporters had noticed that they had slipped away from the pack, hoped none of them got the same idea he had. A few hours earlier, while he was still driving from his home to the CBC newsroom in Halifax, the office had confirmed that it was a Swissair flight with perhaps hundreds aboard. Gordon, who'd briefly gone to school in Europe and who had done his fair share of travelling there, understood the implications immediately. "Swissair was a strong airline," he says. "People used to rearrange their schedules just so they could fly on a Swissair flight. And this one was from New York to Geneva. I knew right away there would be important people on that flight."

By the time he arrived at the newsroom shortly before 11 p.m., his boss, Mike Pietrus, was already there. So was Geoff D'Eon, Gordon's first boss, who'd taught him the "voodoo" of TV news reporting. D'Eon had been working late editing sequences for *This Hour Has 22 Minutes*, a popular satirical sketch comedy show where he worked as a senior producer. As soon as he heard about the crash, D'Eon dropped what he was doing and volunteered to help out with the coverage. "You can't kill a news guy," Gordon says admiringly. Other reporters and cameramen began arriving shortly after Gordon did.

At this point, they still knew very little about the story, including where the plane had crashed. "Let's get a boat," Gordon urged Pietrus. "Let's charter a boat from here and head down there right away."

No one had to say out loud what Gordon was thinking. Westray. When the mine exploded in 1992, the police had very quickly cordoned off the site and the surrounding area, making it impossible for journalists to verify independently what authorities were saying. And — at Westray at least — the authorities had often been lying. If the plane had gone down on the water, their best bet was to approach it from the ocean, slip in before the police had time to set up their no-go zones and see for themselves what was going on. Here, Gordon's mental Rolodex proved invaluable. He knew a guy named Eric Haynes. Haynes and his wife ran a charter service called New Dawn Charters out of Purcell's Cove on Halifax's Northwest Arm. Gordon called him at home. At first, Haynes thought Gordon must be joking. "I had to call him three times before he finally agreed to go out," Gordon remembers. "By the end, I was practically pleading with him. 'Look,' I said, 'This is real, it's happening, we're going to need you for two days.'"

By the third call, Haynes realized this was no joke. He and his wife, Ellen, were also members of the coast guard auxiliary and they'd just been asked to join in the search. Gordon could come with them if he wished, he said. But since it would take time for Haynes to get to his boat and get it ready, and then several more hours after that to motor to the scene in his Cape Islander, the *New Dawn III*, it was decided that Gordon and Carmichael should drive down to St. Margarets Bay to see what he could learn from shore while Lisa Taylor and Dave Archibald, another reporter-cameraman team, would go with Hayneses.

Gordon and Carmichael drove first to Bayswater Beach, largely because they'd found out that fire trucks from volunteer brigades all over St. Margarets Bay had assembled there to await further instructions. So had ambulances. As Carmichael gathered footage of the firemen in full gear standing by their vehicles, Gordon could see off in the far distance in the night sky a Labrador helicopter hovering over the water, its spotlights casting an eerie glow on the sea below. But he could see no sign of an airplane. Gordon wasn't the only reporter on site. There were, it seemed, dozens of them there already. And every one of them ended up doing the same thing he was: interviewing local bystanders while they anxiously waited for some official, or even unofficial, word about where the plane had gone down and what had happened to it. What did you see? What did you hear? No one had seen anything, but plenty of people had heard something: a sound like "low thunder, louder but not stronger," that rattled windows and shook roofs. Some people even reported feeling a pressure on their ears from the intensity of the noise. While Gordon was conducting his interviews, the CBC *Newsworld* satellite truck arrived from Halifax and began setting up shop near the church so Gordon could feed his videotape and live reports back to the station.

Finally, just before 1:30 a.m., word spread that the RCMP and local emergency measures authorities had established their command post at Peggys Cove. Even though it would not turn out to be the closest area of land to where the plane went down, the choice made sense for a number of reasons. For starters, there was only one road into and out of the tiny cove, which is home to just 60 families. Controlling access to it would be fairly easy. And because Peggys Cove was one of Nova Scotia's most popular tourist destinations, it already had more amenities and facilities than any other comparable community in the Bay. The restaurant and gift shop could easily be turned into a command centre, and the tour bus parking lot could accommodate helicopter landings. When the sun came up and — everyone hoped — the fog and cloud lifted, the cove also commanded an unobstructed view across the head of St. Margarets Bay and out into the ocean. Though no one probably considered it at the time, there was another good reason for choosing Peggys Cove as what would become the visual reference point for the disaster. Its lighthouse, one of the most photographed tourist attractions in Canada, would serve as part of the backdrop for television news reports beamed round the world. In the months after the crash, provincial tourism officials would report a spike in interest in visiting Nova Scotia. Much of it would come from people who'd seen the news reports about Swissair from Peggys Cove.

But no one at this moment was thinking about the implications of where the command post would be located. Instead, everyone at the Bayswater location — the volunteer firefighters, ambulance drivers, satellite truck operators, reporters — urgently began packing up for the 35-mile drive to Peggys Cove. Everyone except Rob Gordon. "I was about to follow when I saw these two parachute flares go off," he recalls. He realized from earlier stories he had done that they were search and rescue flares. Perhaps they'd found something out there. How far out was it? Not far. A few miles, maybe. Thirty seconds later, the sky lit up again with two more flares. And then two more. There was definitely something important going on, he thought. Gordon telephoned his office and told them about the command centre being set up in Peggys Cove. "I don't want to go," he said. "I want to get a boat." Gordon knew there would be fishing boats tied up at the government wharf at New Harbour just a few miles down the road. He could go there, perhaps find a fisherman — despite the hour, everyone on the Bay seemed to be out and about on this night — to take him to where he'd seen the flares. His bosses agreed; they'd send another reporter to the command centre.

Finding a fisherman to agree to take them to the scene had been the easy part, Gordon realized now. Getting there would be more problematic. The lightweight boat was being buffeted and bounced as it made its way through 6- to 10-foot swells. "I began to think maybe it was all going to be too much for his boat."

Halfway out, Gordon saw what he at first thought must be lights from the houses on Tancook Island. But he suddenly realized it wasn't. There were already dozens of boats off in the distance — coast guard vessels, fishing boats — all with their spotlights playing over the water. Overhead hovered two navy Sea King helicopters. More flares were lighting up the sky. "They looked like yellow harvest moons," Gordon remembers. "They'd shine directly down, creating these weird shadows on the water." Beyond the boats and the helicopters, Gordon could make out the silhouette of HMCS *Preserver*.

"Can you turn on the VHF?" Gordon asked the fisherman. The radio crackled to life.

"I found somebody. I got a survivor! —"

"I need a body bag —"

"More body bags over here."

"It's not a survivor."

"We got a piece of the plane."

The response from the disembodied voice of Cmdr. Rick Town, the captain of the *Preserver*, was calming, almost soothing, Gordon says. "It was, 'Yes, we hear you. Don't worry, we'll get to you.'"

As they drew closer, Gordon could smell the distinctive odour of JP4, jet fuel, hanging in the air. He could see what looked like pieces of airplane too.

The fisherman began to get nervous. "If we hit one of those things, it will go right through the boat," he warned Gordon. He cut back on the throttle and, as the rain spit down on them, they began to drift through what looked like a floating field filled with debris. "Most of it was surreal," Gordon says, "like being on another planet, another world. It was not anywhere where I lived."

They saw a life raft floating past them, empty. "We should get that," Gordon said to Carmichael, but he was already filming it. Since it was half-inflated, Gordon imagined there could be survivors nearby. He and Carmichael began to use the camera's sun-gun floodlight to search the waters around the boat for any sign of life. Instead, they saw pieces of people: arms, legs. What looked like a baseball cap floating nearby turned out, on closer inspection, to be someone's liver.

Carmichael didn't film the body parts. As they had been getting on the boat back in New Harbour, he and Gordon had made a pact "not to do anything we'll regret," Gordon says now. "We knew there was a real good chance our stuff would be going out live on the satellite and, once it's on the bird, every news organization in the world would have access to it. It would be in the ionosphere forever. The only way we could control what went out was by controlling what went into the camera."

Gordon knew too that the only way he could remain in control of his emotions was to not look too long or too closely at what he was seeing. "I look, I see, I look away." He'd learned that lesson years ago as a young reporter covering the trial of a woman who had gruesomely beaten and murdered a toddler. "At the break one day, I made the mistake of asking the Crown to let me have a look at the morgue slab pictures he'd entered into evidence. He showed me. I couldn't stop looking. I'd just had my first kid then. Those pictures have haunted me ever since. I still dream about them sometimes. So ever since then, I've trained myself so that, once I know what something is, I move on. If you look too long, you'll never be able to let it go."

It was time to get to work. He got out his GPS indicator to try to pinpoint the boat's exact location.

"Where are we?" he asked the fisherman as he fiddled with the device.

"Off Pearl," the fisherman replied.

Pearl Island! Gordon suddenly remembered he'd been on this very spot on the water only a few days ago. When had it been? Sunday? Three and a half days ago now. It had all seemed so different then. They were at the spot where he and Jeffers had been when he cut the engine on his Nordica 20 and raised the sail. Just off Pearl. A glorious sunny summer day.

He picked up his cell phone, called the CBC newsroom and asked them to put him through to *Newsworld* editor Dan Leger. "I can tell you what's going on or I can give you a first-person account of what I'm seeing," he told Leger.

"First person," Leger answered quickly and patched him through to the *Newsworld* host, who was then broadcasting live from Vancouver. "Rob, tell me where you are and what you see," the host began after introducing Gordon as the CBC's reporter on the scene.

After giving his location, Gordon described clearly

but discreetly the carnage he was seeing. "When I look out the port side, I can see a half-inflated life raft," he explained. "But there are no signs of survivors there."

Or anywhere else, for that matter. Best not to think about that yet, Gordon thought.

Emergency Committee Room, Swissair Operations Centre, Zurich Airport
7:30 a.m. CET

Beatrice Tschanz stepped past the hordes of reporters, photographers and camera crews milling about in the grey dawn outside the building where Swissair pilots and cabin crews normally assembled for their pre- and post-flight briefings. CNN, Sky, Swiss TV. How had they all found out about this before she had? She noticed the faces of the local reporters. They were as shocked as she was. For Swiss journalists, she instinctively knew, the crash of a Swissair airplane was more than just another news story: it was a slap in the face to their notion of what Switzerland was as a country. She understood that, because she felt the same thing. A former Swiss newspaper editor, she'd joined SAir Group, Swissair's parent company only two years ago. "There will be a press briefing at eight o'clock," she announced, then hurried into the building. Nothing had been scheduled yet, of course, but she knew it would be critical for the airline to answer questions, and quickly.

Tschanz, the company's high-powered 54-year-old head of corporate communications, had originally planned to sleep in that morning. She'd earned it. She'd spent the previous evening entertaining a group of visiting Turkish journalists and hadn't gotten home until after eleven. Since she wasn't scheduled to be on call for overnight public relations emergencies, she'd turned off her cell phone and almost immediately fell sleep. "I slept like a bear," she says now. "I always do. I'm not what you call a morning person, so it's sometimes hard for me to wake up."

She says that, when she did finally rouse herself, "I had the feeling that the whole house was ringing. There were phones going off in the bedroom, my fax line was ringing, there was ringing, ringing everywhere." She picked up the closest phone.

"There's been an MD-11 crash, Beatrice, you have to come immediately," said one of her colleagues in investor relations.

"No, it can't be true."

"Come quickly," he repeated. It was 5:45 a.m.

"For two seconds," Tschanz says now, "I had to think: am I awake or am I asleep? I switched on CNN. They already had an infographic of Swissair on the screen. I thought, it's true. Then I had a real 10 seconds of panic. I knew that communications would be of the utmost importance today. This would be the most professionally and personally demanding day of my life. Could I do it? Then I took myself to order. 'Now calm down, girl,' I said. 'You have to function well.' I woke up my husband. I said, 'My God, the nightmare has become true.' Then I took something dark from the closet. I forgot to do my hair. It was a 20-minute drive from my house to the airport. I got there in seven."

Inside, passing through the airline's crewing centre, she could see the shock on the faces of pilots and cabin crews as they arrived from their overnight flights from North America and South Africa and heard the first, sketchiest outlines of what had happened to Flight 111. This would all have to be explained to them too, she knew. And at least as quickly as to the outside world. People sometimes forgot that internal communications were as important as getting your message out to the rest of the world. Indeed, the airline's future could depend on those crews continuing to function at a high level in spite of the disaster.

Most of the other members of the airline's 12-member emergency committee — plus all of SAirGroup's top executives, including Hannes Goetz, the chair of SAir's board of directors, Philippe Bruggisser, the CEO of SAir Group, and Jeffrey Katz, the CEO of Swissair itself — were already gathered inside the emergency committee room. "What were the chances that all of this huge, global company's top executives would be in the same city at the same time?" Beatrice Tschanz thought to herself. That, at least, was good.

The mood among everyone around the table was the same: shocked, stunned, utterly disbelieving. Matthias Mölleney, Swissair's executive vice-president of human resources, had been at his son's school for a meeting the night before. Afterwards he'd ended up talking with some of the other parents about their fall vacation plans. One was going to the Caribbean, another to the U.S. One woman, seated beside Mölleney, confessed she wasn't planning to travel anywhere. She was desperately afraid of flying. "You have to fly Swissair," he urged her. "It's completely reliable. I'd put our entire senior management team on the same plane and not have the least worry that anything would happen to them. Fly Swissair and nothing can go wrong. I guarantee it." But this morning, as he looked around the room at the very executives whose safety he had been so absolutely confident about the night before, he confesses now, "I thought to myself, 'You should never say things like that.' "

By 7 a.m., chaos reigned in the cramped, windowless committee room. All the members of the emergency committee, including everyone from the airline's executive vice-president of operations to the vice-presidents of maintenance, flight safety and cabin crews were seated around the oval table in the centre of the room. Most of the dozen telephones on the table were ringing, making it virtually impossible to know which one to answer. A phalanx of legal, security and marketing specialists clustered around another table at the far end of the room while the airline's top executives found makeshift seats for themselves on tables lining another wall. There was barely space for anyone to move. The walls were already almost completely papered over with taped-up sheets of flip chart paper covered with handwritten to-do lists and flow charts. One committee member was talking to the Rescue Coordination Centre in Halifax; someone else was on the phone to Delta officials in Atlanta, who had taken charge of the immediate North American response; someone else was monitoring CNN on the TV that had been set up in one corner. Swiss radio was playing in the background, just below the din of frantic conversation.

"CNN says it went down seven nautical miles off Peggys Cove," someone shouted.

"That's not my information," said Captain Christian Stussi, the chief pilot for the airline's MD-11 fleet, who was talking into another telephone. "My information is that it was 70 miles."

The truth was that no one knew much yet.

Reality was so much different from what Jürg Schmid had expected it to be. Swissair's head of flight safety, who'd helped train the airline's emergency committee by devising simulated crash response exercises, had waited impatiently for his early-morning caller to give him the code word. "We always used code words," he explains. "We'd begin the phone call with, 'This is . . . and then say the exercise code name so they'd know they were being called in for an exercise." But his caller this morning didn't use any code name. It wasn't until he turned on the radio during the rushed drive to the airport and heard the sombre classical music the station played only to indicate someone very important had died — instead of the Swiss folk music usually heard between five and six in the morning — that he finally realized for certain this wasn't an exercise.

Not like Bombay. In April 1998, Schmid had put the emergency committee through its paces. Some of them had grumbled when he refused to tell them exactly when the exercise would take place. We have important meetings, they said. But it wouldn't be an emergency if you knew when it would happen, he told them. In the end, the call had gone out to the committee members' emergency beepers shortly after 10 p.m., at exactly the time when a real Swissair 747 was scheduled to take off from Bombay for Zurich. In the exercise, an engine fire had broken out just as the plane was taxiing down the runway for takeoff. The pilots decided to abort the takeoff at the last second, but the big jet overshot the runway, plowing into a populated area and bursting into flame.

Schmid, as the mastermind of the simulation scenario, had dribbled information out to the emergency committee members and forced them to respond to events as they happened. There have been some injuries among passengers, crew and those on the ground, he told them at one point. Then, a few minutes later, he added that some of the injured had died. And then, a few minutes after that, he provided the first hint that the aircraft had been carrying dangerous goods in its cargo hold. Soon after, the flight engineer, played by Schmid himself, telephoned the emergency committee, supposedly from Bombay. "I have to make this quick," he told them. "I'm being arrested."

The idea was to teach the members of the emergency committee to expect — and react to — the unexpected.

But in real life, Schmid was beginning to realize on the morning of September 3, even the expected would turn out to be fraught with unanticipated twists and complications.

The airline's disaster response plan, for example — which had been updated three months earlier and filed with both the U.S. Departments of Transportation and the National Transportation Safety Board in order to comply with tougher, family-centred legislation passed by the U.S. Congress — called on the airline to immediately notify each passenger's next of kin in the event of an accident. But how could the airline now be sure who'd actually boarded the plane in New York? The 80 volunteers on Swissair's new Special Assistance Team, which had been set up to deal with the emergency needs of family members, which finished their final training sessions only the day before. The training could not prepare them for the reality. Now, while some members of the hastily reassembled team compared information from reservations in the airline's computer system with the names of those who'd officially boarded the plane in New York, others tracked down copies of the I-94 forms all non-U.S. citizens have to file with American authorities when they arrive in the U.S. Those forms include spaces for people to indicate where they plan to stay while in the United States. In the case of non-U.S. citizens, that could help the airline to track down next of kin. Provided, of course, that the person listed on the passenger manifest, or passenger list, was really the person who had boarded the plane. It wasn't unknown for people to occasionally pass their tickets on to someone else. To further complicate the difficulties of tracking down the names of the real passengers, the spellings of names often varied from form to form. The reservations system, for example, allowed for only so many characters per name, meaning some longer or hyphenated names had to be truncated, and because the names were entered using capital letters only, they were often missing accents and other critical distinguishing information. Then there were the human errors, such as misspellings.

Yet finding out who was really on the plane — and quickly — was becoming more urgent by the moment. Although airline officials had wasted little time in putting their emergency family assistance plan into action — within an hour of learning that the plane had gone down, Swissair and Delta had each mobilized dozens of telephone operators in Zurich, Geneva and Atlanta and had set up toll-free hotlines for families to call — they had little information to share with the thousands of desperate callers (48,000 on September 3 alone) who wanted to know if their relative was on the plane. Instead, the operators began collecting from each caller whatever information they could — birthdates, home addresses, and so on — information that could ultimately link the caller with a passenger. Or, preferably, reassure a caller that a family member wasn't on the flight.

That brought up still another question no one on the special assistance team had considered before. In these complicated, modern times, exactly who is a next of kin? As Franz Bucher, Swissair's manager of the airline's emergency and care team, puts it: "Is it the wife or is it the girlfriend?" Or the first husband or the current one? The estranged brother or the close-as-brothers cousin? The ex-wife or the adult daughter?

The airline's policy was to notify one next of kin per passenger or passenger group and let that person take responsibility for notifying the others. But almost immediately officials were forced to make exceptions. The parents of one couple who died in the crash, for example, refused to speak to one another, so Swissair had to make sure both sets of parents were notified separately. And in several cases, more than one relative demanded to be the designated family member.

Identifying the appropriate next of kin was only the first step. All the operator could say on the telephone that first night was that a family member had been a passenger on Flight 111. In most countries, it would then be the responsibility of the police to formally notify the next of kin that their loved one was dead.

But, thanks to the proliferation of 24-hour-a-day news channels pumping out live pictures from the scene of the disaster, most of the world — including most of the victims' families — would learn the grisly truth that no one had survived Swissair Flight 111 long before the police could reach them with the news. And they would learn it from Swissair itself.

"I've scheduled a press conference for eight," Beatrice Tschanz had told Philippe Bruggisser as soon as she'd arrived in the emergency committee room. He nodded. Despite the company president's well-earned reputation for coldness, Tschanz could see he was deeply troubled by the human dimensions of what was happening to his airline. Though she certainly wouldn't have put it so bluntly, she realized that the genuineness of the emotion she saw on his usually boyish face would strike just the right tone with the Swiss public. And that would be critical for maintaining the airline's hard-won reputation as one of Switzerland's best-managed companies, a reputation that would be severely tested that day.

There would not be a lot that Bruggisser could say, of course, at this first press conference, but it would be important that he establish the company's message from the beginning. The approach, says Tschanz, was to be a simple three-pronged one: "Number one, that our first concern is for the victims and their families; number two, that Swissair supports and will cooperate fully with the official investigators; and number three, that we will communicate everything we know as quickly as and transparently as possible."

A solemn Bruggisser delivered precisely that message as he stood in front of the more than 200 journalists who'd crowded into a too-small classroom at the airline's training centre for the first of what Tschanz promised them would be hourly briefings on the developing situation. As cameramen climbed onto desks to get a better angle, Bruggisser confirmed that a Swissair MD-11 on a flight from New York to Geneva had gone down off Nova Scotia.

"Do you expect any survivors?" a reporter demanded as soon as he'd finished his initial statement.

Bruggisser knew that Canadian officials were adopting a stoic don't-abandon-hope approach in their search for survivors. But he knew too what reporter Rob Gordon was describing in his telephone reports from the crash site on CNN, and he'd also gotten his own briefings from emergency committee members about what they were hearing in their calls to Nova Scotia. He knew he couldn't hold out false hope.

"We don't expect survivors," he said quietly. "For all of us it is a very sad day. All our hearts and souls are with the friends and relatives of the people who lost their lives this morning."

Within minutes, CNN reported that Swissair officials were now confirming that there were no survivors from Flight 111.

Despite the reality that the world had shrunk to the point where comments at a press conference in Zurich — based at least in part on live televised reports from half a world away — could be flashed back to the originating location as accepted fact within minutes, Beatrice Tschanz knew the world was still too big, and Zurich too small, for the entire complex communications effort needed to cope with the crash to be handled from Zurich — or even by Swissair — alone. "We had a nice lady at Swissair in New York," she would explain later, "but we knew one person there would not be able to handle everything that needed to be done."

Jeff Katz had already made much the same point to Bruggisser. "Philippe, we've got to get a New York PR agency right away," he argued.

Though he would concede later that it might seem "macabre" to outsiders, Katz admits he was already dealing with the crash as a corporate crisis that would need skilful managing if the company's shareholders were to be protected from financial disaster. "I'm a pretty emotional guy, high strung," Katz would marvel later, "but I found myself in the first few days after the crash pretty much without emotions. There were things that had to be done and I did them. I'm a multi-tasker, I don't focus on just one thing, ever, and so I knew that while other people in the company were dealing with the human side of this, I had to be thinking about the business. We'd been having an excellent financial year, and I remember at one point turning to Lee Shave" — Swissair's British sales and marketing boss — "and saying, 'Lee, this is going to be bad for business, isn't it?' "

To try to make it less bad, Tschanz's staff swung into action on several fronts. In addition to promising to release whatever information they learned as quickly as possible, they also immediately replaced the airline's upbeat marketing-oriented Internet home page with one that simply announced that a Swissair plane had crashed off Nova Scotia and listing numbers for family members to call. And they cancelled a just-launched advertising campaign featuring the contented faces of sleeping people, which was supposed to promote Swissair as a "restful" way to fly.

Tschanz herself called a contact at Hill and Knowlton, the huge American public relations firm, to ask them to set up a press conference in New York for later in the day.

The question of who would speak there was a no-brainer. Jeff Katz was not only an American who could speak the language comfortably and well but he was also the airline's most senior official. Who better to bring reassurance both to the families of the victims and government regulators as well as to the investment community? The emergency committee decided that Katz should leave immediately with a squad of Swiss journalists and the airline's own emergency "go team," flying first to Halifax for on-site briefings and to meet with the media there, and then on to New York to hold a press conference in time for the U.S. networks' evening news shows.

New York City
2 a.m. EDT

Mark Rosset could hear the telephone ringing as he pushed open the door to his hotel room. The 27-year-old Swiss tennis player was an 11-year veteran of the professional tennis tour who'd won the gold medal in singles competition at the 1992 Olympics in Barcelona and was currently ranked number 47 in the world. He had just spent the evening relaxing with friends in Manhattan. It had been his first chance to unwind after the disappointment of the U.S. Open.

On Monday, he'd lost to Dominik Hrbatry of Slovakia in the tournament's opening round. Rather than return home to Switzerland immediately, he and his coach, Pierre Simsolo, had decided they should hang around New York for one more day to take advantage of the quality of practice opponents available during the Open. But the courts at the tournament site had been completely booked Tuesday, so they decided to stay in New York one more night, practise at Flushing Meadows on Wednesday and then catch the evening flight back to Switzerland. Simsolo booked them on Swissair Flight 111.

By the time they arrived back in their hotel room to pack, however, it was already late in the afternoon. "It would have been a big rush to get to the airport," Rosset would explain later, "so I decided to stay another night and go out to dinner with friends." Simsolo agreed.

Rosset picked up the telephone. It was a friend from New York. "You'd better turn on CNN," the friend said. "That plane you were supposed to be on just crashed."

Rosset would not be the only person watching television that night feeling "a little bit lucky, but strange, and a little bit afraid. When you realize you were that close to dying ..."

A week ago, Jill Tannenbaum Korn, a New Yorker who worked in PR in the health care field, had moved her reservation on Wednesday's Swissair Flight 111 forward a day. She says, "I decided I didn't really have to be there as early as I thought." Helio Takai, an experimental physicist at Brookhaven who said he travelled to Geneva aboard Flight 111 about a half-dozen times each year, was also scheduled to be on the flight that night but had cancelled a few weeks before so he could attend a retirement party for his mentor at the University of Pittsburgh. "Obviously, I am glad that I wasn't on the flight," he told reporters the next day. "Today, I keep thinking I could go home tonight and have a car crash on the William Floyd Parkway, and that would be it. You never know."

Like Rosset, he knew he was still alive and others weren't. After watching the reports on CNN for a few minutes, Rosset reached for the telephone again and dialled the number of his parents back in Switzerland.

Goldens Bridge
2:20 a.m. EDT

Lyn Romano stared at the 1-800 number on the screen. She knew she should call. Upstairs. In her purse. The itinerary. She should go get it first. Then she'd know for sure. She didn't want to know. She didn't want to call, either.

Ray would be telephoning her in a few hours. From his room in Geneva. He'd be pissed when he found out. He'd say she was overreacting. Again. There it was again, on the TV. Swissair ... Crash ... Flight from New York to Geneva ... She'd flipped on the late news a few hours earlier, more out of habit than anything. And there it was. Oh, my God, she thought absently, another plane crash. She hated flying ... Swissair ... Wait a minute! Ray was flying Swissair. Ray ...

She went upstairs to their bedroom, found the itinerary Ray had left for her, brought it back downstairs and put it beside her. She didn't read it. She couldn't.

Terminal 3, the man on the TV said. Was that where Ray's plane had taken off from? She couldn't remember. But she couldn't reach down and open up the paper with the itinerary on it either.

Instead, she reached for the telephone.

1-800-

Her whole body was shaking. She knew she was in shock. The woman at the other end of the line couldn't give her any information. There was no information yet. Perhaps in a few hours. Do you have family around? the woman asked. Lyn called her sister. "Mary Jo," she said, "can you turn on the TV? I have a feeling Ray's plane's gone down but I think I may be overreacting. Ray's right, you know. I always overreact. Can you come over?"

Twenty minutes later, Mary Jo was there.

"Read this, will you?" Lyn said, handing her the itinerary.

Mary Jo looked at it for a moment, then at the TV.

She began to cry.

Lyn was crying too. Everyone in her husband's family died too young, but always from heart attacks. Ray's father had died from a heart attack just before she and Ray got married. That's why she shoved baby Aspirin down his throat every day. So he wouldn't have a heart attack and die on her. And now—

Should they go to Kennedy? Lyn asked.

There was no point in going to Kennedy, her sister said. No one there would know what they needed to know. So Mary Jo kept calling the 1-800 number, but no one there seemed to have any information either.

Halifax
3:20 a.m. ADT

The loudspeaker in the ambulance bay finally crackled to life as dozens of doctors, nurses and other staff stood in clusters, waiting anxiously for the first casualties from the crash to arrive at the emergency entrance to the new QEII Health Sciences Centre in Halifax. They'd heard reports that some passengers had already been airlifted from the scene to CFB Shearwater for the 15-minute ambulance ride to the emergency room.

"We can handle as many as will come in," Chris Power, the vice-president of nursing services, had explained to the clutch of waiting reporters. "We have contingency plans to set up various stations throughout the hospital."

"We're preparing for the worst," added Dr. Doug Sinclair, the head of emergency services at the hospital.

Suddenly, the voice of the dispatcher broke in over the loudspeaker. "Thanks for coming," he said in a calm, clear voice. "You can go home."

The ambulance bay doors slowly closed and the faces of the waiting emergency staff, as Halifax *Daily News* reporter Chris Lambie described it the next day, "fell like hail from a black sky."

It was left to Power to tell reporters the obvious. "There are no survivors en route to us. We have called off our alert within the hospital."

Two minutes earlier, across town at the Rescue Coordination Centre in the naval dockyard, Major Brisebois had put in a call to his superiors in Ottawa, asking them to call off the MAJAID alert. They wouldn't be needing a mobile military hospital dropped on to the crash site tonight.

Still, Brisebois wasn't ready to give up hope yet. "We knew from everything we were hearing that this was a catastrophic hit," he says today. "In my own mind, I knew the likelihood of finding 150 people alive was not possible. But maybe there'd be one or two. The philosophy of search and rescue is always to err on the safe side, to give the benefit of the doubt to the possibility of survivors."

Cointrin Airport, Geneva, Switzerland
9:30 a.m. CET

The sign on the arrivals board at Cointrin Airport was deliberately bland, initially announcing only that Swissair Flight 111 had been "delayed," but then the message changed: those waiting for passengers should proceed straight to Swissair counters — "See Agent," it said. There, Swissair officials ushered more than 100 family members into a lounge normally used by businesspeople relaxing with coffee and newspapers while they waited for their flights to be called.

"We do not expect any survivors," Jean-Claude Ducrot, the airport chief of police, announced solemnly before he carefully began to read aloud each of the 215 names of those on the passenger list. "We share your grief," he said. "You must be strong."

As he spoke, reported Reuters News Agency, racking sobs and anguished cries "rose above the din of airport announcements of flight departures and arrivals and busy duty-free shops."

"He was there, oh, my God, he was there," cried one elderly man as he heard his son's name read out.

"I invited her, I paid for her ticket, and now she's dead," wept Lidia Picco, whose sister had been flying from Mexico to visit her in Geneva.

As religious leaders, nurses and social workers gathered in the lounge to offer what comfort they could to the families at the airport, 20 or so young men and women, members of Swissair's catastrophe unit, were already ensconced in an office on the fourth floor of the airport surrounded by banks of telephones, trying to answer questions no one wanted to ask.

Crash site
3:30 a.m ADT

He'd known as soon as they reached the crash site that there would be no one to save out here tonight. The devastation was so astounding, Harris Backman would find it impossible to speak about it, even months later, with anyone who wasn't there.

He and Steven had been the first fishermen to reach the crash site nearly two hours before. The debris field, a small, roiling patch of water and wreckage in the middle of the darkest nowhere, could have been a scene from a Hollywood disaster epic. Only worse. Much worse. Helicopters hovered at about 150 feet, their spotlights playing over the wreckage, the pieces all so small you had to wonder — Best not to do that now. The smell of aviation fuel was overwhelming at first, but he could get used to that. It was the rest that he'd never get used to.

The *Preserver* was already on the edge of the crash site when he and Steven arrived. Harris spoke to the captain, got his instructions. The instructions weren't complicated: look for survivors, call in what you find.

Things quickly became more complicated as dozens of other fishermen from up and down the coast, alerted by the noise, by the news on the television, by neighbours, descended to join in the frantic search for survivors. "Everything that could move was out that night," Harris would marvel later. Coast guard cutters, Cape Islanders, draggers, gillnetters. Forty-five-footers, 50-footers, 60. A passing Dutch-American cruise ship, the *Veen Dam*, had volunteered to join in the search. He could see it now, anchored just outside the debris field. Harris didn't count them then, but he'd guess later there might have been as many as 150 boats on the water that night. More than a dozen of them, he would note proudly, were flying the coast guard auxiliary pennant. They were all trained in search and rescue techniques. Unfortunately, neither the training nor the techniques would matter on this night.

In the eerie glow of his boat's spotlight, the object in the distance on the water looked to Robert Conrad like a doll. He manoeuvred the *Jubilee* closer, then used his eight-foot gaff to pull the object alongside. But it wasn't a doll.

It was a baby, "unlike any I had ever seen." The child's naked body had been so mangled in the crash that Robert Conrad couldn't tell whether it was male or female. Strangely, he would say later, he felt no particular horror at this moment. "It was just like it was a mechanical act," he would explain. "You function because you need to function." He lifted the child aboard, put the body on the deck and radioed his find to the *Preserver* on Channel 8, the channel set aside for the fishing boats to communicate with the on-scene commander.

"Flash your spotlight so we know your location," Cmdr. Rick Town radioed back calmly.

"There was something about his voice," Conrad says now. "No one who was not there can appreciate what the sound of the right human voice is. There was something about that voice that night that made you feel like you're doing the right thing, that everything would be okay. I took that sound with me and I remember thinking, if I ever find out who that person is I want to seek him out and thank him for what he did that night. I want to get acquainted with that voice." (When they did meet, two months later, at a seminar on the crash, Conrad says he was surprised to learn how hard-won Town's radio-controlled calm really was. "He had 50 men on the bridge with him and it was chaotic, he told me. They weren't trained to manage anything like this either. But then, none of us were.")

Whether it was Town's soothing voice or his own determination to do the right thing for those who had died that night, Conrad managed to keep the horror of it all at a distance at the time. As he waited for the *Preserver*'s barge-like recovery vessel to make its way to him, he looked down at the child lying on the deck, naked. "I thought it shouldn't be so undignified, even in death." He radioed the *DCD Rocker*, a fishing boat owned by a friend, which was circling nearby. "Do you have anything on board I can use to wrap a child's body in?" he asked. The crew came close, tossed him a blanket. "I didn't understand the significance of it yet, but I knew that this was Providence. I'm a great believer in Providence. I was out there alone. I had a limited capacity to help. That little child was the only one I could have managed to bring aboard. It was like an honour I had been bestowed, to be with that child at that moment." He took the blanket, spread the covering on the deck table he normally used to dress tuna, then gently picked up the child, put it on the blanket, wrapped it "reverently" in the covering and held it close. When the recovery vessel finally managed to manoeuvre alongside in the choppy waters, Conrad took one last look at the child in his arms, then handed it over to the waiting arms of the sailor from the *Preserver*. "It was a moment of significance for me," he says simply.

And then he went back to work. There was more, much more, to do. He could see a partly opened black suitcase floating in the water. He gaffed it over to the side of the *Jubilee*, but the soft-sided case was already too heavy with water and too slippery with fuel for him to bring it aboard. As it slipped away from his grasp, he noticed a piece of clothing sticking out of it. Perhaps at least he could salvage that, he thought. He used his gaff to hook it, pulled it in and dumped it on the deck. It was a woman's brown suede jacket. He didn't wonder whose it was then. "There wasn't time to think about the significance of anything that night," he says now. "You just did what you did. And the night passed."

After doing his first live report from the debris field for *Newsworld*, Rob Gordon remembers, "the world went nuts." It turned out he was the only reporter who'd managed to get out to the scene of the disaster, and every television network in North America and Europe wanted to interview him. Since he'd taken both his personal cell phone and his CBC cell phone with him on the boat, he says, "I'd start talking on one and the other one would go off." He did "live hits" from the scene for CNN, ABC, NBC and CBS as well as his continuing reports for *Newsworld*. As he talked, Carmichael continued to take carefully composed pictures of the scenes of carnage they were seeing all around them.

It was, in fact, in the middle of one of those live hits with CBC *Newsworld* anchor Norma Lee MacLeod that the immensity of the disaster he was seeing in front of him finally dawned on Gordon. Despite the evidence in front of him, Gordon had continued to imagine "we were still looking for a live person. But then Norma Lee asked me if there were any signs of life out there and I said no. And then it hit me. What I said was true. There was no life. There weren't going to be any survivors. The navy was still talking about a search and rescue operation, but the fact was that there had been 229 people aboard that plane. And every one of them was dead ... I'm not a religious person but, as that was setting in in my mind, I can remember the words to that Dylan song going through my head — 'knock, knock, knockin' on heaven's door.' I was thinking, right above me, there's all these people knocking on heaven's door."

Emergency Measures Organization, Halifax 3:30 a.m. ADT

Mike Lester knew right away that it would be bad. During his previous career in the RCMP, he'd worked one plane crash in Gander "where there were a hundred-odd casualties, so the magnitude wasn't lost on me." Ten years ago, after a 25-year Mountie career, he'd retired to take on the seemingly thankless job as head of Nova Scotia's Emergency Measures Organization. At the time, the EMO was in disarray. Volunteers had just botched a high-profile search for a little boy in woods near Halifax so badly that the case is still used at international emergency preparedness workshops as an example of how not to respond in a crisis. In the aftermath of that tragedy — the boy was eventually found dead — Lester replaced the EMO's executive director and slowly began to upgrade the operation.

Though it doesn't provide what Lester calls "first response" in the event of a major catastrophe, the EMO's role essentially is to coordinate everyone else's efforts. The EMO develops disaster plans and then trains those who will have to make them work in a crisis. The training often includes simulations of possible disaster scenarios, which bring together a cross-section of front-line emergency workers — police, firefighters, municipal planning officers, corporate safety officers, search and rescue volunteers — and put them through their paces in realistic situations. "We always work the worst-case scenario," explains Lester. "The power is out all across the province. Now what? It's not always an easy sell," he concedes. "People ask, 'How likely is that?' 'Never mind,' we tell them, 'we have to extend it to the end to make sure we can handle whatever comes along.'" Provincial EMO trainers have simulated floods, evacuations of senior citizens' homes, fires in industrial complexes, but never an airline accident. "We always figured an airline accident was too narrow an event for us to get the best bang for our training buck."

In fact, disasters of any sort, as Lester would be the first to happily say, are exceedingly rare in Nova Scotia. "Hurricanes occasionally threaten our coast, only to disappear out to sea," he says. "We've had emergency disaster assistance legislation on the books since 1990, but we've only used it once."

That's not to say something terrible couldn't happen: "All it would have taken was a couple of degrees in the difference and we would have been the one with the ice storm a few years back. Instead, Quebec got the worst of it. And we just sent aid."

The only way to make sure the very unlikely terrible event didn't turn into an even worse mess was to be prepared. Mike Lester thought he was. Lester was relaxing at his home in Musquodobit Harbour, an hour outside Halifax, when he'd received the call from the EMO duty officer shortly after 11 on September 2. His own first call as he pulled out of the driveway was to his wife. "I'd left in such a hurry, I needed to tell her where I'd gone." By the time he arrived at EMO's nondescript headquarters in a downtown office building overlooking Halifax Harbour, five regional EMO coordinators were already at work in the boardroom trying to cope with the constant incoming calls while not only finding outside telephone lines to coordinate the efforts of all the other various agencies already responding to the disaster but also getting supplies the front-line emergency workers would need to do their job. As at the RCC, most of the calls were from the international media. Luckily, however, the EMO boardroom had been equipped with wiring for extra phone lines they could drop from the ceiling in case they were needed.

They were certainly needed that night. But they couldn't just drop phone lines from the ceiling at Peggys Cove, Lester knew. Until the telephone company managed to scramble its workers to provide extra land lines for the command centre and other key sites — they were already on their way — he would have to depend on the local ham radio operators, "the unsung heroes of any disaster," to set up communications sites. "The amateur radio operators can run an aerial up a tree and be in business before you can bat an eye," Lester says with admiration. "And they work for coffee." By quarter to three, the local ham radio club's volunteers had established communication sites at Peggys Cove and Shearwater and were busy setting up a net control centre to coordinate the traffic among the sites.

Even as that network was being patched together, the province's chief medical officer, John Butt, arrived in Lester's office with his own lengthy — and esoteric — shopping list of supplies, equipment and material he needed immediately if not sooner: a morgue, portable X-ray equipment, refrigeration trucks to store the bodies, air changers, latex gloves, 1,000 body bags ...

One thousand body bags? The scope of the disaster he would be dealing with finally began to dawn on Lester. One thousand! Where do you find a thousand body bags in the middle of the night? Surprisingly, it wasn't all that difficult. Within minutes of the first news reports on CNN, a Georgia-based manufacturer of body bags that had previously done business with the provincial medical examiner's office telephoned to offer its products. Maybe he would have to call them back eventually, but, in the short term, Lester already knew where to start looking for body bags closer to home.

One EMO official contacted the Department of National Defence for body bags. Someone else called the provincial department of health to ask them to round up every available latex glove they could lay their hands on. No one worried about how much any of this would eventually cost. "If you have to ask, you don't understand the situation," Lester says simply. "We were operating at that point with an open chequebook. The important thing was to get what we needed and get it quickly." Besides, he adds, in this business "there's no such thing as an end to resources." The province already had a mutual assistance agreement in place with the other Atlantic provinces, and Lester had been in the process of negotiating a similar arrangement with the New England states. Even without a formal pact, however, offers of assistance came pouring in. By late morning, Lester would receive offers of aid from New York, New Jersey, Maine and Manitoba as well as the other Atlantic provinces.

The most immediate need was to find and build a temporary morgue to handle what now seemed certain to total several hundred bodies. The military quickly gave its approval to use Hangar B, a huge beige and white building at CFB Shearwater, on the outskirts of Dartmouth, that was used as a helicopter testing centre. The building was the right size, and the proximity of the air base would make it convenient for helicopters to ferry bodies from the crash scene.

Lester knew he'd still need to find someone to organize building the lab, transforming the cavernous empty hangar into a city of cubicles, complete with all the necessary plumbing and electrical services that Butt's pathologists and technicians would need to conduct autopsies. Chris Moir, the provincial department of transportation and public works emergency services coordinator, took responsibility for turning Hangar B into a fully functioning morgue. Even though Moir, like other departmental emergency officers, kept his own list of all the home phone numbers he thought he might need in the event of any emergency, he quickly discovered he would also need to be able to improvise to cope with the demands from the Swissair crash. And fast. At one point during the 24-hour-a-day construction of the morgue, for example, his crews ran out of plywood at six a.m. Moir called the Halifax Police Communications Centre. "Imagine somebody has broken into a building supply company," he began. "Who do you contact?" Within minutes police were calling the home numbers of their emergency contacts at building supply dealers, and not long after that, trucks loaded with plywood were rumbling out of a Beaver Homes lumber yard on the way to Shearwater.

He was not the only one to discover that morning that even the best laid plans are often no match for reality. When Red Cross director John Byrne, who had his own command centre and was working closely with the EMO, passed along the request for some refrigeration trucks to Halifax's emergency measures coordinator Barry Manuel, "I thought, no problem, I'll go to my resource book and I'll find five refrigerator units, no problem," Manuel says. Over the years, Manuel had carefully compiled a list of every type of resource he thought he might need in any conceivable type of emergency. "Do you need hotel rooms? Do you need shelters? Do you need people? And with what specialties?" But there was no listing in his book for suppliers of refrigerated vehicles. "What saved me," he would recall later, "was a firefighter standing outside my mobile command bus who overheard me say, 'Where am I gonna find five reefer trucks?'"

"Well, it's simple," the firefighter said. "My brother works at Agora Foods. I'll call him. He'll have their supervisor call you."

Within the hour, Manuel marvels, the company had dispatched five trucks to Shearwater and one to Peggys Cove. "Now, that," he would later tell a debriefing on emergency preparedness, "you can't put in a plan."

Goldens Bridge
4:30 a.m. EDT

He's not on the plane, Lyn told herself. He's not. At four-thirty, the Swissair rep finally called back. Ray Romano was listed as a passenger on Swissair Flight 111.

Wednesday! It had happened on a Wednesday, Lyn thought suddenly. She'd been born on a Wednesday, she'd met Ray on a Wednesday. And now Ray was dead. On a Wednesday.

"Darlene, it's Lyn."

Even though it was four-thirty in the morning and her friend Lyn Romano's call had just woken her from a deep sleep, Darlene Goncalves responded almost as if by cheerful rote.

"Hi, hon, how are you?" But then she caught the tremulous tone of Lyn's voice, realized the time.

"Ray was on that Swissair plane," Darlene heard her friend say. "He was on the plane that crashed."

"Okay," Darlene said, reacting, not letting herself think, "I'll be right down and I'll go with you." She didn't know where they would go, only that she should be with her friend.

"It's okay," Lyn said, "my sister's here now. I just need you to let the neighbours know. Okay?"

"Okay."

Darlene woke up Tony.

"What do you want?"

"Tony, get up. Ray was on that plane." Tony knew right away what she meant. He'd stayed up the night before watching the news about the Swissair plane that had crashed off Nova Scotia, not thinking for a moment his friend Ray might be on it. That's not to suggest he hadn't thought about Ray as he watched the news. They were both into aviation, both into airplanes, both loved to fly. When they'd get together, they'd often talk about what they'd seen the week before on *Wings*, a Discovery Channel series about the history of aviation. The plane crash was the kind of news he and Ray would almost certainly have talked about later.

Ray on that plane? "There were survivors," he told his wife suddenly. When he'd turned off the television, he remembered the announcers were saying there had been survivors. Ray was a survivor. He would be all right.

They turned on the TV.

But now the news had changed. There were no survivors.

No survivors at all.

He and Darlene hugged one another and cried.

"This can't be real," she said. "It can't."

The insistent ringing of the telephone woke Moira Devey shortly after 6 a.m. Matt, still sleep-puzzled himself, picked it up first.

"Ray?" she heard him say into the telephone. "Airplane?"

And then she knew. It was as if someone had punched her in the stomach. She'd been up with the new baby until after midnight and had been watching the news. She'd watched the bulletins about the crash, seen the fishermen in their boats.

It was all too horrifying to watch, she told herself as she turned off the TV. Thank God I don't know anyone travelling tonight. But she did. She'd forgotten that Ray Romano was supposed to be flying off to Switzerland someday this week. Was it? It was. Last night. By the time Matt got off the telephone and returned to their bedroom, she was sitting in a chair, crying hysterically.

St. Margarets Bay
6 a.m. ADT

Robert Conrad had never before in his life felt quite this tired. Or this angry. He could understand the tiredness. But the anger? The anger surprised him. He'd finally left the debris field just before dawn to begin the hour-long journey back to the wharf in Northwest Cove. There was nothing between him and land now but 40 minutes of open water, plenty of time to think again, this time to reflect on just what he had experienced.

That's when the anger had washed over him. "I guess it's because of my background," he would explain later. "I had to be able to attribute blame for this tragedy. So I directed my feelings at that old feller we call Lucifer."

By the time he reached the wharf, the anger had been replaced by an even more profound sense of sorrow. "I was overwhelmed with it. I had never in my life experienced anything like that. I knew I was overwhelmed, but there was no understanding it. I could only experience it."

When he finally got home, he tried to explain what he was feeling to his wife but he had no words to describe it. For days afterward, the feeling would not leave him; it would fade from time to time, but then sweep back over him "just as intense as that first time on the water."

His wife made him breakfast but he had no desire to eat. "I wasn't repulsed by food or anything," he says. "But it was like my digestive system had just shut down." He nibbled at his food, couldn't eat it. Finally, he got up to clean the food off his plate and to put his dishes in the sink. "When the kids were growing up, we had a rule in our house that everyone had to pick up after themselves and at least put their dishes in the sink. I got up from the counter and took the dishes over and put them in the fridge. When I realized later what I had done, I thought, 'Boy, I'm not over this.' "

To make matters worse, as tired as he was, he couldn't sleep. "There was no such thing. The only thing I felt capable of was replaying in my mind the events of the past few hours. Any idea I was a fisherman was gone, fishing was gone. It was just those few hours on the water, playing and replaying in my mind."

Peggys Cove, Nova Scotia
6:30 a.m. ADT

Rob Gordon would remember it later as a kind of "stop the presses" moment, a throwback to an earlier journalistic era. When he learned that the *New Dawn III* with the reporter-cameraman team of Lisa Taylor and Dave Archibald aboard had finally reached the crash site, Gordon decided he and Carmichael should rush their own video — the first from the scene — back to shore at New Harbour as quickly as possible.

"We got off the boat and hightailed it to Peggys Cove to feed it out," he recalls. By the time they reached Peggys Cove, the idyllic little fishing village cum tourist attraction had been transformed into both a chaotic search command centre and a bustling international media community. "The world was there." There were satellite trucks from everywhere, everyone staking out their camera positions on the rocks near the lighthouse. CNN and *Good Morning America* both had cameras set up waiting for Gordon to do live on-camera interviews with their hosts in the U.S. They would have to wait. He had the video. "And there we were, running up to the [*Newsworld*] truck, 'I got the tape. I got the tape.' And that's what went out. Raw. Just the way we shot it."

Gordon was even more grateful now that he and Carmichael had decided not to shoot some of what they had seen. There were scenes he would not want the world to see, some scenes he wished *he* had not seen.

Haverford, Pennsylvania
6 a.m. EDT

Barbara Fetherolf looked again at the clock by the bed. Tara should have called by now. It wasn't like her. She woke her husband. "She should have called," she told him.

"Okay," Mark replied, "I'll go to the computer and find the Swissair web site." He would double check the arrival time and maybe get a number they could call.

When he opened the Swissair site, however, there was a press release on the opening screen:

> Press Release — 09:30 AM (CET)
> Swissair aircraft involved in accident
> Zurich, September 3, 1998 — A Swissair aircraft crashed off the coast of Nova Scotia, Canada at 03:20 this morning (Central European Time). The aircraft, an MD-11, was operating flight SR 111 from New York to Geneva, and was carrying 215 passengers and 14 crew.

When Mark didn't come back to the bedroom, Barbara, imagining he'd probably fallen back asleep at the computer, went downstairs to check on him.

She found him slumped over the computer, but he wasn't asleep. He'd passed out from shock.

East Brunswick
7 a.m. EDT

"Mommy, Mommy," Dylan said, running into the bathroom, "George is here, George is here."

George? Rich's boss, George Feehan? Why would he be stopping by their apartment at seven in the morning? Maybe Rich had forgotten to take one of the CD-ROMs for the trade show, Peggy Coburn thought. Again. She'd been standing at the bus stop waiting for Dylan to arrive home from school the day before when Rich and a few of his co-workers had pulled up in a station wagon filled with computers and equipment packed to take to Geneva. Rich had forgotten some stuff then, and had had to stop by the house on his way to the airport to pick it up. Perhaps he had forgotten something else.

Peggy had gotten up earlier than usual that morning so she could shower and dress before their three small kids woke up. Lucky, she thought to herself now. It would just take her a minute to finish with her hair. She just hoped she'd be able to figure out which CD-ROM George was looking for. She hurried to the door to greet him.

"Peggy," he said, "I'm afraid I have some terrible news."

At first she didn't catch the ache in his voice, the ashen look on his face. "What?" she said lightly, not thinking. "Did Rich's plane crash?"

George nodded numbly. He wasn't smiling. He wasn't kidding.

Panic now. "Is he still alive?"

"There were no survivors," George told her. "None."

Peggy could feel herself begin to hyperventilate. She couldn't move. "It was like being on Jupiter," she would say later. Her arms felt like they were attached to lead weights.

George stayed with her while she called a neighbour-hood mother to come and take Dylan and Kira to school. "I told Dylan to get dressed. Thankfully, he was in a coopera-tive mood. Kira came into the kitchen. She too obliged me to get dressed all by herself." Then she called her parents in Long Island. And her sister. She got her sister's machine. "Richard's plane crashed," she said. "You've got to start praying that if he's alive he gets saved. Hurry!"

She turned on the television. CNN was showing images of a place called Peggys Cove. Why did she know that name? Though searchers were still looking for sur-vivors, the announcer said, officials now held out little hope they'd find any of the passengers alive. The death toll: 229. Two hundred and twenty-eight, you idiot, she said to herself, 228. Rich is not dead. He's smart. He knows how to survive. They'll find him. He'll be floating on a seat cushion somewhere off Peggys Cove.

Peggys Cove ... Peggys Cove. She went out into the kitchen. Yes, there it was, on the refrigerator. A postcard from Peggys Cove. Her aunt had visited there and sent her a postcard. When was it? She lifted the postcard from the magnet, flipped it over — 1991! She'd kept that post-card on her fridge for seven years. Why? Was it a sign?

What was the message?

Aboard HMCS *Preserver*
8 a.m. ADT

As John Butt silently, carefully examined each of the 16 bodies the *Preserver*'s sailors had brought aboard ship overnight, he couldn't help but remember that illustrated talk he'd attended at an American pathologists' association convention a few years back. He couldn't remember now whether the person giving the lecture was an investigator from the Armed Forces Institute of Pathology or from the FAA but, "whoever he was, he was someone who dropped planes on runways for a living. And I can remember him saying to us, 'The physics of landing on water are exactly the same as crashing into a concrete runway.'"

Perhaps worse. These weren't really bodies at all, he could see now, just pieces of bodies in 16 bags. Every one of the torsos had been decapitated at either the neck or the jaw. Only one or two still had all their limbs. All of the long bones in the limbs that remained had been fractured. "There wasn't one that was intact." In some cases, the impact had "de-gloved" a limb; what looked like an intact leg attached to a shoe would, on closer examination, turn out to have no bones in the leg at all. They'd been sucked right out of the body. "It was incredible," the pathologist in him would marvel later at what the violent force of the impact had done to these human bodies. "As the plane hit the water, it was as if everyone was sprayed with a fire hose shooting water at a velocity of five to six hundred miles per hour."

He'd only seen anything even approximating this level of carnage twice before in his career. As a student in England in 1967, he'd helped pathologists sift through what was left of a train that had gone off the rails at more than 70 miles an hour, killing 50 people aboard. "That was," he begins, then stops for a moment, "very bad." In 1986, he'd been the pathologist in charge when a VIA Rail passenger train collided with a CN freight near Hinton, Alberta, killing 23 people. That was "a lot cleaner," Butt says today, but awful in its own way too. The crash sparked a fire, disfiguring half a dozen bodies so badly that they couldn't be identified by conventional means.

As horrific as those two incidents had been, John Butt

knew now that Swissair would turn out to be much more gruesome. And scientifically more complicated — not to mention interesting — too. He could not and would not be able to ask family members to identify these pieces of their loved ones; in the end, he knew, he might not even find all of the pieces in order to put their bodies back together again. Two hundred and twenty-nine of them!

"At first," he says now, "you say to yourself there's this massive job ahead of you and you're all alone. You think, what are your options? One of the first things you want to do is to run away. But you know you can't. And then you step back and look at the bigger picture. It's like any crisis. You realize when you think about it that you're not really alone."

And despite what he'd said to his boss the night before, he wasn't really without a disaster contingency plan either. In fact, he'd written a chapter about coping with disasters in his book, *Investigation of Sudden Death*. He'd remembered it almost as soon as he'd hung up from his conversation with Gordon Gillis. He'd started writing the chapter manual in 1977, just after he became Alberta's first chief medical examiner. He'd finished it nine years — and one Hinton train wreck — later.

As soon as he helicoptered back to land, he would stop by his office, photocopy half a dozen copies of the chapter and jam them into his briefcase to hand out to whoever needed one.

"Oh, and by the way,' he said to Commander Town before he boarded the helicopter to take him back to Halifax, "I'd be careful about how you describe what you're bringing aboard." The TV networks were reporting that there were 16 bodies aboard the *Preserver*. There were 16 *body bags*. How was he going to explain that to the media? Butt wondered. Worse, how would he explain it to the families?

Ramada Plaza Hotel, JFK International Airport
10 a.m. EDT

It was almost too smooth, too practised, Ali Chiani thought to himself. Within five minutes of Delta's call to the hotel's security manager early this morning, every one of his key executives had been notified and was en route to his general manager's office off the lobby of JFK's Ramada Plaza Hotel. After getting his own unwelcome wake-up call shortly after four, Chiani skipped his usual shower and headed directly for the office too.

Some of his staff were already there and coolly taking care of business by the time he arrived. Someone had thought to call the telephone company to ask for 40 more direct lines into the hotel. The switchboard operator, Chiani had noticed on his way past, was already "going crazy" trying to deal with the flood of incoming calls. Someone else was busy designating meeting rooms: the airline would need one, of course, and the Red Cross, the FAA, the Port Authority, the police. Religious leaders would want quiet space to meet with family members individually and in small groups. Chiani's staff seemed to know, without having to discuss details, which group would need which size meeting rooms. Another staff member cancelled long-standing, confirmed reservations for those rooms. Sorry, they'd say, it's an emergency. The press centre? This time it should be set up in the parking lot, a veteran staffer suggested to Chiani, so the reporters can get their pictures and information but not get in the way. But that meant the journalists would need to be fed and, oh yes, they'd need a portable john.

Chiani, who'd been appointed the Plaza's general manager just three months ago, was new to all of this, although most of his staff had been through it before: two years earlier, when TWA Flight 800 exploded over the ocean off Long Island shortly after taking off from Kennedy, the Ramada Plaza had also been designated as the gathering place for grieving relatives.

It was still a logical choice. The largest of Kennedy's airport hotels, it was just down the road from the Delta terminal and it boasted a large parking lot as well as a dozen meeting rooms of various sizes. And now, there was also a staff experienced in dealing with the bereaved.

Delta had already called to ask that the Ramada's first two floors — more than a hundred rooms — be set aside for family members. Shortly after eight, the hotel's rooms director had quietly begun shifting the few long-term guests on those floors to rooms elsewhere in the hotel; luckily, because it was an airport hotel, most of the customers stayed only one night.

Chiani's staff weren't the only ones who knew from painful experience just what would be expected of them today. By the time the first stunned families had begun to trickle in to the hotel lobby shortly after 7 a.m., the Red Cross had five counsellors on site, some of whom had been there to comfort the families of Flight 800 too. "You can never understand what people are going through," the Red Cross's Michelle Auster told one reporter, "but counsellors certainly draw on that experience of helping people in a different disaster."

Sometimes there seemed little anyone could do to help. Capt. Darren Mudge of the Salvation Army spent two hours with one young Greek woman. "Why didn't she take another flight?" the woman cried. "Why not another day?" She was a student at Rutgers. Her mother had flown over from Greece a few days before to help her settle into a new apartment. The night before, she'd brought her mother back to Terminal 3 to board Flight 111 for the journey home.

If there was anything positive to say about what was happening inside the hotel, Mudge told inquisitive reporters later, it was that the Delta/Swissair care centre was much better organized than the one for TWA 800. "There's not so much chaos," he said. It wasn't much, but Ali Chiani, who would spend much of the day feeling overwhelmed by the grief around him, took comfort in hearing it.

Even the 70 journalists waiting in the parking lot weren't complaining. As Abigail Pogrebin, a writer for *Brill's Content,* described the scene in the magazine's November issue: "The parking lot looks from afar like a tailgate party. There are round white tables with sun umbrellas and chairs, platters of sandwiches and tortilla chips, soda, a water cooler. There is a trailer with portable toilets. Swissair and the Ramada have been impressive hosts, reporters say, an improvement over 1996 when many of these same journalists covered the crash of TWA Flight 800 and were given a more chilly and chaotic reception."

Still, despite the proliferation of uplink trucks and satellite transmission trucks in the parking lot, there was little for the journalists to report live from the Ramada Plaza. Grief-stricken families were hustled in and out of the hotel's rear entrance, often under police escort, while the 50 cameras remained trained, almost pointlessly, on the lobby doors. The few people who did stop to talk to reporters turned out to be the usual suspects: Rabbi Edgar Gluck, the Port Authority's police chaplain who, one reporter noted tartly, had never been considered camera shy, and New York mayor Rudolph Giuliani, who arrived in a limousine, spent a few minutes inside and then stepped before the waiting cameras to confide that a friend of his had a brother on the flight.

A few reporters, frustrated by the slim pickings outside

the hotel, wandered through Terminal 3 looking for employees who might have something to say. Skycap Stanley McKenzie remembered how one arriving passenger had left him a generous tip. "We watched these people say goodbye to their families and then spent some of their final moments on earth with them," he told Canadian Press solemnly. "That creates an unusual bond when we find out they're gone. Then, it's almost like they become part of our family."

Back at the hotel, Ali Chiani would echo those sentiments. And hope he never had to see such grief again. "It was heartbreaking," he says.

Swissair Operations Centre, Zurich Airport
11:30 a.m. CET

Christian Stussi sat in his office and stared again at the computer printout in front of him. He still couldn't believe it.

Urs Zimmermann?

Stephan Loëw?

He knew them both. Zimmermann had joined Swissair in 1970, the year before he had. Later, Zimmermann had been Stussi's instructor during some of his captain's training. Two years ago, Stussi, by then the chief pilot for Swissair's MD-11 fleet, had persuaded Zimmermann to switch from flying the Airbus A320 and join his fleet full time as a captain and instructor. Stussi had long admired Zimmermann's approach to teaching. "He was the kind of instructor who could make of a weak pilot a good pilot," Stussi would say. "He took the soft approach but he had a way of gently building up the self-confidence of people, of making them better."

The Swissair MD-11 aircraft HB-IWF, nicknamed Vaud, before the September 2, 1998 crash. The force of impact shattered the 200-foot long, 600,000-pound plane into more than one million pieces, some as small as a fingernail.

Flight 111 Captain Urs Zimmermann (left) and co-pilot Stephan Loëw were not only experienced MD-11 pilots but also highly regarded instructors. Fellow Swissair pilots found it difficult to believe they could have been responsible for the tragedy.

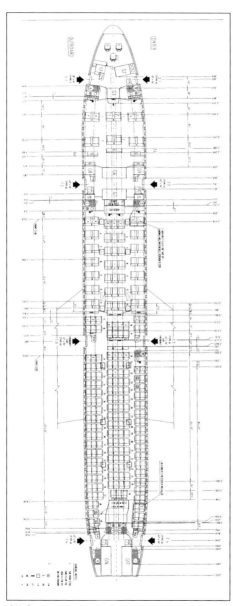

The floor plan of the MD-11 showing the cockpit, First Class, Business and Economy sections. Before the crash, the pilots reported smoke in the cockpit and investigators later discovered signs of fire in the ceiling above it. Since a bulkhead and galley separate the cockpit from the first-class section, it's possible only a few — perhaps none — of the passengers would have understood the seriousness of the problems aboard the plane in its final minutes.

SAir Group

SAir Group

Members of Swissair's Emergency Committee meet at the Flight Operations Centre in Zurich. When they were awoken in the early morning hours of September 3, some initially thought it was only an exercise. Swissair planes, they believed, didn't crash. They soon discovered how wrong they were.

SAir Group

Swissair volunteer care partners in Geneva field calls from anxious family and friends September 3. Call centres in Zurich, Geneva and Atlanta logged over 45,000 calls that day.

Lyn Romano, whose husband Ray was killed aboard Flight 111, at the inaugural meeting of the International Association for Aviation Safety in her home in Goldens Bridge, New York, February 1999. Romano planned to use the proceeds of her lawsuit against Swissair to fund the organization.

CBC-TV reporter Rob Gordon was the first reporter on the scene of the crash on the night of September 2. His reporting of the tragedy, which has since earned him several awards, was seen and heard all over the world.

Eighteen-year-old Rowenna White (inset) was on her way to Switzerland to study hotel management. Four days after the crash, her mother took this photo of her backpack, passport and the few personal effects officials had recovered.

On the afternoon of September 6, 1998, Nancy Wight (centre) visited with St. Margarets Bay residents Peggy Conrad and Bob Walkowiak, two of those who'd reached out to the families after the crash.

Sixteen-year-old Tara Fetherolf, a gifted math student, discovered a school in Switzerland she was keen to attend. Barbara Fetherolf didn't want her eldest daughter attending school so far away from their Pennsylvania home, but Tara was insistent.

Three key figures in the Swissair tragedy — family member Nancy Wight, pathologist John Butt and fisherman Robert Conrad — at lunch in Vancouver in April 1999. The crash was the genesis of their unlikely friendship.

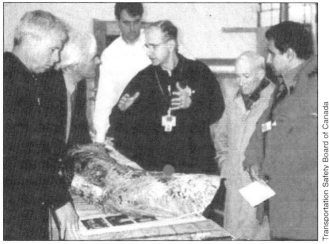

Transportation Safety Board investigators brief members of the Families of Swissair Flight 111 on their findings. From left to right: Deputy Chief Investigator Larry Vance, Miles Gerety, Unidentified, Chief Investigator Vic Gerden, Hans Ephraimson-Abt and Myron Ratnavelle.

Investigators use a specially built frame to try and reconstruct the cockpit area of the shattered aircraft in their search for clues to the cause of the crash.

DND, Canadian Forces photo by Master Corporal Richard Sirois

Canadian divers are lowered into the waters off Peggys Cove as part of a joint Canadian–U.S. effort to recover human remains. One diver said going down to the dangerous, ghastly crash scene was like descending into "hell."

Stussi didn't know Loëw quite as well, but he remembered that the co-pilot was very serious about flying. Like many Swissair pilots who'd received their initial flight training in the military, Loëw continued to be active in the reserves and was even scheduled to take over his air force squadron the next year.

"If these two couldn't handle whatever happened," Stussi thought to himself, "could anyone have managed it?"

Stussi certainly didn't have to be told the statistic that three-quarters of all aircraft accidents are caused by human error. But for Zimmermann and Loëw to have both made some fatal mistake? It seemed impossible. And yet he'd seen the debris on the television screen in the emergency committee room. Something terrible must have happened.

He picked up the phone and dialled Zimmermann's home number. He had known since he'd taken the job as captain of the fleet nine years ago that he might someday have to do this. He just never imagined he would, and certainly not for someone like Urs Zimmermann.

Though their families didn't socialize — Stussi, who'd been an engineer, didn't come from the same military background as the two Flight 111 pilots, and the military pilots travelled in different social circles — he knew Prisca Zimmermann well from her days as a Swissair flight attendant during the mid-seventies. "She was very pretty, young but with a strong personality," he recalls. Shortly after marrying Urs in 1980, Prisca abandoned the first-class cabin for full-time motherhood. Stussi knew that the Zimmermanns' first child, a boy named Philippe, had drowned in the bath when he was just three. That must have been terrible enough, he thought to himself. And now this.

"Prisca," he began when she picked up the telephone, "it is Christian Stussi." But Urs Zimmermann's wife already knew. Their 15-year-old daughter, Andrea, had heard it on the radio. She knew her father was due home that day; she needed his help with a math assignment. When she heard the news, she had immediately woken her mother. "Daddy's plane has crashed," she said.

"It doesn't look good," Stussi admitted. "I'll be there within the hour."

Then he called Stephan Loëw's wife. Sonja Loëw had been so busy taking care of her three small children — the oldest was almost five, the youngest not yet one — that she hadn't heard the radio or watched TV. She knew nothing about the accident at all. "She was in a state of shock," Stussi remembers. He sent his deputy to be with her.

By the time he arrived at the Zimmermanns' house in Winterthur, just outside Zurich, Prisca's and Urs's family were already gathering. They'd all heard Philippe Bruggisser's press conference, heard him say there were no survivors.

"We must expect the worst," Stussi told Prisca Zimmermann gently.

"You took him away from us," Prisca replied harshly, a reference, Stussi knew immediately, to his recruiting Urs for the MD-11 fleet two years before. "You have to get him back."

What could he say to that?

Command Centre, Peggys Cove
2 p.m. ADT

Before September 2, 1999, Everett Densmore had no idea that there were 365 islands — most of them uninhabited, some of them rarely ever even visited by humans — in the waters off Nova Scotia's South Shore between Chester Basin and Prospect. He did now.

Within 12 hours of the crash of Swissair Flight 111, in fact, Densmore, an RCMP constable who is the search master for the province's volunteer ground search and rescue teams, had teams on every one of those islands. Not to forget combing the miles of rocks and beaches and shoreline that edge St. Margarets and Mahone Bays.

Densmore's middle-of-the-night call for assistance had already generated 1,500 trained volunteers from 23 ground search and rescue teams around the province — people who'd willingly abandoned their everyday lives as lawyers and store clerks and construction workers to help out for as long as it took — as well as 350 ground troops supplied by the military's Land Forces Area Atlantic.

Even though this was still officially a search and rescue, everyone knew better now than to expect survivors. The real — and daunting — task of this massive effort would be to find, catalogue and bag every single piece of Swissair Flight 111 that drifted to the shore, from a child's beret to a battered piece of luggage to an unidentifiable scrap of metal to a bloated piece of body.

It would not be easy or pleasant or rewarding, Densmore knew, but someone had to do it. They would. And they would do it well. That was what they had trained for.

Peggys Cove
2:15 p.m. ADT

"You're Rob Gordon." It was a statement, not a question. Gordon nodded, sizing up the man in front of him: big, pockmarked face, heavy New York accent. Gordon was already deep into the trough of this day of virtually nonstop live reporting. He had lost count of the number of interviews he'd done, the number of foreign networks he'd been on. CNN, ABC, CBS, German TV ... When the man with the New York accent approached him, in fact, Gordon had just finished yet another "live hit" for CBC *Newsworld* from the search command centre at Peggys Cove.

"I want to shake your hand," the man said. He didn't tell Gordon his name; Gordon didn't ask.

Gordon was wary. He'd seen the man earlier, hanging at the edge of the army of journalists, watching, listening. Gordon could still recall, with sandpaper-rubbed-raw freshness, the hatred so many ordinary people seemed to feel for reporters in the first few days after 26 men died in the Westray mine explosion back in 1992. "We were the bad guys there, especially in the beginning," Gordon says of the days when the mining company was still ostensibly looking for survivors. "The company was staging these fake press conferences and trying to keep the families from talking to us. We knew the families knew about the unsafe conditions, so we had to go after the families ... and people hated us for it."

He remembers the emotional, sometimes frightening night he and his cameraman spent in a small apartment in nearby New Glasgow with six miners who had just been down in the depths looking for the missing men. "They were crying and whimpering and threatening me and hugging me and kicking the walls. They talked about the things that went on in the mines, the coal dust up to here, the jammed methane meters, the guilt that if only they'd gone public earlier ..." But they'd also been warned that they might not be allowed to go back down to search for their lost friends if they talked to the press. Gordon cajoled and pleaded but to no avail. After six hours, they told him to leave.

"Get the fuck out, parasite," one angry draegerman told him.

Gordon's news reports, which suggested just how dangerous the mine was, had made him a target for public anger, especially in the early days when most people were unwilling to consider that the accident was anything but an act of God. He was spit on in the streets of New Glasgow and passing motorists flashed him the finger. "It was a very strange, difficult time," he allows.

Swissair was different. Though the police weren't ruling out anything yet, it seemed unlikely that this disaster had been caused by a terrorist bomb or some obvious act of negligence or malfeasance on the part of the airline. So far, in fact, Swissair appeared remarkably open in its dealings with journalists. The company president was already on his way to Halifax to talk to reporters. And the Mounties, who had acted more like an old-time company police force during Westray, were far more even-handed this time in protecting families from too-intrusive reporters. The reporters were more discreet too. "The situations were very different," Gordon says. "At Westray, the families knew how bad things had been in the mine and the cops kept us from talking to them. Here, the families didn't know anything more about the accident than we did, so you didn't have to go after them. You could leave them alone unless they wanted to talk to you."

Now, as he tentatively reached out to shake the hand of the intense-looking New Yorker, Gordon wondered to himself: What does this guy want?

"You told me my girlfriend died," the man said simply. He had been engaged to a Greek woman who was a passenger on the plane. He'd learned of the crash while watching television. In the first few eerie hours of confused, scrambling-to-find-out-anything TV coverage, he told Gordon, some of the news reports had suggested there might be survivors. Finally, the CNN anchor announced that they had managed to contact a CBC-TV reporter named Rob Gordon who was at that very moment on a fishing boat in the middle of the debris field off Peggys Cove.

Gordon had simply told the anchor what he was seeing.

"I knew then she was dead," the man told Gordon now, adding quietly, "I needed to know that."

Gordon nodded gratefully. At that moment, he would tell friends later, "I needed to hear him say that as much as he needed to say it."

"What did you see out there?" the man wanted to know.

"You mean the body parts?" Gordon asked.

"Yeah."

"Do you really want me to tell you that?"

"Yes."

Gordon looked at him. There were all sorts of pieces, he offered carefully, not wanting to get more graphic. "Whatever happened," he said to the man gently, "happened incredibly quickly. I don't think anyone suffered."

The man was satisfied. So was Gordon. Telling the man about what he had seen, he later explained, made him feel less like a parasite. "It said to me that I did something useful in a terrible way," he said.

They talked for another 15 minutes. At one point, Gordon thought briefly about interviewing the man, asking him to tell his personal story on camera.

It would have made a good story. But Gordon couldn't bring himself to ask. He never did find out his name.

Aboard SR1138 over the North Atlantic
1:30 p.m. CET

Luckily, the photographer, who'd slipped unnoticed into the plane's first-class section just as Jeff Katz was swallowing two Aspirin to ease his raging headache, had managed to snap only one quick picture before a flight attendant pushed him back beyond the curtain. Normally such an intrusion would have bothered Katz — as would the fact that the unflattering picture would be on the front pages of Swiss newspapers in the morning — but today he barely noticed.

Swissair's president did notice, however, that the worst seemed somehow to be getting even worse as this terrible day wore on. When he'd taken his first cryptic call early that morning from an airline official informing him that they'd lost contact with a plane, he had asked for details about the flight number and how many people were aboard. "I couldn't believe it could be possible. Then I went right to the operations centre but, even as I was driving there, I still half-expected it all to be fixed by the time I got there."

It wasn't. Such an awful crash. So many people. He tried not to think about such things now, but it was almost impossible not to indulge in a little introspection as the plane flew over continents and oceans and time zones on its way to Halifax. For Katz, there was little else to do now.

Even though everyone on the emergency committee agreed it was imperative for Katz to get to Halifax and, more important, New York as quickly as possible, the plane had sat, fuelled and ready to depart, on the tarmac at Zurich that morning for more than two hours before finally taking off. First, they'd had to wait while nearly two dozen local journalists scrambled to find passports and pack for the trip to Halifax, and then while members of the airline's care team arrived from Geneva for the flight.

Katz knew such holdups were unavoidable. The company needed local reporters on site to provide coverage of this major event to viewers back home almost as much as the journalists needed to cover the unfolding story. And the care team absolutely had to get set up in Halifax that day in order to handle the influx of family members who would be descending on the area over the next 48 hours.

But Katz knew as well that he had to get to New York in time for that evening's network newscasts if his airline was to have any chance of putting its own spin on the critical first night's television news coverage of the crash. To do that effectively, of course, he would need to know exactly what was happening back in Zurich so that when he landed, "we'd all be on the same page." The problem was that he couldn't communicate with the emergency committee in Zurich directly from the plane. It wasn't until they were airborne that it finally dawned on anyone that the old Airbus 310 they'd pressed back into service for the journey to Halifax and New York had no satellite telephone communication system. Up in the cockpit, Jürg Schmid, Swissair's head of flight safety, used the high-frequency radio to try to find out more information about what was happening back at the emergency committee meetings.

When they got to Halifax, Schmid would head up the airline's initial investigative "go-team." The small group of about a dozen employees, which included pilots who could help decipher cockpit conversations and engineers who could brief the authorities in Halifax on the inner workings of the aircraft, would work with the investigators to figure out the cause of the crash. For now, however, Schmid tried not to think about the cause. He simply worked the HF radio in the cockpit, trying to pick up whatever new scraps of information about the crash he could over the crackle of the radio and pass them back to Katz in the first-class cabin.

There'd been no out-of-the-box drills quite like this in the neatly plotted simulations Schmid had devised for the emergency committee. Perhaps there should be. But there should never be reporters like the ones back in the economy section. "They were disgusting," Schmid remembers. "We'd lost friends, not just an aircraft, and I could hear them saying things like, 'Do we have to take an A310?' 'Why couldn't they get us a better aircraft?' 'I hope we can smoke on this flight.' For us, we were angry and desperate and upset. For them it was another job. I told someone, 'Don't let them anywhere near me.' "

Jeff Katz wouldn't have minded talking to the reporters. If only he had something to tell them. But he didn't yet.

Friday, September 4, 1998

Rescue Coordination Centre
10:30 a.m. ADT

Maj. Michel Brisbebois had known, almost from the moment he heard the first distressing reports from the crash site two nights ago, that the final outcome was inevitable. But in his heart he had refused to accept what his mind told him. He'd done everything possible to postpone the inevitability for as long as possible.

At seven o'clock the evening before, Brisebois had briefed his boss, Admiral Dusty Miller of the Canadian navy, on the status of the search for survivors. "I'm not sure we should quit yet, sir," Brisebois said.

He told him about a conversation he'd had with his opposite number at the American rescue centre in Norfolk, Virginia. The man had been in charge of the search effort off Long Island during TWA 800. "I asked him what mistakes they'd made, and he said they'd called off their search too early, that people were upset that they hadn't really tried hard enough."

He also informed Miller about the results of computer modelling exercises his officers had done during the previous 24 hours. Shortly after the search began, coast guard aircraft began dropping self-locating data buoy markers into the choppy waters around the crash site. The sophisticated gizmos, which beam signals indicating their

position up to satellites every 90 seconds, can be config-
ured to mimic the effects of wind and tide and current on
people or life rafts floating in the sea, helping searchers
zero in on how far and how fast something or someone
might have drifted from a crash site. Since the markers
also send back detailed information on water temperature
and other variables, searchers could also use the computer program to figure out how long someone could survive
in particular conditions. "We ran 21 extreme models,"
Brisebois recalls. "We found out that a frail, 60-year-old
lady could only have survived one and a half hours out
there, but a 25-year-old male in good shape and with
some fat on him could last up to 36 hours."

"If someone like that survived the crash itself,"
Brisebois told Miller, "he could still be out there."

Miller agreed and gave Brisebois the go-ahead to continue looking for survivors until at least morning, when
they would get together again to reassess the situation.
By 8 a.m., however, Brisebois had nothing new to report.
"The question then became how far could we go?"
Brisebois says now. To complicate that question, his
overtaxed staff had already had to deal with a number of
other major incidents. The night after the Swissair crash,
in fact, a fisherman from Yarmouth, Nova Scotia, had
been killed when the *Cat*, a high-speed ferry arriving
from the U.S. on its daily passenger run, plowed into his
boat. RCC staff had had to deal with that even as they
continued their increasingly unlikely search for anyone
who'd escaped the carnage of Flight 111.

At 10:30 a.m. on Friday, September 4, 36 hours after
the crash, Brisebois reluctantly gathered up his maps and
charts and notes and carried them across the hall to the
navy officer who would now take command of what was
no longer a search and rescue operation. It was a search
and *recovery* operation. From now on, responsibility for

the crash of Flight 111 belonged to others: to the navy, which was charged with coordinating the recovery of bodies and wreckage; to the RCMP, which was responsible for determining whether any criminal acts had been committed; and to the Canadian Transportation Safety Board, which would have the daunting task of trying to figure out exactly what had gone wrong on the night of September 2, 1998, and — perhaps even more important — to then figure out what could be done to make sure it never happened again.

Halifax
11 a.m. ADT

Larry Vance had arrived in Halifax early in the afternoon the day before. As the Canadian Transportation Safety Board's deputy chief investigator looking into one of the biggest air disasters in Canadian history, he had to be there. But he also *wanted* to be there. "I'm like a fireman when the fire bell rings," he admits. "If someone calls and says there's been an accident, I say, 'Pick me, pick me.' The bigger it is, the more I want to be involved." And yet, he knew he also needed to be at home right now. He had finally given up pretending he was just putting in a few seasoning years in Canada's capital before moving back home to Moncton, New Brunswick. This past week, he and Charlotte, who'd abandoned her teaching career to raise their three kids 20 years ago, had taken the first steps in preparing for Larry's post-retirement years by purchasing a Sylvan Learning Centre franchise in Nepean, an Ottawa suburb. The centre had opened on September 1 under its new ownership, even though there was still some legal paperwork to complete. Although the plan was for

Charlotte to run the centre, which provided tutoring services for students, and Larry to keep his day job at the TSB. But Larry had promised he'd be around to handle the business and banking end of their new joint venture.

He'd been at home relaxing Wednesday night when Charlotte told him she'd just seen a television report about an aircraft accident. "There wasn't much information — just an airliner missing in the water — but you could tell right away it was serious," he says. Because of his experience, "Vance was sure he'd be involved in some way, perhaps as the deputy, perhaps as the operations guy. "So I was torn between getting some sleep and wanting to find out more about what had happened."

He watched the news reports until after one, then packed a suitcase and tried to get at least a few hours' sleep. The call he'd been expecting, hoping for and dreading finally came, shortly after 4 a.m. Ottawa time. "Bring your stuff and come on down," he was told.

"How long do you think you'll be gone?" his wife asked.

"Could be two weeks, could be a year," he replied. Like every investigator, Vance hoped against hope that "we'll find that magic BB on the second day, we'll come up with that one key thing that will show us the direction and lead us to all the right answers." He hoped, but he knew better.

The Swissair investigation would be the first large-scale one since Ottawa created the TSB in the aftermath of the bungled investigation into the crash of a chartered DC-8 carrying soldiers from the U.S. 101st Airborne Division home for Christmas. The Arrow Air flight crashed shortly after takeoff from Gander International Airport on December 12, 1985, killing all 256 people aboard. But members of the Canadian Aviation Safety Board, the Transportation Safety Board's predecessor, couldn't agree on what had gone wrong. While the CASB's professional investigators had quickly zeroed in on the problem of ice on the wings, some politically appointed members of the CASB championed a more sinister theory that the plane had been brought down by a terrorist bomb. A few even hinted that the government was covering up the cause of the accident. The ensuing furor became so embarrassing in international aviation safety circles that Ottawa eventually abolished the CASB and replaced it in March 1990 with the Transportation Safety Board.

Vance himself hadn't been involved in the Gander investigation. At the time, he was still a newcomer to the craft of crash investigation and enrolled in an investigators' course at the University of Southern California. But he is quick to defend that probe today as a "high-quality investigation conducted by capable people that came to the right conclusions. The problems," he argues, "were all at the board level."

Still, Vance knew that a lot of "armchair quarterbacks" and media second-guessers would be keeping a close eye the Swissair investigation to see whether the new board could avoid the in-fighting of its predecessor and reach conclusions that would withstand critical scrutiny. That was one reason he wanted to be part of it. Even though he had begun to spend more time pushing paper since his promotion to head office eight years ago, he was still one of the board's most senior investigators. Besides, he knew his way around Atlantic Canada better than almost anyone else at the TSB's national headquarters.

Until he moved to Ottawa in 1990, in fact, he'd spent his whole life in the Maritimes. Born in Amherst, Nova Scotia, in 1949, the middle child of a CN rail worker and a homemaker, Vance discovered his fascination with flying by chance. Although he was a member of his high school's air cadet group, he says "it was mostly just a social thing to do with my friends." When one of his friends wanted to apply for a flying scholarship offered through the nearby Moncton Flying Club and was looking for someone to go with him, Vance agreed to apply too. He won the scholarship. "I was pretty good at it," he says simply. "It was just one of those things that came naturally. And I thought to myself, 'This would be a pretty good way to make a living.' It certainly beat the alternative of working in a foundry for the rest of my life."

By the summer of 1969, he'd earned his commercial pilot's licence and landed a full-time job as an instructor at the Moncton Flying Club. He's not sure why, but he says he never harboured any ambition to become a commercial airline pilot. "I just wanted to be an instructor."

Besides, he wanted to stay in Moncton, where his parents had settled and where his new bride's family lived. But he soon realized he'd be hard pressed to raise a family on the modest wages of a flying club instructor. In 1978, he took a more secure and better-paying government job as a civil aviation inspector at Transport Canada's regional operations centre in Moncton. His role was to make sure commercial pilots maintained their skill levels.

In 1984, when Transport Canada decided it was time to separate its potentially conflicting roles of regulating the aviation industry and investigating aircraft accidents, Vance became a regional pilot-investigator for the newly minted CASB. "It seemed to me to be a great opportunity to combine my flying career with detective work." He says he especially liked the respect and recognition that came with his new territory. "You walk into a situation that's often quite chaotic and you bring calm and control to it. It's like, 'Oh, the pros are here now.' You get that even from police agencies. They cordon off the area and wait for you. It gives you a buzz, no question."

Although Vance says there are plenty of courses that

teach the techniques of accident investigation, "you really learn it on the job in a mentoring situation." On major investigations, the newbie's role might be as mundane as finding out what the weather was like when the accident occurred — "something that's pretty hard to screw up" — but the junior investigator also picks up the tricks of the trade so he'll be ready when his turn to investigate solo comes along.

Vance's turn came in October 1984, when he was dispatched to Goose Bay, Labrador, to investigate why a medevac flight had crashed into a mountain south of there. All those aboard the Twin Otter, which was evacuating an injured man to hospital in Newfoundland, were killed. Vance's initiation was made more difficult because he knew both of the plane's pilots. One had been a student of his. "It was pretty traumatic," he allows now, but that, he says, is "part of the process of learning how to do the job professionally. When you start into accident investigation of any type, you have to decide for yourself how you're going to deal with death. Can I make this part of the job? You know that there has to be an investigation, that someone has to do it, so the question becomes can you handle it? In the end, I didn't really have a problem with that. I was able to put it in a compartment. Here's the aircraft and here's what I have to do. You tell yourself, 'There's tragedy here, but I'm helping. I'm not gawking, I'm not ambulance chasing. I'm helping.' "

Out on their own on a relatively small accident like the one in Goose Bay, investigators hone the many and various skills they need to tackle bigger and more complex accidents. They learn not to touch anything before taking photos, and to document the accident scene from all angles. They learn to deal with cops and reporters and the relatives of the victims. They learn how to interview witnesses, survivors, co-workers, family members. They learn to recover wreckage and analyze what they find.

They even figure out how the companies that built and flew the plane operate their businesses.

But perhaps the most important lesson they learn is not to assume anything. The trick, Vance says, is to not allow yourself to become trapped too quickly into a theory or set of assumptions that will lead you to a premature or wrong-headed conclusion or will make you miss some critical connection in the chain of events that led to the accident. Most major aircraft accidents, he says, are the result of a complex series of sometimes seemingly unrelated events, and it often takes months or years to trace the chain back to its beginnings. Nothing can be overlooked. If an investigator decides not to pursue one link, Vance says, "he'd better be prepared to explain why. You do things in anticipation of being challenged about your choices later on. One of the things you learn is to formulate those questions other people will ask you a year from now."

In the Goose Bay accident, Vance determined that the pilots had been flying in bad weather, become confused about how far they were from the airport and descended too soon. "They ran into the last mountain before the airport," he says sadly. "They hit just 20 or 30 feet below the top of the mountain." That finding, while important in providing answers for those most directly involved, had no safety payback: the pilots had gallantly gambled in an effort to save someone's life and they'd lost the gamble.

But the real purpose of accident investigators isn't just to determine what caused a particular accident. It is to figure out what should be done differently to prevent a similar tragedy from happening again. When accidents turn out to be unavoidable or, as often happens in incidents involving private planes, "some buddy had 'get-home-itis' and took off in lousy weather conditions, there's no safety payback. You may spend $15,000 to $20,000 investigating it for the practice, but how do you fix something like that from a safety point of view?" The issue had recently become a more critical one at the safety board. Because of federal budget cutbacks, the TSB had lost one-third of the 300-person workforce it started with back in 1990. So, says Vance, "you focus your attention on those accidents where there's likely to be a safety payback. Or where there's a high profile."

Swissair offered plenty of both. The investigation would not only attract worldwide media attention but its safety implications could be staggering. There were 178 other MD-11s in the world, many of them still flying passengers for a dozen airlines from Alitalia to China Airlines. On any given day, 30,000 people flew in the Boeing jet. If there was something wrong with the aircraft that investigators could discover and determine how to fix, hundreds, perhaps thousands of lives could be saved. Vance liked the thought of that.

In his nearly 15 years on the job, he had taken part in more than 200 accident investigations, from glider accidents in which the extent of injuries was a broken toe to the 1991 crash of a DC-8 near Jidda, Saudi Arabia, that killed all 263 people aboard — 34 more than died on Swissair Flight 111. Canada participated in that investigation because the aircraft's operator, Nationair, was based in Montreal and the crew was Canadian. But officially, at least, Vance served only as an adviser to the Saudi Arabian Presidency of Civil Aviation investigating team that headed the inquiry. Although the *Globe and Mail* would later claim that "TSB investigators did almost all the work in determining the cause" of the crash, Canada hadn't been able to claim credit for their efforts.

But now Canada, and the TSB, had a chance to take centre stage in an important, high-profile investigation that could go a long way to polishing — or not — its international image. Even though this accident involved a Swissair plane that crashed on a flight between the United States and Switzerland, the fact that it had gone down in Canadian territorial waters meant Canada — and by extension Larry Vance and the rest of the TSB — was ultimately responsible for answering the question of what went wrong and why.

John Maxwell, the Transportation Safety Board's director of investigations, had appointed Vic Gerden, a 55-year-old former military jet fighter pilot who'd headed TSB's regional office in central Canada and the Northwest Territories for the past nine years, to lead the investigation. Larry Vance would serve as his deputy. Though Vance tended to be more outgoing, the two investigators were cut from the same precise, careful and considered professional cloth. Both were experienced pilots who understood airplanes from the inside out, and both had been rigorously trained not to allow themselves to speculate in public.

"In a perfect world," Vance suggests, "you wouldn't say anything about anything to do with an investigation until it was all done." Vance was of course savvy enough to know that this was far from a perfect world and that much of what he and Gerden would have to do over the next year or two, perhaps even more, was to dampen expectations and insulate themselves and their investigators from the understandable demands of the media, the families, the airline, the airline industry, the politicians and the public for too-quick, too-easy and, most likely, wrong answers to the question of what caused the accident. It wouldn't be easy. It was already, Vance could see just by looking around him now at the media-crazed scene at Peggys Cove, an international media event.

After checking in early Thursday afternoon at the Dartmouth Holiday Inn, which would serve as both headquarters and home for investigators, Vance and other members of the TSB's go-team, which included experts in operations, human factors, cabin safety, weather, and fire and safety analysis, had headed straight to Peggys Cove to be briefed and take over from local TSB officials. They'd been on the scene there since three o'clock the morning of the crash. Mostly, though, says Vance, they simply wanted to "show the flag, take charge, get the lay of the land." The reality is that the crash site is rarely the sole, or even main, focus in an accident investigation. "Everything is," Vance says. Thanks to years of practice on smaller accidents, the TSB go-team had become a smoothly functioning unit that was able to hit the ground running, even on an investigation as huge and complex as Swissair promised to be. Investigators quickly divided up responsibility according to their assigned roles: some scrambled to hitch rides out to the ships involved in the recovery operations so they could oversee procedures for collecting debris and searching for the plane's critical flight data recorders; others fanned out to begin interviewing "ear witnesses" to the crash. Others flew to New York to take control of dispatch records, or to Zurich to get the aircraft's maintenance records. Another investigator set up liaison with key officials at Swissair, Boeing and Pratt & Whitney, the company that had supplied the engines for the aircraft. Jim Harris, a former newspaper reporter who was the TSB's chief spokesperson, arrived to begin briefing the press — "keeping the wolves at bay," as Vance put it. There would be plenty of wolves, and the best way to keep them at bay, he knew, was to come up with answers to their question about why Flight 111 had crashed.

It would not be easy. Vance looked out at the distant vessels plying the waters around the crash site. It could take months to recover the wreckage. And some critical pieces might never be found at all.

St. Margarets Bay
Noon ADT

Rob Gordon saw the wallet floating in the water near the boat. "Let's get that," he said to Capt. Eric Haynes.

It was his second trip out to the debris field, his first in daylight, and Gordon found himself fascinated with the floating sea of flotsam. "I just wanted to know who these people were," he says now. He had gone out on the *New Dawn* with Eric and Ellen Haynes, the charter operators whose boat had brought reporter Lisa Taylor and cameraman Dave Archibald down from Halifax two nights before.

Taylor had arrived on the scene just as dawn broke and the intensely human reality of the tragedy finally became apparent. "You've made reference to the debris field," Taylor told one CBC *Newsworld* anchor during a live report, "but 'debris field' is a rather antiseptic term for what we're seeing here. We're seeing the fragments of what people brought with them on that flight — suitcases, briefcases, wallets. There are shoes, children's toys. There was a postcard with someone's best wishes written on it. Everywhere you look there's one more piece. Some of it is horribly mangled, some intact. And every one of those pieces seems to tell a story of the people who went down on that flight."

For reasons he couldn't quite articulate, Rob Gordon wanted to know those stories for himself.

Over the course of the first full day, more and more of them had emerged. Stephen Kiley, a charter boat captain who'd agreed to take a Swiss TV crew out to the crash site, scooped up a diary whose final entry was dated September 2 at 8:50 p.m. "J'écris," it began, then stopped — possibly because the cabin crew had begun serving dinner. According to the diary, the woman, who was travelling with a man, had come to North America three weeks before, flying from Switzerland to New York to Montreal. The couple vacationed in Quebec and had caught the New York flight back to Switzerland. They had visited Central Park before going to the airport. Kiley turned the diary over to the RCMP in the hopes that the police could figure out who it belonged to and give it to the woman's family.

Brendan Elliott, a reporter with the Halifax *Daily News*, reported seeing "a semi-inflated, red balloon bob past our boat with the inscription Happy Birthday. It hit me. Someone had celebrated a birthday in New York and had boarded a plane carrying this small gift."

Gordon had decided to return to the debris field with the Hayneses to see for himself what he could find. But Ellen Haynes wasn't interested in carrying non-working passengers, even reporters. On the first night, in fact, she'd put Taylor and Archibald to work, instructing them at one point to put down their camera and notebook and take up fishing nets so they could retrieve whatever they could catch of the personal belongings floating by. "The families will want it," she told Taylor, "and if we don't get it now, it'll be gone forever." Taylor didn't argue. Neither did Gordon. For journalists who almost always regarded themselves as detached observers, it was a strange, revelatory moment. "I realized I was a human being first," Taylor wrote later.

So did Gordon. As he scooped up assorted bits and pieces floating on the water — torn seats, ripped luggage, lone shoes, dresses — he tried to imagine the people who had belonged to the items. This was so different from Westray, he thought. Westray had been sanitized, purged of its reality. You couldn't see the inside of the mine where the explosion had taken place. You couldn't see what the explosion had done to the miners. You never saw their bodies, even when they were removed from the mine. The cops and the mining company officials wouldn't even let you get close enough to the families to ask for photos of their loved ones so you could print a face with a name. Here, everything was sprawled out before you. You could see — and feel — everything. There were even photos of people — passengers, perhaps? — in happy vacation snapshots taken 36 hours ago, and then developed and brought aboard to show someone who might have been waiting at the airport in Geneva. My summer vacation in America ...

There were still body parts on the water, a sea of them, in fact, but they no longer resembled even pieces of human beings, Gordon thought. The first night, the flesh had been fresh and still pink; now, drained of blood, "it all looked like pieces of pork."

Cmdr. Rick Town's voice was still as calming as it had been two nights before, but the chaos of two nights ago had been replaced by a structure. "If you see any human remains," the *Preserver* captain declared over the VHF radio, "please bag them, mark your co-ordinates and note the time the item was found. Then notify us, and we'll arrange pickup."

Gordon reached out with his net and hauled up a red leather box. It was a box for an Omega watch. He opened it up. There was a card inside, a sales slip from the duty free shop at JFK, with a man's name on it. The name was German. But the box was otherwise empty. "That's when this wave came over me," Gordon says. "I'd been in England on a story not that long ago and I bought this Swatch watch at Heathrow. When I got on the plane, I remember I took it out of the box, I put it on and I played with it. And I thought, that's what this guy did. He'd bought this watch and he was probably excited with it, and so he opened it up and put it on. That's what this person did. And all that was left was the box."

Peggys Cove
3:30 p.m. ADT

At first, Miles Gerety had thought he was going to Nova Scotia by himself. But just before the buses arrived at the JFK Ramada Plaza to ferry family members to the waiting aircraft, Little Pierce showed up, and then Miles Jr. too. Tommy drove down from his home at Amherst College in Massachusetts. Sebastian, Pierce's younger son, a university student, flew in from California. And suddenly, Peter, the second-youngest of Pierce's brothers — who'd initially said he didn't plan to go to Nova Scotia with them — showed up at Kennedy too, just in time to catch the charter plane. The Gerety boys were together, all heading to Nova Scotia to say goodbye to Pierce, the best and brightest of them all.

Like many of the nearly 150 other American relatives aboard the flight out of New York that day, Miles Gerety admits he wasn't absolutely certain what compelled him to make this strange odyssey to the place where his brother had just died. "I just felt that I had to go."

"At first I couldn't see the point," agrees Peggy Coburn, who was on the same plane. Peggy even telephoned a specialist in child bereavement in Boston to ask whether she thought it would be wise for her to take her three young children to Nova Scotia. "She encouraged me to go up and take them with me," Peggy says. "She said if you don't go, you'll regret it. So I decided it was probably better to go and think afterwards that it had been a waste than not to go and feel badly about it later on."

She recalls the tenderness of the grief counsellors and clergy who hovered nearby — but never intruded on her private moments — while she wandered across the rocks at Peggys Cove, the two Mounties who not only seemed to understand why she needed to do it but also offered her a life preserver and then held on to her so she could stand as close as humanly possible to the cove's rocky edge and let the sea wash over her, so she could be as close to Richard — myhoneymylove — as she could possibly get.

It didn't matter to her that the moonscape rocks and postcard-picture-perfect lighthouse that have helped make Peggys Cove Nova Scotia's most photographed tourist landmark were shrouded in an almost impenetrable fog that day. Or that it was difficult to see anything beyond where the thundering surf smacked up against the sea-worn granite boulders. It was enough for now just to know that she and her husband were connected by the ocean.

She only wished that Rich could be here now to share it with her. He loved natural wonders. She remembered Rich telling her about how, before they met, when he was still in the navy, he used to just get in his car on his days off and drive deep into the countryside. Once, he told her, he'd been driving through Zion National Park in Utah and got out of his car just to admire the mountains. "He told me he had to lean against the car for support for 10 minutes. He was just in awe looking at those mountains." He should be here, she thought, he should be in Peggys Cove.

"Feeling the water touching me was almost spiritual," she says now. "And the people we met were wonderful. That visit turned out to be incredibly healing for me. In the middle of all of this terrible time, it was like a revelation: the world is teeming with wonderful, caring people."

Beginning — even though she would never meet them personally — with the pilots of the charter plane that took them to Nova Scotia. Air Canada pilots were in the midst of a bitter strike, but the pilots' union and the airline had immediately agreed to a temporary halt to their dispute so the pilots could fly family members back and forth each day. It was what they could do, they explained later.

Immigration officials set up special areas at the Halifax International Airport terminal so family members could clear customs in private and with a minimum of fuss. Volunteer drivers in donated buses and mini-vans, provided by everyone from local car dealers to volunteer fire brigades to individuals, lined up at the curb to ferry them to their hotels, Shearwater, Peggys Cove or almost anywhere else they wanted to go.

During the first 48 hours after the crash, more than a thousand ordinary Nova Scotians even called the province's Check In service — usually used to book commercial tourist accommodations — to offer rooms in their homes, even their entire homes, if necessary, for the families to use. Those rooms turned out not to be needed; other teams of volunteers from Tourism Nova Scotia had already deftly juggled bookings out of the major downtown hotels, eventually freeing up 943 rooms for families, airline officials and accident investigators. The one group who may have had trouble getting rooms was the media. Tourism Halifax director Lewis Rogers later deadpanned to a debriefing session, "We got calls from six different presidents of Swissair demanding a room and from three different Tom Brokaws."

Halifax's venerable Lord Nelson Hotel, which had been partially closed for renovations, reopened within five hours of getting a 4 a.m. request from Swissair the day of the crash. The once elegant 70-year-old hotel, which had played host to everyone from Fidel Castro and Louis Armstrong to the world's media during the 1995 G-7 summit, became not only the main hotel for family members during this and subsequent visits but also the command centre for all of Swissair's family support activities. Its adjacent Georgian Lounge and Admiralty Room, more often the scene of political conventions and election-night parties, were transformed into a place where family members could gather in comfort and security. Inside each guest room someone had placed an unsigned printed message "To The Families and Friends of Swissair Flight 111":

> The people of Nova Scotia share your sorrow and pain. We pledge to take care of the waters around Peggys Cove for they have become a part of your lives just as they are a part of ours. Our hearts go out to you and we will never forget. We are tied to you in sorrow and in friendship. We hope that one day you will feel strong enough to return to our province and that you will always feel that you are coming home.

Overworked hotel staff willingly put in 16- and 18-hour days for weeks after the crash. The housekeeping and sales staff did double duty as informal care workers, serving as everything from a shoulder to cry on to the person who would track down rain gear for a three-in-the-morning trip to Peggys Cove, no questions asked. "Any request was granted," David Clark, the director of hotel services, says proudly. "No was not an option."

The desire to help was infectious. In the immediate aftermath of the crash, about 600 other Nova Scotians called the province's public enquiries service offering everything from translation services to grief counselling to even the gift of an already consecrated 12-hectare cemetery if family members needed a place in the province to bury their dead.

"Nova Scotians' outpouring of generosity and support for the families of the crash victims has been extraordinary — but not surprising," Premier Russell MacLellan told reporters a few days after the crash. It was, he suggested, just the Nova Scotia way.

The Nova Scotia way touched a chord with many of

the relatives and friends of the victims. Tom Gerety would later write an open letter to the Halifax *Chronicle-Herald* thanking the president of a local software company for handing over his nine-passenger van to the Geretys for as long as they needed it.

Richard MacDonald had been flying home to Halifax from Toronto when he struck up a conversation with his seatmate, Nigel Fisher, a United Nations official on his way to Halifax to assist the families of UN staff killed in the crash. When Fisher told MacDonald about the problems he was having lining up a van big enough to transport one large family group, MacDonald simply handed him the keys to the van he'd left at the Halifax airport parking lot. When the plane landed in Halifax, MacDonald called his son to come pick him up. "It was no big deal," he says today. "It was something any Nova Scotian would have done." Tom Gerety thought otherwise. "Your impulsive generosity made a tremendous impression on all of us in my family," he wrote. "Perhaps one day we can meet you when we visit St. Margarets Bay. I enclose Pierce's obituary notices so that you may know just a little bit about him. Thank you again." Other family members would later take out ads in local newspapers offering their public thank yous for the way Nova Scotians treated them that weekend.

It was, Miles Gerety later recalled, a weekend for impulsive acts of kindness. The Geretys were among the first to arrive at Peggys Cove on that first Friday afternoon. "We all ended up getting wet," he remembers. He was sitting on the rocks, sobbing, when he suddenly realized someone had wrapped a blanket around him, "so gently I didn't know where it came from." He looked around and there was a young woman, a volunteer from the local Red Cross whose hair — like his own — was prematurely grey. "Don't ever colour it," he told her.

And then he looked back out into the fog, his eyes still wet with tears, and thought about the older brother he'd looked up to for so long. "I thought about how good he was and I thought I needed to do something to make this better. I wanted to do the kind of thing Pierce would have done if he were here."

His chance would come soon enough.

Lord Nelson Hotel, Halifax
8 p.m. ADT

Nancy Richard took a deep breath, walked over to the man and two women standing together awkwardly in the hotel lobby and began: "Hi, my name is Nancy and I'm a care partner with Air Nova."

She'd been at a friend's house for dinner the night before when Laurel Clark, the airline's vice-president, called her to ask if she'd be willing to act as a care partner for one of the families who'd lost a loved one in the crash. In the past five years — spurred partly by legislation and partly by a growing recognition of both its importance and its public relations value — airlines around the world had set up these one-to-one programs, using employee volunteers to provide for the immediate needs of passengers or their families in the first difficult, confused and confusing hours after a plane crash. The volunteers were not grief counsellors, though they almost inevitably did some of that, but they were trained to recognize when people needed that kind of help and to find it for them — along with anything else they may need, from forgotten toothbrushes, to information on the next official briefing, to advice on where to find a quiet place to be alone for a while. Air Nova, the regional partner air-line for Air Canada, had established its care partner pro-gram just that spring, shortly after an Air Canada jet crashed while landing at the Fredericton airport in December 1997.

Richard, whose day job is in the human resources department at Air Nova, volunteered for the program as soon as it was announced. Since then, she'd taken a course, done some role playing, read the manual. But this was different. In spite of the training, she says, "you really don't know what it will be like until you go through it."

Still, she answered Clark without hesitation. "Sure," she said. The 27-year-old daughter of a Canadian Airlines pilot, her brother is also a pilot and flight instructor in the military. Richard says she grew up in airports. In a sense, she saw herself as part of the tightly knit worldwide culture and comradeship of those who fly. "It's hard to pin down, but whatever job I did, the airport always felt like home." As awful as this accident was — and as daunting as the prospect of trying to help a stranger cope with their private grief — she says it just felt right for her to be involved.

When she got off the phone with the airline that night, she remembers, her friend was nonplussed. "I couldn't do that," she said. "I just couldn't."

"It was hard," Richard agrees today, "the hardest thing I've ever done. But it's common sense, really. You just have to try and be a compassionate person."

That was easier said than done. Standing in the hotel lobby on that Friday night, looking out into the sea of shocked, pained, desperate faces, Richard admits she wasn't sure at first what she should do. She was one of about a dozen Air Nova care partners, but there were dozens of others too, from Swissair and Delta and other airlines and volunteer groups. Many had flown in with the families on charters from New York and Zurich and

had already hooked up with the families they would comfort through this first, worst weekend of grieving in a
strange place and in the company of strangers.

To this day, Richard can't explain why she singled
out Nancy Wight, her former husband, Paul, and his current wife, Judith, from among the milling, stunned crowd
at the Lord Nelson Hotel that Friday night. "Nancy was
wearing a hat, I remember that," Richard says. And she
needed help.

Nancy Wight had never felt so alone. She was divorced.
Her father and mother were dead. Ariel, the family dog
she and Rowenna had doted on, had passed away the
month before, after a lingering illness. Row had wanted
to take the dog to the vet, but Nancy knew it was a lost
cause. They'd spent most of the summer just coming to
terms with the dog's death. Now, with Rowenna, her only
daughter, suddenly gone too, Nancy found it impossible
to even remember what that sort of grief had felt like.

She hadn't been there for any of them, she realized
with a guilty start. Her father, an engineer who designed
fish meal plants — during her childhood, he'd often spent
time in Halifax on business, sometimes telephoning home
from his hotel — had died of a heart attack in Montreal
during Expo 67. She hadn't been there for him. Nancy's
mother, an extrovert, bubbling over with "noise, drama
and sociability" — very much like her granddaughter —
had died the year before at her home in Maine. Nancy had
been at home in New York when it happened.

And now Rowenna, dying in Nova Scotia, alone on
the plane. Nancy hadn't even accompanied her daughter
to the airport Wednesday night. Paul had done that, along
with Judith and Rowenna's boyfriend, Adrian. Nancy had
stayed home alone and read.

The truth was it had not been a good summer for

mother and daughter. None of what happened between them, viewed from a broader perspective, was unusual in mother–daughter relationships, especially during the teenage years. Nancy knew that. But the problem was that now there could be no broader perspective, no opportunity for reconciliation down the road. Rowenna was dead.

Nancy and Rowenna were competitive. It sometimes surprised Nancy to realize how true that was. Growing up, Nancy had witnessed the competition between her own mother and her older sister, and she'd vowed the same thing wouldn't happen with her and Row. But it had. They'd butted heads from childhood. Nancy loved reading, Rowenna hated it. After Row was tested as a borderline dyslexic, Nancy made sure she got the special attention she needed, even putting her in a special program at school where a resource teacher spent half an hour with her each day coaching her in reading skills. "She felt like the odd person out in her class," Nancy says now, "and became even less interested in reading." But that summer, Nancy noted with some satisfaction, Rowenna had, on her own, begun to read *The Scarlet Pimpernel* because she and some friends were thinking of going to see the Broadway play. Perhaps she would have grown interested in reading as she—? No, best not to think of that now.

Nancy, who'd once been a dancer with the Boston Ballet Company and then, briefly, the New York City Ballet Company before knee injuries ended her career prematurely, had encouraged Rowenna to study ballet too. She did so for a while, Nancy says, but only "under duress." Just as Nancy, who has a passion for choral music, had to virtually order her daughter to join the school choir at I.S. 44 in New York. "In the end, they won a national choral contest and she was very happy to have been part of it," Nancy says now. Still, "if Mommy liked it, Row was against it."

Rowenna was born in 1980, the only daughter of Nancy Wight and Paul White ("our friends used to call us the Wight Whites"), an electrical engineer whom she divorced in 1987. They'd called their daughter Rowenna from a mishearing of the name Mawrenna, one of the heroines of *Poldark*, a British television series from the seventies. Nancy suggested it to Paul, who liked the name too, "so that's what we called her. Of course everyone thought it was from Scott's *Ivanhoe* but that heroine is Rowena." Rowenna herself liked the name, "if not the mispronunciation and constant misspelling that attended it." She signed herself Rowenna L. White, even though the name on her birth certificate read Rowenna Lee Wight White.

Nancy had been against Rowenna's plan to go to the Hotel Institute Montreux in Switzerland. She telephoned her ex-husband. "I don't think Row should go," she told Paul. "Switzerland is so far away, and it's so expensive."

Paul dismissed her objections. Everything would be fine, he said. And he was more than prepared to pay his half of the cost. Judith even flew to fly to Switzerland with Rowenna in March so they could check out the school.

Standing in the lobby of the Lord Nelson Hotel now beside Paul and Judith, Nancy tried not to remember how she and Rowenna had argued over when Row would leave, tried not to remember that, in the end, she'd been the one who refused to accompany her daughter on the flight to Geneva, that she'd been the one who didn't go with her daughter to the airport to say goodbye.

Instead she tried to bring back other, sweeter memories. Like the time, after ignoring her mother for a long period, Rowenna had impetuously placed three pictures of herself on Nancy's bedboard along with a note on the pillow that read: "I LOVE Mom." Or the words she'd written in her journal during her first year at boarding school: "I miss my mom. I always feel this way after I've spent a weekend with her. I'm going to take her to Aruba when I start working after college ... I hope God will tell my mom that I love her tonight in her sleep."

On Wednesday night, after Paul had picked up Rowenna for the ride to the airport, Nancy had gone to bed early to read a book. At one point she looked over at the clock beside the bed. It read 9:30. That was, she realized later, 10:30 Nova Scotia time, just a minute before the plane went down.

She found out about the crash a few hours later, when Lillie Rovno, an elderly musician friend who knew Rowenna was leaving for Switzerland that night on Swissair, telephoned her to tell her what she'd just seen on the news. "I knew immediately it must be her plane," Nancy would recall. "I was shaking so hard I had trouble turning on the TV."

Nova Scotia? Joe Nye, a friend in her apartment building, was vacationing with his family in Nova Scotia right now. He'd called from there earlier in the week just to check in. She had the number where he was staying. She'd call him. He could take care of Rowenna for her until Nancy could fly up to be with her — "I was thinking she'd have a broken arm or something small like that" — but when she phoned, he'd already left the place where he'd been staying. She called her older brother Garrett out on the West Coast.

She also called Paul.

Judith answered. "He's asleep," she said.

"Wake him." Nancy needed to ask him something; she still wasn't absolutely certain Rowenna had been on that particular flight.

"What?" he growled when he picked up the phone.

"What was the flight number of the plane Rowie was on?" As he said the numbers — one-one-one — she wrote them down in pencil in big letters on the front page of her *New York Times*.

"You'd better turn on CNN," she said. And then she hung up.

The three of them had flown up together on the Air Canada flight that Swissair had chartered from New York, but Paul and Judith had been in a different part of the plane. Nancy sat with Richard Cameron, a psychologist from Halifax who'd flown down to accompany the families from New York. They'd talked about Rowenna. Nancy found it comforting somehow. But now she was in the hotel beside Paul and Judith, and Cameron was gone.

She was alone again.

That is, until Nancy Richard approached her from out of nowhere and began to talk to her. Although Richard initially focused on the three of them, it quickly became apparent that, while Paul and Judith had each other to lean on for emotional support, Nancy was on her own.

On the surface, Richard, a young married and childless Maritimer, and Wight, a middle-aged divorced New Yorker, couldn't have been more different. But in the mysterious, mystical atmosphere that cloaks tragedies, the two Nancys bonded instantly. "We're Nancy-squared," Wight began to tell people they met in the hotel.

Now Nancy Richard was coaxing her toward the hotel ballroom. There was going to be a briefing, she said.

What could he say? What could anyone say? And yet someone had to tell them. *He* had to. John Butt stared out at the news-numbed faces of more than 300 relatives and friends of the victims of Swissair Flight 111. They'd crowded into the ballroom to hear the president of Swissair and representatives from all the key agencies that had responded to the crash — including Butt as the province's chief medical examiner — tell them the grimmest-of-grim news about the fate of their fathers, mothers, sisters, brothers, sons, daughters, aunts, uncles, friends, colleagues.

He would be the last speaker, after Vic Gerden of the Transportation Safety Board, Capt. Roger Girouard, the military commander for the recovery operation, and Chief Superintendent Steve Duncan, the head of the RCMP for the province.

When Swissair president Jeff Katz, who was chairing the briefing, had called that morning to ask him to speak at the meeting that night, Butt had assumed it would be a small gathering to discuss policy and that, if there were next of kin present, there would only be a few representatives to talk about process. Even after he met with Katz and Lee Shave, another Swissair representative, at RCMP headquarters before driving to the hotel, he says, "I still didn't have a sense of what kind of meeting it would be. When we got to the hotel, I could see there was a lot of security around. I thought, well, that must be to keep the press away. And then we got inside and there were all these very upset people around. And I had to talk to them."

Despite his role as the province's chief identifier of the dead, Butt himself rarely talked face to face with next of kin. In Alberta that had been the job of his office's nurse-investigators. But in Nova Scotia at the time when Butt first arrived, there were no nurse-investigators. "I think I'd been here a week when someone came in and said to me, 'Dr. Butt, the family of So-and-so called.' I said, 'Well ...?' "

"Could you give them a ring back?"

"Do I have to?" he asked.

"There's no one else," he was informed.

And so he did. He was far better at it than he ever thought he could be. One of the first relatives he talked to, in fact, came back to see him months later to give him a Christmas gift — an angel figure.

But that at least had been one to one. To stand in front of a room full of hundreds of family members and tell them their loved ones were not only dead but broken and mangled ...

It was even worse than Butt had first imagined. The day after the crash, he had instructed his lab team to "DNA everything." But less than 24 hours later, he'd had to rescind that order. It turned out there was just too much small, unidentifiable "material," as it was called, being brought to shore to justify using the sophisticated and expensive DNA technology to identify it. The role of the medical examiner's office, he had to remind himself, was not to identify every piece of every victim but to identify those individuals who had perished. To simplify matters, he'd created a four-part classification system to help technicians catalogue what they were finding. Type 1 was for intact bodies. So far, at least, there was only one of them, a woman who'd been found the first night and whose body was now in Billet #1 at the temporary morgue at CFB Shearwater. Type 2 included all identifiable body parts, which could range from a human navel or fingernail to an obvious piece of an arm or a leg. Type 3 was the designation for body parts that couldn't be visually identified as a specific body part but that searchers considered significant pieces of bodies. Type 4 — or Type X, as it became known in the lab — covered all other human "material," some of it no bigger than half an inch square. That afternoon, Butt had reluctantly issued instructions that pathologists shouldn't bother trying to identify Type 4 remains; they were simply too small and there were too many of them.

Could he really tell the families that? "No honest person could have bullshitted them," he says now. "As awful as it was, they had to know. I had to get it across."

It was, he admits, the worst moment of his professional life. And perhaps also the finest.

"I am very sorry about the situation," he began, his voice heavy, slow, halting. He then told the relatives, as gently but as firmly as he could, that they wouldn't have intact — or even necessarily complete — bodies to identify, to bury, to take home with them. Their loved ones were gone.

"Suddenly," Katz would recall later, "you could hear people shouting for doctors in so many languages. There were people fainting, people screaming. Sitting there in front of that audience that night, I could see every range of human emotion on display — from totally out of control to total calm."

Butt managed to say everything he had to say, emphasizing the terrible problems that remained in identifying each of the victims and the important role next of kin could play by gathering information that would help identify the victims — old X-rays, operations, scars, tattoos, even unusual earrings or body piercings — as well as providing blood and other samples that could be used for DNA testing.

Finally, he asked if there were any questions. "This woman stood up, a black woman from Montreal, and asked about a relative of hers who'd been on the plane and did we known anything about her," Butt recalls. "Incredibly, she turned out to be the aunt of the one person who had been recovered intact. By midnight, some friends of the family had gone over to the chapel at Shearwater and identified a Mrs. Benjamin," — who had died in the crash along with her three children. In the end, hers would be the only one of the 229 bodies to be identified visually.

When the meeting finally ended, more than an hour later, many in the room came up to the front to talk to Butt, to ask him more questions, to shake his hand, to hug him, to thank him for so obviously caring about their loss.

For a man who didn't believe he was emotionally equipped for the job of dealing with the next of kin, it was a revelation.

"Somehow," Butt says, marvelling, "I was given a gift."

Nancy Wight didn't go up to speak to Butt that night, but she says she could sense how deeply he cared. And how much that mattered to her. She would speak to him later.

Saturday, September 5, 1998

Crash site
9:30 a.m. ADT

By the end of his second sleepless day on the bridge of the *Preserver*, Cmdr. Rick Town could no longer even remember whether he took cream in his coffee. It was not just that the commander was more tired than he'd ever been in his life. It was simply that, as he put it later, "if it didn't have anything to do with rescue, I didn't want to think about it." He wasn't the only one. George Robertson, a chief petty officer on the ship, would later tell a *Globe and Mail* reporter that his most difficult job "was to persuade sailors to go off duty on the first day after the crash, even though many of them had been up for more than 28 hours."

That all-consuming moment had passed now with the seemingly simple decision by their military superiors to change the name — and nature — of the operation from "rescue" to "recovery." There was, of course, nothing simple about it. "The emotional moment of [the crew] having to strike down all the gear that was set up to receive survivors [and] quickly switch into processing human remains ..." Town stops. "You know, you try to put a human face on things, and gain an understanding that way. In this instance, you just can't. It just defies description and it just doesn't work."

Now, maps on the wardroom wall showed where divers had found various pieces of the aircraft and, of course, "HR" — human remains. Often "Multiple HR." The ship's helicopter hangar had been turned into a temporary morgue filled with body bags and bleach, rubber boots and boxes of freezer bags. The tools of their new grisly trade were everywhere. There was no escape for anyone.

"We're doing, I think, a very good job of taking care of each other," Town reported in one ship-to-shore interview with a reporter. "All the men and women are being careful of each other to ensure that the other person's doing okay ... They stop each other in the flats, and they look each other in the eye and what you hear from them is 'how are you?' instead of 'hello.' "

When he got home, he told the reporter, the first thing he planned to do was cry.

Peggys Cove
10:30 a.m. ADT

Darren Wilkins threw yet another flower into the ocean, then watched it disappear into the receding surf. "You know what I think Monte would like better than me throwing flowers into the water for him?" Darren finally said to no one in particular. "I'd bet he'd like it if I hit some golf balls into the ocean instead."

Their shared passion for sports in general, and golf in particular, had helped bring Darren, 27, and Monte, 19, much closer together in the last few years. "We began to interact as equals," Darren says, instead of just as little brother–big brother. That summer, while Monte was living at home with their parents in Yucaipa, California — between his spring semester at Walla Walla and his planned year in France at Saleve Adventist Institute, the same college Darren had attended seven years before — he and Darren had managed to get in at least a couple of golf games each week. Mostly, they played at what Darren calls "nine-dollar courses" in the neighbourhood.

That made the previous weekend — the last weekend before Monte left for Europe, the last weekend, in fact, of his life — seem so special now. A grateful patient had given their father, David, an eye surgeon, the gift of a free weekend of golf and relaxation at the famous PGA West course in Palm Springs. The family had turned the weekend into an impromptu going away party for Monte. While their mother, Janet, and Darren's wife, Yvette, enjoyed the condo that was part of the weekend package, Darren, Monte and their father played two complete rounds of golf, despite a blistering heat wave and the realization that "this course was way too hard for us." Nevertheless it was, Darren would recall, "a special time."

Three days later, Monte was dead. Four days later, the whole family — Monte's father David, mother Janet, two sisters Shannon and Marci, brother Darren, brother-in-law Dan, sister-in-law Yvette, and two family friends, Darla Klokeid and S.A.M. (pronounced "Sam") Cantrell — were on their way to Nova Scotia. "Mom and my wife didn't really want to go at first," Darren says, "but Dad and I did, so they decided to come so we would all be together."

The first night in Halifax, he recalls, "we sat around and cried a lot. My wife and I and my little sister walked around the Public Gardens for a while and then we went to the briefing. It was hard. We all saw it as just this horrible thing that had happened, but there were other people there who were very angry and wanted someone to blame. The authorities were very good — they were there to answer any questions we had — but it was hard to be with these people who were so angry about it all."

That's what had made this morning's visit to Peggys Cove so much better. They'd met some other families, shared some stories. "It was real bittersweet." A local Seventh-day Adventist minister had photocopied some hymns for them to sing. "We decided before we left that we were going to sing," Darren recalls. John O'Donnell, a Canadian Forces chaplain, escorted them down onto the granite face of the tiny peninsula, and there they began to sing "It Is Well With My Soul" and "Nearer My God To Thee."

"It was beautiful," remembers O'Donnell, "but after four, five verses, I start to think, 'Oh my goodness, we're taking a lot of time here because there's lots of families waiting.' I looked up and everyone — all the firemen, all the police, all the other families — was just sort of trans-fixed on this family down there singing away. They fin-ished that hymn and broke into 'Amazing Grace.' It blew me away."

Afterwards, the Wilkins family and friends had all gone down to the water's edge to toss into the water the flowers the Red Cross volunteers had given them. That was when Darren began to think about the kind of tribute he was sure his brother would have preferred.

He only wished he'd brought his golf clubs.

Swissair Training Centre, Zurich
8:30 p.m. CET

Reudi Bornhauser stepped through the doorway and entered the second-floor catwalk that ran along one side of the training centre's cavernous, gym-like simulator room, walked past the unmanned external computerized command centre and then gingerly made his way along a suspended steel walkway to the entrance to the MD-11 simulator's cabin. The simulator was a gigantic box-like structure mounted halfway between the floor and the ceiling on spider-like legs from which thick cables snaked to unseen controls that could rock and shake the structure in response to whatever commands the pilot issued from inside the faux cockpit. It had been carefully constructed and expertly programmed to mimic in every way possible the sound and feel and sense of an MD-11 cockpit.

Swissair used the simulator to train and test MD-11 pilots, its own as well as those of other airlines. You could do things in simulators you simply couldn't do in the air: surprise a pilot in the middle of a requalification test with an unexpected engine fire, or some sudden smoke in the cockpit. How fast could he react? Would she remember to follow the proper checklist? The simulator could also be programmed to train pilots to land at specific airports. Projectors on the top of the simulator beamed amazingly life-like computer-generated images of airports and terrain and landing strips on screens just beyond the cockpit. Looking out through the cockpit's windscreen, it was possible to believe you were taxiing down a runway at the new Hong Kong airport.

Reudi Bornhauser wasn't interested in Hong Kong that night. Or in any other world airport currently programmed into the simulator's data bank. Bornhauser, Swissair's chief technical pilot for the MD-11 fleet, was more interested in trying to figure out whether his friend and colleague Urs Zimmermann could have landed an MD-11 with a bellyful of fuel and cargo and passengers at the Halifax International Airport on Wednesday night.

The speculation and the second-guessing about that had already begun in the media. Some reporters were blaming the aircraft, trotting out a 1996 U.S. Federal Aviation Administration Air Worthiness Directive that warned of a wiring fault in the MD-11's aft console that could lead to a fire and make it difficult for the pilot to control the plane. But Bornhauser knew SAir Technics, the subsidiary responsible for Swissair plane maintenance, would have followed the FAA's instructions to American carriers for fixing the problem. As for suggestions in the media that the MD-11 itself was a problem-prone aircraft, Bornhauser begged to differ. His job involved putting each new MD-11 that Swissair bought through its technical paces. He did the same for every individual MD-11 in the fleet after it had undergone major maintenance checks or repairs. He trusted this aircraft with his life — and still would today.

The other early speculation in the press was that the pilots were to blame for the crash. Arthur Wolk, a prominent American aviation lawyer who described himself as a pilot and crash expert, was being quoted in the media criticizing the Swissair pilots for not taking the cockpit smoke warning seriously enough and for deciding not to land immediately at Halifax. "The capabilities of the MD-11 to descend safely and swiftly, and land overweight, without risk, makes this crash wholly preventable," Wolk said in a statement.

Could Zimmermann and Loëw really have landed safely in Halifax? Bornhauser didn't believe so, but he wanted to try it out in the simulator anyway, just to be certain. He didn't attempt to replicate all the weather conditions that night or the specifics of the Halifax International Airport, except for creating a generic computerized landing strip the same length as the Halifax one, but he did program into the simulator Flight 111's fuel, passenger and cargo weights. Then, beginning at 33,000 feet, the same altitude Flight 111 was flying when it reported its initial pan-pan-pan, Bornhauser tried to bring the aircraft in for a safe landing within the same 70 miles Zimmermann and Loëw had to work with that night. He couldn't. He tried again. And again. It simply couldn't be done.

That wasn't quite true, of course. Bornhauser had strictly and precisely followed the manufacturer's and airline's procedures for landing an overweight plane. It's possible, of course, that he just might have been able to bring the plane in for a safe landing by pushing the plane's tolerance envelope a little, something other pilots had occasionally done, and which critics argued the pilots should have done in this case, too.

Despite that unmentioned caveat, Bornhauser's failed attempt to land the MD-11 in the simulator that night was more than enough for SAir Group CEO Philippe Bruggisser, who would tell a Zurich press conference the next morning that Swissair had reconstructed the final phase of the flight and concluded that the plane was simply too high and too heavy for a landing. He insisted to reporters that the plane would have required another 60 miles of flying time to have had any hope of a safe landing.

It had been less than four days since the plane crashed, but already everyone was staking out their turf.

Sunday, September 6, 1998

Lord Nelson Hotel lobby
3 a.m. ADT

S.A.M. Cantrell couldn't sleep. After their friends the Wilkinses had gone up to their rooms a few hours earlier, she and Darla Klokeid went to have a quiet drink together. Cantrell says that, because of their religious convictions, none of the Wilkinses drank alcohol, "but I like a glass of wine now and then, and that night, I needed a glass of wine. I was just spent."

They wandered around the corner from the hotel to a basement bar called the Oasis. "Could we get something to eat too?" Cantrell asked. Though there'd been plenty of plates of food for the families back at the hotel, she says "we hadn't felt like eating all day. Now we did."

"Kitchen's closed," the waiter replied.

"So we started to drink our wine, but then, after a few minutes, he came back over to us and asked if we're with the Swissair families. We say yes but we tell him we don't want to talk about it right now. So that's okay. He goes away again." But he returned a few minutes later. He'd gone to a restaurant next door and bought them each a sandwich. "And, you know," Cantrell says, shaking her head at the memory, "he wouldn't take our money, not even a tip."

It wasn't the first time Cantrell had had such an

encounter with what she still calls, months later, "the most outstanding collection of people I've ever met anywhere." Earlier, she'd gone out to Peggys Cove without the Wilkinses. "I tried to pick my spots so I'd go when no one else was around," she says. She'd taken along one of the teddy bears the Red Cross had been handing out to family members. Many had been throwing the stuffed animals into the ocean in memory of their loved ones. Cantrell wanted to do the same — for Monte, with whom she'd been very close, but also in memory of her own son who'd died years earlier in a car accident. But she didn't toss her bear quite hard enough, and it fell short of the water, landing on a rocky ledge above the crashing waves. It was too dangerous for her to try to reach it on her own. "I don't know why, but that just hit me really hard at that moment," she explains. One of the recovery workers saw her distress and clambered over the rocks to the bear. "I know the workers had all been working very hard and they were tired because it was the end of a long shift," she says now, "but he came anyway." He went out on the ledge, got the bear and threw it the rest of the way into the ocean. "I just want you to know he's in the water now," the man said gently as he headed back up to rejoin his fellow workers.

In the hotel lobby on their way back from the bar, they ran into two police officers assigned to keep the press at bay. They got to talking and Cantrell had happened to tell the officers about the Wilkinses' visit to Peggys Cove: about the hymn singing, the flower-throwing and Darren's offhand remark that he'd prefer to honour Monte's memory by hitting golf balls into the sea.

"I just wish I could find a store open now so I could buy him a golf club and some balls," Cantrell said.

"Wait a minute," one of the officers, Const. Pam Winters, said suddenly. "I think we probably have some golf clubs in Abandoned Goods."

"I'll buy you a pizza if you go and get it," the other policeman said.

Winters did just that, rounding up a golf club and some balls that had never been claimed from the department's evidence locker and bringing them back to the hotel, along with a police engraving tool.

Cantrell spent an hour carefully inscribing everything, including the golf balls. On the shaft of the golf club, she wrote: "Monte, We Love You." It wasn't easy. She had to stop from time to time because she was crying too much to see what she was writing. The next morning, Cantrell and Klokeid would present the club and balls to Darren. It was strange, Cantrell thought, how good she felt in spite of this horror. She credited Nova Scotians for that.

CFB Shearwater, Nova Scotia
10:30 a.m. ADT

As they approached the shelter where the passengers' personal effects had been collected, Peggy Coburn suddenly felt like she was walking into a kind of "spiritual Jell-O."

"Wow, did you feel that?" she asked her brother.

"I don't want to talk about it," he said quickly. "It's too 'out there.'"

So he had felt it too! They were here. The souls of some of those who had died on Flight 111 were here in this place, she thought. "It was like they had formed a 'soul cloud' that was now filling up the space around the shelter," she would explain later. "I didn't have a feeling of terror or sadness. It was serene and peaceful, and I could picture what they looked like."

Peggy and her brother, Fred Newman, were among

the latest group of families to be bussed over to Shearwater to this tent shelter beside the hangar that had become the temporary morgue so they could look at, and perhaps identify, items that had once belonged to the passengers. Handbags, photographs, wallets, passports, driver's licences — all manner of things had been carefully laid out on long tables covered with white tablecloths. Some were so badly mangled they were scarcely recognizable as what they had once been; others looked as fresh and unused as the day they were acquired. Some of them were already identified and grouped, with the person's name handwritten on a card in front of it.

Peggy's brother had decided to accompany her into the shelter because, Peggy says, "he was worried about how I might react if I saw Richard's stuff." Her sister, Ronnie Newman, who'd come with them, stayed on the bus with the baby, Alea.

"If you see something that you recognize, please don't touch it," the man in the white space-like suit with the orange gloves told them outside the shelter. He was so tall and he walked so fast she practically had to run just to keep up with him. "Just call one of us over and we'll make a note of it," he said. He explained that the personal effects were all still part of the police investigation. They'd been rinsed, tagged and dusted for evidence of explosive chemicals. Just in case. Everything, he was quick to add, would be returned to the next of kin as soon as it was no longer needed for the investigation.

Peggy had already been interviewed by the police, the night before at the hotel. Everyone had been, she guessed. It was all so clinical — Had Richard ever had any broken bones? Were there any identifying scars or tattoos on his body? Could she describe his body hair? — and yet the policemen who talked to her were so compassionate, so caring. They asked her to describe Rich's wedding ring

— three gold ribbons braided around each other — and they took the photograph of him someone had asked her to bring along to Halifax. They asked if there were two family members who could donate some samples for DNA testing.

Richard's wallet! There on the table! It was his, she was sure of it. She called someone over. But seeing the wallet itself mattered less now than what she felt as she walked around the tent. Later, she would try to describe it: "It was like these little bubbles sticking together to form multi-bubbles and they were all pulsing like they were alive. I couldn't actually see anything but I could definitely feel it — wispy, ephemeral like the feeling you get when hair blows around your face. I felt like I was walking into it."

Was it Richard's soul she was feeling? she wondered.

"Nancy, over here." Nancy Wight looked up. It was her new friend, Yvette Wilkins, calling her from the other end of the table, pointing to a collection of personal effects.

Nancy had been staring unseeingly — for how long? — at an assortment of unidentified handbags clustered together on one of the tables. For some reason she couldn't quite figure out, the bags reminded her of nothing so much as the old-fashioned ladies' handbags that were popular during the forties. What were they doing here? Then she saw it in among the handbags. A tiny photograph, no bigger than a postage stamp, of Rowenna and her friend Elizabeth Rinaldi. It had been taken when the girls were about 12. Rowenna loved that picture. She'd shown it to her mother again shortly before she left on Wednesday. She kept it in her wallet.

"I've found something." Yvette was by her side now, guiding her by the arm along the table to where there was a sign: "White, Rowenna," it said.

Nancy had come out to Shearwater on the bus with Nancy Richards, her care partner, who'd barely left her side since they'd met on Friday. Whenever they met someone new, Wight would now introduce Richard by saying: "She's my guardian angel."

But now, of course, she was less alone. She'd met other families who'd lost loved ones aboard Swissair Flight 111. Like the Wilkinses. Monte Wilkins, like Rowenna, had been on his way to school in Europe when he died.

Monte's father, David, had met Nancy first. He'd seen her standing alone by the elevator in the lobby of the Lord Nelson Hotel. "She was alone," he recalls, "and it was clear she wasn't doing well."

"Who did you lose?" he asked, putting his arm around her shoulder.

"I lost my mother, my dog and my daughter all in the same year," Nancy answered softly. "I'm all alone now."

Within minutes, the Wilkinses had adopted Nancy as one of their own. Despite their loss, the Wilkins family did not feel quite so alone. They had not only each other but their Seventh-day Adventist faith as well. It created a wider circle, even here in Nova Scotia, 3,000 miles from their California home. On Friday night, Glen and Susanne Mitchell, the local Seventh-day minister and his wife, had stopped by the hotel to spend a few hours with the family. And then on Saturday, another Seventh-day Adventist couple from Halifax, Bob and Sirje Walkowiak, had called to invite them to spend some time at their home in Hubbards, on St. Margarets Bay. Sirje Walkowiak, Wilkins explains now, was "some sort of shirt-tail relative" of his family. There'd even been a message left on their hotel telephone from another local Seventh-day Adventist, a fisherman named Robert Conrad, expressing sympathy for their loss and inviting them to come out to their house in Fox Point on Sunday afternoon.

Wilkins accepted, and then invited Nancy Wight to join them. What was one more?

Before that, however, they'd all decided to go out to Shearwater to see whether they could identify anything that had belonged to Monte or Rowenna.

Though the Wilkinses found nothing at all of Monte's on the table, Yvette, Monte's sister-in-law, was quick to bring Nancy to the collection bearing Rowenna's name.

Nancy stared at her daughter's things, all neatly arranged around the card with her name. There was her new green backpack she'd bought for the trip, and her yellow wallet that had once belonged to Nancy's mother. The wallet, which was bulging with travellers' cheques, was open. Nancy could see a recipe sticking out from a pocket; Rowenna had been taking it with her to school. Her black address book and passport were there too, both in pristine condition. They did not look like they'd been in a plane crash. The passport was open to the page with Rowenna's picture on it. So beautiful.

"Can I touch it?" she asked the attendant, pointing to the backpack. She thought it still looked wet.

"Okay," he said reluctantly.

She ran her fingers over it. The backpack was actually dry. It just looked wet. The chemicals, perhaps? She stared at it all for a long time. Yes, she decided finally, there really had been a plane crash, and this was all that was left of her daughter.

She and Nancy Richard then walked to a nearby Quonset hut where other workers in white suits and orange gloves were sorting through bins of aircraft debris. She could see only three tiny shards from the plane itself.

"Where is the morgue?" she asked one of the workers suddenly. He ignored her, so she asked again. He self-consciously cocked his head in the direction of Hangar B, then went back to his work. She looked over, looked away. She just wanted to know. And now she did.

She told Nancy Richard she should go home. She was going to spend the afternoon with the Wilkinses visiting friends of theirs. She'd be all right. Richard should go home, get some rest. She was okay, she said, she really was.

Fox Point
3:30 p.m. ADT

Robert Conrad had expected they would arrive as traumatized as he still felt. Perhaps they were. Perhaps these Californians just had different ways of expressing their grief. Truth be told, he thought to himself, he preferred their way to his.

As the Wilkinses and their friends spilled out of the two cars the Walkowiaks — fellow parishioners of the Conrads at the Seventh-day Adventist church in Fox Point — had had to use to bring them all out from the city, they ran up and began to hug Robert and Peggy like long-lost friends.

David Wilkins introduced himself, his wife and children and their spouses, as well as their new friend, Nancy Wight. And then they all helped Sirje Walkowiak bring in the food.

Nancy Wight, who was hungry for any scrap of information about the crash that killed her daughter, had quizzed Sirje, a school principal who'd been an "ear witness" to the crash, on the drive out. What time? How loud? What did it sound like? She was just as keen to hear Robert Conrad's story about what it had been like on the water that night.

In truth, Conrad needed to talk about that too — with people who had lost someone in the tragedy and might understand the awful feelings of sadness he was still having. It was one of the reasons he'd called Wilkins in the first place. Incredibly — Conrad would call it providence — Conrad's wife, Peggy, had been in email correspondence before the crash with a cousin of hers in Washington State, a retired doctor, who had a friend named Wilkins. After the crash, the cousin contacted Peggy to suggest she get in touch with the Wilkins family when they arrived in Nova Scotia. Peggy happened to mention it to Sirje, who'd already been making plans to invite the Wilkinses, her distant relations, to her house. They decided to combine forces: the Conrads would provide their house, the Walkowiaks would bring the food. Neighbours pitched in too. The Robsons, who lived down the hill from the Conrads, brought more food.

If the circumstances hadn't been so awful, it could have been wonderful.

Robert Conrad didn't need much prompting to recount the sanitized version of what he'd seen and done the night of the crash: about finding the body of the toddler and, later, the black suitcase that was too heavy to bring aboard. But he had, he told them, managed to rescue a brown suede jacket from the case as it drifted by. He'd turned it over to the police the next day.

Brown suede jacket? Black suitcase? What did the jacket look like? Nancy Wight wanted to know. Rowenna had packed a brown suede jacket in her black suitcase. In the end, there was too little information for either of them to be absolutely certain, but it seemed likely that Robert Conrad had fished Rowenna's jacket from the ocean that night. It was another bit of providence, another tie to bind them together. Robert and Peggy had already noticed how alone Nancy was; they knew, without having to say anything to one another, that they would try to keep in touch with this sad, lonely woman from New York.

The Conrads and Walkowiaks were as keen to hear about Rowenna and Monte as the others had been to hear their stories about the night of the crash. Darren told them about the last weekend of golf he and his father had shared with Monte, then said to his host: "If you don't mind, Bob, my family has a request to make of you." And he launched into the story of the police officers and the golf club. "I brought the club and the balls with me. Is there some place we could go to hit them into the water?"

Of course there was. They all piled back into the cars for the 12-mile drive to Bayswater Beach, the closest point of land on the peninsula to the site of the crash. During the drive in Bob Walkowiak's car, Janet Wilkins, her daughters and her daughter-in-law spontaneously began to sing hymns. "Bob pretty much had to stop the car," Conrad says. "He was crying so hard."

The sun had finally broken through the fog that had enveloped the bay for most of the days since the crash. It was a "gem of a day," Conrad says, a glorious sunny Sunday afternoon. They all walked along the rocky beach to the point of Bayswater Beach closest to the crash site.

Nancy spotted a group of divers surfacing near the shore and ran after them. "They didn't really want to talk with me," she says now. "I suppose they were very tired, but I was desperate to know what they were finding. I was exhausted and on edge." Later she encountered an army officer beside a military vehicle. "Her name was Martin and she was friendly," says Wight, who had one of the others snap a photo of the two of them beside the truck. "I did thank her for her work."

When they finally reached the farthest end of the beach, Darren recalls, "I realized I didn't have a tee and there was no place I could really use to hit the ball. Finally, I found this bottle cap and I put it down on a rock and put the ball on top of it and that was the tee." He smiles.

"Monte would have laughed really hard. I sliced that ball hard. And I did the same with the second one. Monte and I always trash-talked each other when we played. He would have trash-talked me for sure then." Darren gave their father the last ball to shoot. His drive wasn't much better, but that didn't matter, Darren says. "It just felt right."

He considers for a while. "I know different people have different ideas about the afterlife," he says. "We Seventh-day Adventists believe everyone will be resurrected at the same time, that the afterlife doesn't begin right after you die. But that day on that point of land hitting those balls, I could just picture Monte there looking at me. Right now, I just think someday he and I are going to be together again and we're going to look at the videotape of that day and we're just going to laugh about it."

Darren had originally hoped that, after firing the golf balls into the ocean, Conrad could take everyone out to the crash site in his boat so they could drop that driver — with "Monte, We Love You" engraved on the shaft — over the side at the exact spot where the plane had plunged into the sea. Unfortunately, Canadian authorities had closed off the entire area to all vessels. Darren gave the golf club to Conrad and asked him to complete their tribute when he was allowed to return to the waters around the crash site.

They went back to the Conrads' to eat some more food and sing some more songs. By the time they left it was dark, but the sky was still clear and a fat, full moon hung over the bay. They all stood in silent awe for a moment beside the rock where Conrad sometimes came at night to watch the sky and think about life. "All I could think of," Nancy says now, "was 'Hymn to the Moon' from Dvořák's *Russalka*." When she got back to her hotel room, she says, she turned on the television "and what should I hear but the 'Hymn to the Moon,' one of my very favourite arias." The next day, after she returned home to New York, she immediately took a nap. "When I woke up I turned on the radio and the 'Hymn to the Moon' began to play. It was so coincidental. Strange and comforting."

Like a full moon on St. Margarets Bay. Like providence, perhaps.

Halifax
10:30 p.m. ADT

Nancy Richard just had to talk to her parents back in British Columbia. She couldn't wait, she needed to call them now.

This had been, she would tell friends later, the most emotionally exhausting and difficult two days of her life. Until Nancy Wight went off with the Wilkinses earlier that afternoon, Richard had spent virtually every waking moment with her. They'd talked endlessly about Nancy's dog, her mother, her ex-husband, her life. And especially, of course, about her daughter. They'd shared intimacies people rarely share, even close friends. She and Nancy Wight had become, for these few days at least, the closest of close friends.

"I don't think I could have done this if I had children myself," Richard would later say. "It would have been too hard. You have to be so strong when you're with your partner."

To make matters worse, she couldn't even share her feelings with anyone when she got home. Richard's husband, Troy, a naval officer, was among more than a thousand navy personnel who'd been mobilized to deal with the crash. He was conducting stress debriefings for military personnel who'd been involved in the gruesome recovery operation. It was ironic, really; they were both so busy helping others that they weren't around to support each other.

That's one reason she wanted to call her parents that night. She'd thought a lot about the things Nancy Wight had said, about the argument she'd had with Rowenna, about not being at the airport to say goodbye. Life was so unpredictable. "You suddenly realize just how important every moment is," she says now.

When her parents answered the phone, she simply said: "I love you."

"I just needed to tell them that."

Monday, September 7, 1998

Bayswater

Audrey Backman had long since given up thinking of her house as her home. Since the morning of September 3, the modest bungalow overlooking St. Margarets Bay that she and Harris and their son Steven shared had been transformed into the onshore command centre for the Canadian Coast Guard Auxiliary's Swissair recovery effort. Helicopters landed and took off from the rocky shore in front of the house. A coast guard trailer had been set up next to the house so exhausted searchers could catch a few minutes' rest before heading back to sea. People — many of whom Audrey had never seen before — trooped in and out of her living room office. The kitchen had become a mess hall for anyone who wandered by at any hour.

Gary Masson, the auxiliary's only other full-time staff member in the Maritimes, had arrived in Bayswater from his home in New Brunswick shortly after noon on the day after the plane went down. He was still there now, working with Harris and Audrey to coordinate what had become a massive operation.

It was an unusual assignment for the auxiliary. Normally, its volunteer members are called out for a few hours at a time to help search for a missing fisherman or boater. They rarely get involved in post–search and rescue recovery efforts, especially in cases where there were no survivors. But then the Swissair crash was a rare and unusual situation, unprecedented, in fact. No single agency or organization was equipped to handle it on its own; few even had contingency plans for such a large-scale cleanup. The auxiliary certainly didn't. But coast guard officials knew that the auxiliary's Zone 11 — the area around the crash site — boasted a group of fishermen who not only were well schooled in the ways of searching but also knew the tricks of navigating the area's bays and shoals better than anyone else. In addition, their sturdy 35- to 40-foot fishing vessels were ideal for the jobs they would be asked to take on: pick up floating debris and deliver it to the larger coast guard and military ships, and, later on, ferry divers, TSB investigators and others between the shore and those larger vessels operating at the crash site. Still, when the coast guard asked the auxiliary Thursday morning to assist in the recovery operation, no one quite knew what that would mean.

"The first few days were pretty crazy," Masson recalls. But by that day, five days after the crash, the chaos had become almost routine. Each evening the coast guard operations centre would call the Backmans' house asking them to deploy a certain number of auxiliary vessels to various locations in the crash area the next morning. Harris, Audrey and Gary would in turn call their members and tell them where to show up the next morning at five o'clock. Then they'd call both coast operations and the Mounties — who controlled access to the exclusion zone around the crash site — to tell them which vessels to expect. After that, they'd begin putting together the packages — box lunches, rubber gloves, masks — the crews would need for the next day. Some crews would stop by the house to pick up their supplies, or someone from the house would deliver them to the

wharf, or Steven Backman, who had become the auxiliary's on-scene commander on the water, would deliver
the necessities in his boat the next morning.

The food for the lunches, and the hands to prepare
and pack them, came from everywhere. The Seabright
Legion supplied sandwiches, a woman in Fox Point sent
down a huge pot of stew, families the Backmans had
never met before stopped by bearing pot roasts and pies.
The hordes of reporters who visited the house in search
of a story would find themselves making more sandwiches — "I'd get them to scrub up and put them to work,"
Audrey says with a laugh — and then being invited to
stay for a mug of stew. "But you'll have to serve yourself," Audrey would tell them. "I can't wait on you."
Everyone pitched in to wash dishes. Sometimes too,
Masson says, they'd happen to notice one of the ground
search and rescue teams combing the shoreline in front of
the house. "We'd called them in for food and a cold pop."

The crews from the auxiliary vessels would often stop
by, sometimes to get reimbursed for their fuel expenses,
sometimes to file an insurance claim because some plane
debris had damaged their boat, sometimes just to share
their experiences of the day, so stress counsellors began
to make the Backman house a counselling centre too.
"We encouraged everyone to get counselling," Audrey
says. Some did. Some of the crews could talk only to
each other about the horrors they'd seen on the water.
Others, Audrey says, "decided they didn't need any help.
Most of them did, but they wouldn't admit it."

During the first few days many of them were just too
busy to "take the time to look at the emotional side of it."
That day, in fact, was the first time Audrey had had a
moment to even think about the reality of how close the
big jet had flown over her home on its final doomed circle over St. Margarets Bay. Officials had finally released

information on the plane's flight path, which showed that Flight 111 had passed almost directly over her house, before going into a spiral and plunging into the water four and a half miles beyond the shore. "Gary and I looked at the chart on the wall," Audrey says. "We were always referring to that chart, but I'd never thought about it before. We looked at where the plane went down and where we were and we started to figure how fast the plane had been going. Gary figured it out on the calculator. Thirty-three seconds. Thirty-three seconds different and it would have crashed in our front yard."

She and Masson stopped, looked at one another for a long quiet moment.

Finally, Audrey spoke. "We were lucky," she said.

And then? "Then we went back to work. There was still lots of things to do."

Tuesday, September 8, 1998

Hangar B, CFB Shearwater

He had warned them. During his first Sunday-morning briefing for senior staff, John Butt had told them about his own difficulties coming to terms with the reality of dismembered bodies from a horrific train crash in England in the sixties. After 48 hours working flat out in the lab identifying remains, he said, he'd gone home and wept inconsolably. But back then in stiff-upper-lip England, he added, he couldn't tell anyone except his wife how he was feeling. Today, he made it a point to tell his staff about the critical-incident stress counsellors who were available to talk to them 24 hours a day in rooms attached to the hangar. They shouldn't be afraid to see someone if they needed to, he said.

He had. Several times already. John Butt knew he could use all the help he could get from whatever source. Whenever he would slip away from the temporary morgue to catch a few hours' rest on a bunk in a corner of the base's officers' mess, for example, he'd read from a book called *The Things Children Write to God.* The book had been a gift from one of his neighbours. Later, when he returned to his duties at the hangar-turned-morgue, he would photocopy the section and post it on the bulletin board for everyone else to read. "We all needed something like that at a time like this," he explained later.

The days and nights had begun to tumble into one another. It had been more than five days since the accident and he hadn't been home yet, and wasn't sure when he'd be able to spend a night in his own bed again, or when — if ever — he'd be able to sleep through the night.

The emotional roller-coaster ride continued. One minute he was gently trying to bring a screaming mother around to the reality that her son was dead, the next he was resisting the demand of a pushy young American who wanted him to sign a certificate of death for his very rich father *now*. Soon after, he would be locking horns with an RCMP brass hat over what Butt saw as his too by-the-book way of dealing with the victims' personal effects and then, a minute later, he'd be on the phone to some official at the Transportation Safety Board giving him an earful about his loose use of the term "bodies" in a press release. Despite the pressures, Butt was nonetheless encouraged to realize that the real job, identifying the remains, had finally begun.

Construction was continuing on changing rooms and locker facilities for the hundreds of pathologists, dentists, photographers, Mounties and X-ray and lab technicians who were arriving to work on the identification process at the hangar, but remarkably, the morgue itself was largely operational. The hangar had already been divided into a dozen 16-foot by 16-foot cubicles.

Identification was a four-stage procedure. First, the remains were visually inspected, photographed, and fingerprinted if possible. Then any piece of clothing, jewellery or other identifying item on the remains was removed and recorded in a database. After that, radiologists and dental technicians X-rayed any bones or teeth. Finally, lab technicians collected for DNA analysis samples of tissue — no bigger than one-tenth the size of the head of a pin — from each piece of remains that had been positively identified as belonging to a specific passenger.

If investigators could also get DNA samples from personal items the victims had used before they died — saliva from a toothbrush or a baby's soother, sweat from an exercise sweatband — they might be able to match it with the DNA from the victim. But even if they couldn't make a match that way, there were other options. DNA isn't just unique to each individual; it also acts as a kind of genetic connector that links family members through patterns passed on from parents to children. Investigators wanted DNA samples from at least two close blood relatives of each victim to use for comparison.

If it was possible to speak in such terms, Butt knew that pathologists were luckier this time than they had been during TWA 800, another crash where identifying remains turned out to be difficult. Although the investigators there used DNA analysis to identify a few bodies, the technology was still in its infancy even as recently as 1996. It had taken 14 months to positively identify just 20 of the 230 bodies. Today, the same work could be done in a matter of days or weeks, and many more bodies could be identified using the technology. A good thing because, as Butt conceded to a reporter from *Newsday*, "this is a much more difficult situation, obviously." Since the TWA plane had been blown out of the sky by an explosion rather than shattering on impact, more of the bodies were intact or visually identifiable than those aboard Flight 111.

Investigators had unexpectedly smacked into their first, and what could be biggest, hurdle on Saturday, after the Mounties called investigators from TWA 800 to ask for a copy of the computer program they'd used to catalogue all the pieces they'd gathered from that disaster — only to discover no such program existed.

Given the number, size and condition of the body parts being recovered from Flight 111 — not to mention all of the passengers' personal possessions and the air-craft pieces that were sometimes intermingled with them — Butt knew that developing a comprehensive database would be critically important, not only to help investigators match body parts and tissue samples with the identifying information the Mounties had been gathering from next of kin but also to assist the police and the investigators from the TSB as they tried to figure out what had caused the crash in the first place. In the end, an RCMP computer guru spent several sleepless nights adapting a program the force had developed for use in a sweeping investigation into child sexual abuse.

The jerry-built program seemed to be working well, Butt noted with satisfaction. If the pathologists found an arm with a tattoo of a rose on it, they could use the program to instantly search the transcripts of all the interviews investigators had conducted with family members and come up with a list of all passengers with tattoos on their arms. "We used to write out all that sort of information on a blackboard," one of the Mounties involved in the identification later told a conference on using technology as an investigative tool, "but in the case of Flight 111 there was just too much information for that."

The program would become even more important later on, when researchers had to try to match the DNA samples provided by relatives with the tissue from passengers on the plane. Being able to link the two samples before testing using other information in the database — mention of a scar from an old wound, for example, or an X-ray of a broken bone — allowed the researchers to narrow down the number of possible matches and made identification much simpler and faster.

There was still what Butt would refer to as a get-on-with-it "battle mentality" among those working in Hangar B, but the frenetic pace of the first few days had become slightly more calm as staff settled in for what everyone knew would be a long and difficult process of recovering, cataloguing and identifying the remains. Butt had quickly given up on the idea of staffing the morgue 24 hours a day — "We couldn't depend on getting in enough material to operate that way" — and staff were now working from eight o'clock in the morning, when senior staff got together for their morning briefing, to eight o'clock in the evening, when operations officially shut down, though people often stayed in their cubicles much later trying to fit together some troublesome pieces of the complex identification jigsaw puzzle.

They had already begun to see gruesomely fascinating patterns among the remains. Virtually all of the bodies had been decapitated at the mouth or the jawline, for example, and the skulls were broken in an average of 15 places. Many of the spines had been broken in three pieces, and the top parts of torsos were often in one piece but the pelvis would be found with only part of one leg. While it was interesting to speculate on the causes of all this — perhaps some combination of the effect of seat belts and G-forces — Butt and the others had to remind themselves that such questions were better left for later researchers. Their job — their only job — was to make sure, if possible, that as much as possible of the remains of each and every passenger who had travelled on Flight 111 were positively identified.

Butt himself didn't do many of the autopsies. Inside the morgue, he was the lightning rod — he even wore an orange construction helmet so people could find him easily — who had to answer questions and make decisions quickly. He sometimes had to keep what he calls "my own tendencies in check. You just couldn't be rude or abrupt. Everyone was working flat out all the time and you had to remember that."

Beyond the morgue floor, he had to meet visiting family members and answer their questions as well as deal with all the complex, unanticipated questions such a mass tragedy provoked. At one point, he met with a bioethicist, a funeral director and a lawyer, for example, to decide how to handle remains that couldn't be identified. Eventually, they decided to keep them in freezer trucks until someone else could decide on their ultimate disposition. Although he was later criticized by some families for not using liquid nitrogen to preserve the remains in more pristine condition so they could be identified using more sophisticated DNA techniques later on, Butt says "reconstituting" the bodies wasn't his job. "We're just there to make sure we can identify the people who were aboard that plane. That's our mandate."

He also had to become a quick study in the death rituals of the world's religions. There had been Christians, Jews, Muslims, a Hindu and a Greek Orthodox — not to mention people of no particular faith — on the plane. Jews, for example, can't begin mourning, or shiva, until after the body has been interred or there is absolutely no hope of recovering it. That meant the families of Jewish victims, of whom there were more than 20, were in a Halachic, or Jewish legal, limbo while the search and identification continued. Then there was the longer-term issue of agunah. In Jewish law, the only way a woman can be freed to remarry is through divorce or death. Proving someone has died for purposes of dissolving the marriage requires either the visual identification of a body or a certain amount of time to pass. Moshe Krupka, a New York rabbi, flew to Nova Scotia to start, with Butt, the "presumption of death" process for those wives whose husbands had been identified.

Though John Butt had dealt with death every day of his professional life, this time it was somehow different.

His eyes often filled with tears as he briefed reporters or spoke to family members. And they had only now, after five days, positively identified the second victim from the crash, this one from fingerprints. There were still 227 to go. Could he survive it all?

That's what made moments like the one that morning so important. The key players — senior pathologists and dentists, the RCMP's fingerprinting expert, the computer expert, the person in charge of collecting information for next of kin and a few other morgue managers — were gathering for their morning briefing. Butt was jotting down notes of some of the issues he wanted to bring up at the session when his assistant turned on her laptop computer. Instead of the usual beep, the computer had been programmed to start with a recorded welcome message from her child: "Good morning, Mommy," it said.

Butt looked up from his paper and smiled. "How wonderful to hear that on a day like this," he said.

Wednesday, September 9, 1998

East St. Margarets Elementary School

Nancy Richard needed to be here, to sit among her friends and fellow care workers and finally do what she hadn't been able to do before tonight. On Monday morning, she'd accompanied Nancy Wight home to New York on one of the continuous Air Canada shuttles and then returned to Halifax the same day. Forty-eight hours later, she was still trying to understand and assimilate all that had happened.

But she wasn't alone this night. A week to the day since Flight 111 had gone down, she and a thousand other people — families of victims, care partners, fishermen, police officers, soldiers, sailors, teachers, schoolchildren — were gathered at the ball field beside this clapboard elementary school to remember the 229 people who'd died aboard Swissair Flight 111. The skies, which had been dark and foreboding for most of the day — most of the week, in fact — cleared just as the service began, and the day's last glorious hour of sunshine washed over the mourners.

Nancy Richard watched the sad procession as 175 family members, holding on to each other and to the flowers and the teddy bears the Red Cross had given them over the last few days, made their slow, sombre way across the field to their seats.

Most of the rest of those who were at the service that night had never met a single one of the people whose deaths they were remembering. "Even though we didn't know the people on the plane, we had been with people they knew, and so we felt a personal connection," Richard explains.

Prime Minister Jean Chrétien had flown in from Ottawa to pay his respects, as had Switzerland's president, Flavio Cotti. There were dozens of other dignitaries too — the premier of Nova Scotia, the U.S. ambassador to Canada, the U.S. transportation secretary — along with a variety of religious leaders.

Richard Walsh, the Anglican minister whose parish included Peggys Cove, told the mourners, "Each and every person who lives here wishes we could turn back the clock and change things. To the families and victims, I can only say your loved ones are spiritually part of our community. We will never forget them. We will always remember."

A local choir sang "Stay With Us Through the Night":

> Stay with us through the night.
> Stay with us through the grief.
> Stay with us, Blessed Stranger,
> 'Til the morning brings relief.

During the service, Clare Mortimer — who'd lost her father, John, a retired *New York Times* executive, and her stepmother, Hilda, in the crash — wrote an impromptu thank you to the people of Nova Scotia, which she delivered in a clear, steady voice.

"I most especially wish to thank today the people of these local communities who got out of bed on the terrible night of September 2," she said, "those of you who, without thinking, put on your boots and grabbed flashlights and got into your boats and went out immediately to start searching for our loved ones."

It took close to 10 minutes to read all of the 229 names of those who had died on Flight 111. Nancy Richard, who sat with the other care partners from Air Nova, cried throughout. It felt good, she says. "We could finally cry, we could let it out, we could lay flowers for ourselves. We weren't with our families anymore."

As the service ended, a solitary bagpiper played the "Lone Piper's Lament" and a Sea King helicopter swooped low over the crowd and out above St. Margarets Bay, where it dropped a single wreath onto the water below.

Friday, September 11, 1998

Episcopal Academy, Haverford

Today was their twenty-second wedding anniversary. Mark and Barbara Fetherolf marked the occasion by attending a memorial service for their 16-year-old daughter, Tara.

Barbara could barely remember what had happened from one day to the next during the past week and a half. She knew their house had been filled with people coming and going, expressing their shock and their sympathy. She knew too that her own bottomless well of sorrow was filled as well with a helpless rage: "How dare they do this to my beautiful daughter!" "They" were Swissair and Delta. Barbara couldn't understand why others had been publicly praising the airlines for their efficient and effective response to the tragedy. They were, she believed, typical big corporations: "covering their own asses" was their top priority.

Despite what the press was reporting — spouting Swissair's own PR line, no doubt — no one from Swissair or Delta had even called the Fetherolfs to tell them their daughter was dead. After he recovered consciousness that first morning, Mark did try to call the 1-800 number, but he had to leave a message. Later, Barbara says, she talked to Swissair officials: "I asked them why they had never called. Their response was that they were too busy." Five days later, the Fetherolfs say, they received "form letters" telling them their daughter was dead and asking if they wanted to receive the *ex gratia* payment of $20,000 the airline was offering to all next of kin to help cover their initial incidental costs, for everything from memorial services to publishing obituary notices. Instead she faxed Swissair pictures and articles that had been written about Tara, asking, "How dare you kill my precious daughter?" The airline did not reply.

Mark and Barbara hadn't gone to Peggys Cove — "We knew that Tara was gone; there was nothing we could do for her" — and although they did attend a memorial service at Lincoln Center in New York that morning, Barbara had found it cold and impersonal. Later, after she discovered it had been sponsored by Swissair, she would add: "Similar to Swissair's behaviour since the crash. Frankly, if I had been aware that they were the ones behind it I would have never gone."

But she was comforted to be at Episcopal Academy, where Tara had blossomed into such a fine and happy young woman. The room — the same room in which Tara had graduated just a few months before, the same room in which she had been called up to the front over and over again to receive her awards — was filled to overflowing with students and teachers and family friends. A boy who had been close to Tara tried to read a tribute to her but was too overcome with emotion to finish. Tara's sister, Amy, played a piece by Bach that she and Tara had performed together in the spring. "It took a great deal of courage to be able to do it at such an emotional time," Barbara says proudly, "but she wanted to do it for her big sister."

Monday, September 14, 1998

Crash site

Master Seaman René Poirier checked the hose on his bulky dual-layered 100-pound black-and-red diving suit and awkwardly lifted one weighted foot off the deck and onto the metal elevator frame that would carry him and his partner to the sea bottom. Poirier offered up a silent Hail Mary as the operators played out the cable and the two divers began their careful five-minute descent into hell.

"There is no way to describe it," the 36-year-old Canadian navy diver would quietly tell a reporter later.

Poirier and his crew of 14 divers had been descending in pairs to the Swissair crash site from first light until close to midnight every day since shortly after their ship, HMCS *Granby*, arrived on the scene three and a half hours after the plane went down. There were now close to 200 of them — Canadian, American, military, RCMP and coast guard divers — gathering up what remained of the plane, personal belongings and, more critically, human remains on the square mile of ocean floor 180 feet below where the plane hit the water. Because of the depths, each diver could spend just 30 minutes scouring another 50 to 100 square feet of territory before he had to surface again. It was slow, difficult and awful work.

Even if there were no words to adequately describe what they were seeing, the divers certainly tried: "If you took a windowpane and let it fall to the ground and it shatters in a million pieces ..." "It's like standing in the middle of a landfill." "Tin foil." "A big pile of metal." "Like a pop can that's been ripped open, very sharp and dangerous."

On one of his dives, Poirier had detected the faint ping of the transponder from Flight 111's voice data recorder, but he ran out of time before he could collect it. The next diver brought it to the surface. That was a cause for some celebration — the so-called black box promised to provide vital clues to the cause of the crash — but their elation was soon tempered after investigations found that the machine had not recorded the final six minutes of the flight.

Such moments of even muted celebration were rare. Theirs was an especially grim task. The divers referred only rarely and elliptically to the main goal of their search: the recovery of human remains. When the first bag, tethered to a rope, came up and was laid out, respectfully, on the ship's quarterdeck, the other waiting divers had to force themselves to gather around and look at the contents. "We had to know who could handle it and who couldn't," Poirier says.

The divers were far from the only military personnel who had been asked to work on this massive recovery operation — close to 1,500 Department of National Defence personnel were now assigned full time to what has been dubbed Operation Persistence — but the divers were probably the ones who came closest to truly understanding the horror of what had happened to the plane and its contents. They were the ones who had to collect the child's Lion King puppet that had become embedded in a piece of the fuselage, or the wallet with the picture of the man standing beside the smiling little boy in a cowboy hat or, not to forget — no one could forget — all those disconnected body parts they had to send up to the surface in their mesh bags.

On the bottom, in murky depths where they could see only a few yards in front of them, the divers had to navigate around all the random pieces of wreckage and luggage and human remains with exceeding caution. One wrong move and a razor-sharp shard from the plane's fuselage could, in an instant, slice through their lifeline — the air hose connecting them to the surface ship — adding one more victim to the 229 who had already perished in this tragedy.

Poirier says he tried not to think about the danger, or the awfulness of the deaths of those 229 people, or the incredible strangeness of seeing a $1,000 American bill floating by him to the surface, or the fact that he was sharing those depths with cruising sharks and the remains of what was once a huge aircraft and people. "You need total concentration," he says simply, "so there isn't much time to think about it."

There would be time for that soon enough. When he resurfaced again, Poirier said another Hail Mary, another prayer.

Thursday, September 24, 1998

Halifax

This shouldn't be, Lyn Romano repeated over and over again in her head as she sat on the chair beside her oldest son, Raymond Jr., watching silently while the nurse efficiently withdrew the small sample of blood from his arm. The blood would help the authorities identify, from among all the bits and pieces of bone and flesh they had recovered, the bits and pieces of flesh and bone that belonged to his father. It just shouldn't be, Lyn said to herself again. He's only 11 years old, for God's sake.

Why couldn't the officials have been right when they told her — when was it now? A day or so after the crash? Time had lost all meaning — that they believed there might be as many as 70 complete bodies inside a section of the cabin that had survived the crash intact and was sitting on the ocean floor. They'd asked her to send them, by Federal Express, a picture of Ray they could use to help identify him. FedEx! She'd never gotten a FedEx package in her life, and now she couldn't answer her door without finding someone there to deliver or pick up a package. Swissair. The State Department. The Medical Examiner's Office.

But of course the picture hadn't helped. There were no bodies, no intact section of the airliner. How could they not have known that? Lyn wondered.

Finally, the nurse withdrew the needle from Raymond's arm, covered the tiny pinprick with a cotton swab. Little Raymond didn't flinch. His father would have been proud.

If only Ray had been sick, she thought. Then they wouldn't need to put little Raymond through all this. But Ray had never been sick a day in his life, never once gone to the doctor, never visited a dentist. No one knew his blood type. Even Women's Hospital in New York, where he'd been born, couldn't help. There'd been a screw-up with their computer system, Lyn was told when she called, and they couldn't access records of births there between 1950 and 1955. Ray had been born July 14, 1954.

So now it was up to Raymond Jr. to provide the blood that would help them to put the pieces of his father back together again. It shouldn't be. None of it should.

The day before, at Shearwater, Lyn had stared, transfixed, at the objects on the table in front of her. She couldn't remember how she'd gotten to the military base, to the makeshift tent, to the rows of tables filled with the personal effects of those who'd died on Flight 111, to the table in front of her, the one with the personal effects of one Raymond Romano.

Lyn could barely recall the details of the flight from Westchester Airport near her house to Halifax. Only that she almost had refused to fly at all. She had been supposed to fly from Kennedy with her mother-in-law and her two sons. She remembered being in the middle of saying goodbye to her mother when the Delta Family Assistance man came to her door.

"I'm sorry," he said, "the plane's been delayed. It'll just be a few hours —"

That's when Lyn lost it. "Get off my property," she'd

screamed. "Get away from me and don't come back!"

The man, Lyn could see immediately, was petrified. Here I am, I'm five-foot-five and 117 pounds, she told herself, and this guy, this gentle guy who just wants to help, is petrified of me. I'm sorry, she thought, I'm sorry for making his life a torture. But not sorry enough to stop. I can't help myself, she thought. I can't.

The man did as he was told. But he returned a short time later with a new plan he very tentatively outlined for Lyn.

"Would you be willing to fly out of Westchester in a private jet?" he asked. The local airport was just 15 minutes away. Lyn didn't want to go, but she knew she had to, knew she had to see what there was to see of Ray, of the place he — she still couldn't bring herself to believe he was really dead.

It was an eight-passenger jet. She remembers literally crawling on to it, remembers not saying a word for the entire flight, remembers thinking she didn't care anymore if the plane went down because Ray was already gone and her boys were with her and what more could happen anyway?

Now, at Shearwater, in the trailer with all the pieces of all the lives that had been lost, she looked in the direction the Mountie pointed. That was Ray's carry-on bag, all right. In shreds. And his magazines — his *Journal of Accountancy*, his *Forbes*, his beloved car magazine. There was a yellow notepad too. With Ray's handwriting on it. She'd packed them all for him. And the two shampoo bottles next to his stuff.

How could they be in one piece and Ray ...?

"I don't understand what they're saying about the bodies," she said to the Mountie. "What happened to the bodies?"

He put his arms around her. "You really want to know this?" he asked.

"Yes," she said. "I do."

He picked up one of the glass shampoo bottles. Lyn noticed for the first time that, while the bottle appeared undamaged, it was completely empty. He showed her the small hole in the bottom through which all the shampoo had been sucked out during the crash.

"The human body," he explained gently, "is 90 per cent water. What happened to the bottles happened to the bodies."

Lyn thought about that. Then she took a picture out of her purse. It was a photograph of Ray. She began to tell the Mountie about her Ray. "I knew then that I needed to show them pictures and explain to them who my Ray was," she would explain later. "I knew I needed to do something to make this right. My husband was not going to be a seat number. He was not going to be a name."

Though she didn't realize it at the time, Lyn Romano had already taken the first step in the process that would turn her into the unlikely leader of a new air safety organization, one she would found.

Sunday, September 27, 1998

New York City

At first Nancy Wight couldn't quite figure out what her caller was talking about. He'd seen her letter, he said, and he just wanted to telephone her to tell her he really identified with it. He'd had a brother who'd been murdered when he was 15 —

"Wait a minute," she said. "What letter?"

"The letter in the paper."

Letter in the paper? "How did you get my phone number?"

"It was in the paper."

It dawned on her that the man must be an editor at one of the newspapers she'd written to a few weeks ago, shortly after she came back from Nova Scotia. She'd brought some Canadian papers home with her — the *Globe and Mail*, the Halifax *Daily News*, the Halifax *Chronicle-Herald*. Though she wasn't keen on journalists generally — she'd hung up on an NBC reporter who'd called and asked how she felt about her daughter's death, and been even more upset later when she learned that a reporter had gate-crashed the memorial service for Rowenna — she desperately wanted to tell someone just how much she'd appreciated the kindness of all the strangers she'd met in Nova Scotia. She'd decided to write a letter to the newspapers. She even enclosed photos of Rowenna. "I really didn't expect anyone to publish it," she says now. "I just thought maybe the editors would read it and understand how important people up there had been for me and probably others as well." Still, she addressed her carefully composed letter to the "people of Nova Scotia and Canada."

> My heartfelt thanks to all the wonderful people of Nova Scotia and Canada involved in the rescue and the salvage operations of the Swissair Flight 111 disaster of September 2. I was overwhelmed by the kindness of everyone in Halifax at this most terrible time. I appreciated the quick and well-organized efforts of all concerned from the highest officials at the daily briefing to an attendant at Peggys Cove who placed binoculars in my hands so I could have a better view of the crash site. The constant presence of the clergy was a great comfort.
>
> Rowenna Lee Wight White, my 18-year-old daughter, was killed en route to Geneva and Montreux, Switzerland. She was to begin studies at the Hotel Institute Montreux on September 3, and was brimming with enthusiasm and motivation in this new venture in her life. I am sure that one of her happiest memories was a week we spent with her uncle in British Columbia on a houseboat vacation six years ago. I believe that in Europe she would have represented herself as a truly fine example of a United States citizen.
>
> My everlasting gratitude goes to my caregiver Nancy Richard of Halifax, a volunteer with Air Nova. Her calm demeanor and steady vigilance gave me enormous strength. She was truly

my guardian angel. I also greatly appreciate the hospitality of Robert and Peggy Conrad of Hubbards, Nova Scotia, and regret the loss of his fishing livelihood and all the other fishermen in the area.

I had hoped to bring Rowenna home to New York, but Dr. John Butt informed us in the most sensitive way possible that it would be unlikely most of us could do so. My special thanks to him for his efforts. I enclose two pictures of Rowenna. One is with her beloved dog who died in early August. His death was a great grief to us, which now seems trivial in light of the 228 other people who perished on Flight 111.

All my love to the Canadians and the starkly beautiful landscape of Peggys Cove. My heart lies there forevermore.

Nancy Wight
New York City

It turned out her caller wasn't an editor from one of the newspapers at all, but a reader. The newspapers had all published her letter. But that didn't explain how he'd found her telephone number. It took her a while to discover that the Halifax *Daily News* had not only published her letter in its Sunday edition but reproduced it in full on the front page, complete with her address and telephone number, as part of a story on the emotional impact of the disaster.

Wight was appalled, and frightened. What had she done? What had *they* done?

Friday, October 2, 1998

East Brunswick

"Are you sitting down?" John Butt began. His voice on the telephone sounded so concerned and compassionate. "Is anyone there with you?"

His deep rich voice sounded like her husband's, Peggy Coburn thought. "I'm sitting down," she told him. "But it's okay. Whatever you have to say is going to be fine. I've already heard the worst."

She had. John Butt's task this morning was simply to confirm that worst. The pathologists had positively identified the remains of Richard Coburn.

After the first night, when he'd briefed the families in the Lord Nelson Hotel, Butt had resolved that he would make as many of these calls as possible himself. Sometimes, the calls would have to be arranged ahead of time through the local police force. Often, there would be language gaps that would need to be overcome. And eventually, when the labs began churning out identifications faster than he could make calls — "We had six confirmations by dental one day alone" — he had to abandon the personal touch. But for now, he says, "it was important for them, and for me, that I make the call."

When he finished delivering the official version of the worst news to Coburn, they chatted for a while.

"The experience of going to Nova Scotia changed my

life forever," she told him. "I never expected to find people like this."

Butt knew what she meant. In the aftermath of the crash, Nova Scotians had dropped the reserve they seemed to save for come-from-aways like him. There were touching little kindnesses, such as the mother and her daughter who had moved into his house for several weeks after the accident, taking turns looking after his dogs "as their contribution to the effort." Butt saw such acts as just part of the "general goodness" Nova Scotians had shown since the crash, but now there were also the invitations to dinner, the easy companionship with people. "After Swissair," he jokes, "I couldn't have dinner by myself anymore." It was as if the accident had been the key to open the door to the Nova Scotia he'd been seeking when he first came to the province two years before.

The only question for him now was whether it had all come too late. "I'd betrayed myself," he explains. "I'd come to Nova Scotia and found something I'd thought I might find here but, now that I had, I found it difficult to handle. I'd begun to realize I had gone too far away from the people I really knew, my own family and friends, and you don't develop those kind of relationships so late in life — and that's what life is really all about."

He had pretty much decided, though now with much less frustration, that he would return to his roots in western Canada when his term as chief medical examiner expired in the spring. You can go home again.

To Peggy Coburn, he simply said: "Yes, I know exactly what you mean."

Halifax

Friday night at the Economy Shoe Shop. Familiar faces, friendly faces. Rob Gordon needed to lose himself in those faces. It had been a full month since Flight 111 went down, and this was the first day since then that he hadn't filed at least one Swissair story.

He was more exhausted than he could imagine. And burned out. And — he could admit to himself at least — more than a little haunted by what he'd seen and been through.

Do you need to talk to someone? Everyone asked him that: his bosses, military guys over at Shearwater, Mounties at Peggys, people he interviewed, people he met on the street. Do you need to talk about it with someone?

"I never felt I needed it," he says. "The plane crashed, the people died and I reported that. Yes, I saw things I can never forget but that has happened to me before. I was upset by those things and I should have been. That tells me that I'm OK. If I saw that stuff and it didn't affect me, I'd be concerned about my soul. I'm not."

"No," he would tell anyone who asked, "I talk about it with everyone."

And he did. But not about everything. He still wouldn't discuss the body parts. Everyone asked about that too. Sooner or later, they would find a way to slide it into the conversation. What did you see? He wouldn't talk about it. He *couldn't*.

He hoped no one would ask him tonight. He didn't even want to think about Swissair. He just wanted a drink. He had one beer. Then another. He was halfway through his third when his cell phone rang.

It was the desk. A Labrador helicopter from the 413 Squadron in Greenwood had just crashed in the woods in

Quebec on its way home from a medical evacuation flight. All six crew had been killed. Could Rob come in and do a story?

It would turn out that Gordon had once interviewed one of the airmen, and his cameraman even had footage of the actual helicopter that had gone down, filmed from the water that night during the search for Swissair survivors.

Gordon paid for his beer.

Perhaps they should call this Canada's half-mast province, he thought.

And then he went back to work.

Saturday, October 3, 1998

Oak Island, Nova Scotia

In the days leading up to this weekend, Harris Backman and Gary Masson had been debating whether to cancel the Search and Rescue Weekend entirely. The coast guard auxiliary's annual gathering of 75 delegates from around the region was held to talk business, train, and engage in a little friendly zone-against-zone competition to see who had better mastered their search and rescue techniques. This year, it just happened to have been scheduled to take place at the Oak Island Inn and Marina in Zone 11, smack in the middle of the scene of last month's disaster.

Harris and Gary, as the auxiliary's full-time employees, should have handled the lion's share of organizing for the event, but they'd been so busy with Swissair that they'd remembered only two weeks ago that it was taking place at all. And they were still too busy to put much effort into planning the competitions and banquet, let alone the semi-annual auxiliary board meeting. All the rest of the Zone 11 auxiliary members were also either too busy or too exhausted to give any thought to preparing for mock exercises, and certainly not when they were in the middle of a real one.

"We thought about not doing it at all," Masson says, "but then we realized that, as big an event as Swissair was for the members in Zone 11, it only really affected one of the 16 zones in our region. So we thought it's not fair to everyone else to cancel it at the last minute, so we scrambled and put it together."

In the middle of that, Zone 11 was called out on another, albeit more conventional, rescue: a small fishing boat in trouble off Blandford "on a dark, nasty, dirty night," Harris says. "It was in shoal water, so it could have been dangerous, but luckily no one was in distress." Still, it did divert even more of their — and the Zone 11 members' — attention away from preparing for the weekend.

Which made it even sweeter when the awards were finally handed out at the banquet. The overall winner of the day's search and rescue competitions was none other than Zone 11.

Goldens Bridge

My God, Lyn Romano thought, how is this possible?

That night, she and Ray should have been celebrating their seventeenth anniversary. Instead, Lyn stood by the window of her living room, alone. She lit another cigarette and stared out, unseeing, onto the darkened street below.

The boys were gone, off at friends' houses for sleepovers. The neighbours and friends and family, who had been her almost constant companions since that morning — My God! Could it really be a full month ago today that she'd heard he was dead? — were finally gone too, back to their own homes and families and lives.

Their lives!

They had lives to get on with. She had ... nothing.

Half her heart and soul was gone, ripped out of her. She couldn't stand it when people said they understood when they tried to comfort her by comparing her loss to the death of someone else, someone they knew. Ray wasn't someone else. There could be no comparison.

She'd done a lot of yelling this past month. At the authorities up in Halifax who still hadn't identified Ray's body. At the clerks at Women's Hospital who couldn't tell her Ray's blood type. At the officials at KPMG who thought they knew better than she did how to invest their late employee's — her Ray's — life insurance. Even at the friends and neighbours she knew only wanted to help.

"No more ziti," she'd yelled once after yet another neighbour stopped by with yet another plate of food for the freezer. Everyone wanted to help out. "What do you need?" her neighbour Darlene had asked. "Tell me what you need and I'll get it."

"Lemon seltzer," Lyn had said. Now she had more cans of lemon seltzer than she could use in a lifetime.

People only wanted to help. Lyn knew that. But she couldn't stand some of the comfort words they seemed to feel duty-bound to say. When her friend Denise stopped by one day with flowers, she put her arms around Lyn and began to use the words. Closure. Healing. Lyn stepped back from her embrace. "I don't want to be rude," she began, "and I don't want to throw you out, but ..." They talked for a while longer, and then Denise left. Afterwards, Lyn noticed that Denise had taken the card that was with the flowers. She wondered what the card must have said, what Denise had thought better about giving her.

Lyn made a fire in the fireplace. It was the first fire she'd lit since the accident. She thought of all the fall Sunday afternoons she and Ray and the boys had spent in this room eating the spreads she'd cooked up and laid out on the coffee table for them, warming themselves in the glow of the fire, watching football games on TV. She hadn't seen a football game since Ray died. My God, what would she do on Super Bowl Sunday? They'd always watched the Super Bowl as a family.

Everything reminded her of Ray. The coffeemaker in the kitchen. She didn't drink coffee. Ray drank coffee. The supermarket. There were aisles she just couldn't go down anymore; aisles that contained foods she'd bought especially for Ray. And the GTO in the garage. Reminding her of Ray every time she passed by. She'd asked Raymond Jr. and Randy if she should get rid of the car. No, they both said, they'd want it when they got older. To remember their dad.

Lyn would always remember. The other night, she'd looked at the clock in the kitchen and wondered idly: When is Ray coming home? As if none of this had happened. As if he would suddenly show up at the door and this would all turn out to have been some bad dream.

Lyn tried to remember the last time she'd slept more than a few hours at a stretch. She wasn't sure how she put in the hours she was awake. She couldn't read; her mind couldn't focus. She couldn't watch TV — except for the video of Ray's memorial service in their backyard. She watched that every night, watched it and cried some more.

Her neighbour Darlene Goncalves had tried to persuade her to take some Valium so she could get some uninterrupted rest. But Lyn refused. If she took one, Lyn said, she'd take the whole bottle. Besides, she really didn't seem to need to sleep anymore.

She did spend hours on the computer. Ray had bought the computer. She didn't want it. "Machines are so cold," she had told him. "I mean, I only got an answering machine a few years ago. What would I want with a computer?"

Ray bought one anyway. And then Lyn had ended up becoming a computer wizard. She discovered she loved emailing, loved hanging out in various chat rooms. She'd met one woman through a gardening chat room — gardening was one of Lyn's passions — and, after a year or so of exchanging emails, she'd even invited the woman and her husband to spend the night at their house. Ray thought that was a little wild, but he said okay.

Now she was using the computer to meet other people who'd lost family in awful accidents, people who might possibly understand the hell she was going through. She'd discovered one man from the Netherlands who'd lost his son in a car crash a few months ago. Now they emailed each other regularly. Recently, she'd even found a web site Swissair had set up for the families of people who died on Flight 111. She'd taken it upon herself to post daily messages to the group, updating them on the status of the identification process and on the progress authorities were making with the recovery and with the investigation into the cause of the crash. Making the calls every day to find out what was going on in Halifax gave her a focus. She needed that.

Ray must have known something, she thought, must have known he might not be around much longer. He'd finally put the heater in the pool. How long had they talked about that? He'd wrapped the house in aluminum siding, did what he could to make everything maintenance-free. He'd even taught Raymond Jr. how to mow the lawn.

Ray's little man.

Two days after Ray's plane went down, little Raymond was out in the yard, mowing the lawn just the way his father had taught him. Her Ray must have known. Maybe, in some strange way, she did too. Otherwise, why had she insisted this summer — of all busy, crazy, complicated summers — on finally staging that boys-only poker party Ray had been talking about wanting to have for his birthday? He'd wanted it for years, and for years Lyn had intended to organize it. But something always seemed to get in the way.

Not this year. They'd had to move the date a couple of times and Ray had told her not to worry, there'd always be next year, but she had insisted. "You're going to have your poker party," she said.

And he did. Matt Devey was there, and Tony Goncalves, and a few others. Lyn organized it all, prepared the food. She told Ray she'd sleep at her mother's that night, let them have their fun on their own, but Ray insisted she stay. He wanted her home, he told her. She'd spent most of the night upstairs. She'd entrusted Matt with the job of making sure no one smoked their smelly cigars in the house. But of course they had. She didn't mind. Not really. It was Ray's birthday. And he was happy. He'd told her so when he came up to the bedroom to see her around 11. He wanted to make sure they weren't making too much noise.

They weren't.

And now Ray was gone. She went back to the computer, went back to log on to a new world she was discovering — a world of airline safety experts and aircraft accident chat groups and a million questions about flying and safety she'd never known enough to ask about before. She knew enough to ask now. More important, she was beginning to see exactly what it was she would do to make sure no one ever forgot her Ray. Ever.

Sunday, October 4, 1998

In the skies over Peggys Cove

The night sky was spectacularly clear. From his seat on the captain's left-hand side of the cockpit, Christian Stussi could make out, even from 35,000 feet above the earth, the faint glow of the beacon from the Peggys Cove lighthouse and the random beams of searchlights from the vessels playing over the water nearby. The boats were still out looking for remains and debris, still searching for answers. So was he.

The chief pilot of Swissair's MD-11 fleet found it difficult to believe that more than a month had passed since the accident. This was his first actual flying assignment since September 2; it just happened to be the Geneva–New York–Geneva run. He spent the previous night in the same New York hotel where his colleagues had spent their last night on earth. "It gave me some heavy thoughts," he admits now.

Swissair Flight 111 had a new number — it was now known as Flight 139 — and the name of Halifax had been deleted from the progress map that allowed passengers to follow the plane's flight path on video screens. The map of Canada's eastern seaboard now listed two smaller Maritime centres — Sydney, Cape Breton, and Saint John, New Brunswick — but not Halifax.

Of course, the flight path, north along the U.S.

Eastern Seaboard and then, near Halifax, swinging east for the flight to Spain and Europe, had not changed considerably since Swissair began flying this route in 1962. Most transatlantic flights from North America to Europe followed a similar route. Nevertheless, Stussi had never noticed the Peggys Cove lighthouse beacon before. But then, there were many things he'd never noticed before that he noticed now. For Stussi, the deaths of Zimmermann and Loëw had changed nothing — and yet had changed everything.

No one knew for certain yet what had caused the accident, so Swissair's MD-11 fleet continued to operate as before, and the fleet's 450 pilots and co-pilots continued to fly the planes just as they did before, without exception. In the first few days after the accident, not one pilot booked off sick or asked not to fly the plane. As the chief pilot, Stussi was extremely proud of that. He'd heard rumours that between 20 and 40 per cent of TWA pilots had refused to fly in the wake of the 1996 disaster off Long Island. By contrast, he believed, Swissair's MD-11 pilots had confidence in their airline, in their airline's maintenance team and in the aircraft itself. And why not? The MD-11 was a pilot's dream machine. "Look around you," he would say as he showed a visitor the inside of the aircraft. "The cockpit is huge, the windows are big. It has a nice presentation, and it's a workhorse too. Nice to fly, nice to handle. And see this," he would add, running his fingers over the banks of switches and buttons on the panels above him. "There's not one switch with a tape over it saying 'inoperative.' You may find that sort of thing on other airlines but not on Swissair, not on the Swissair MD-11. It's a most reliable aircraft."

And yet ... it had crashed. That was the puzzle. On the one hand, Swissair's pilots could not believe the plane itself had been responsible for the accident. To back up his contention that Swissair pilots had complete faith in the plane, Stussi would point to a lengthy waiting list of pilots still eager to join his fleet. But on the other hand, neither could they credit suggestions that the two pilots themselves might have been to blame. Most of them knew Zimmermann and Loëw too well — by reputation if nothing else — to believe they would have been inattentive, or done something stupid. Something terrible must have happened. But what? And why?

Within days after the accident, Stussi had set up open forums so the pilots could talk to him and each other as well as with two company psychologists; Stussi did his best to fill them in on what little anyone knew about the investigation. "Everyone wanted to talk about it," he says. "The first few times lasted four hours each. There were a lot of tears. It was interesting. A lot of these were people I thought of as tough guys. I never expected them to show their emotions. But people just had to talk about how they felt."

Stussi couldn't stop talking about the crash either. Or thinking about it. He'd spent the previous four weeks immersed in the details of it: sitting through the endless meetings of the emergency committee, attending enough funerals and memorial services to last a lifetime, talking on the phone at least once a day, sometimes more, with the widows, thinking about death. His own. He had only recently turned 50 and had never considered the possibility of his own death before. "I have a good life," he says, "a job which is demanding, a lot of friends, a wife I've been with for 24 years, two good kids and ... and it could happen to me today, tomorrow, now. It has happened to two people like me, two families. You just never know."

In the cockpit that night, Stussi took a last look at the lighthouse beacon below, now fading into blackness.

Saturday, October 10, 1998

Goldens Bridge

If he says that one more time, Lyn Romano thought, I'm going to explode. "He" was the priest at her mother-in-law's church, and "that" was the phrase that had become his mantra during this memorial service: "closure and healing."

Lyn had already organized one memorial service for Ray, two weeks earlier. That one — for their friends and Ray's colleagues — had taken place on a sunny afternoon on the deck Ray had built by the pool in their backyard. One of Ray's childhood friends had told stories about Ray's boyhood, about the day they'd turned Ray's father's lawn mower into a go-kart, got it going and then couldn't figure out how to stop it until it crashed. Some of the men Ray worked with didn't just talk about how "very friendly, very caring, very fun to be with" Ray had been; they told stories. About the day that Ray had taken one of them for a drive in his GTO before he got the muffler working; about how they'd put the Rolling Stones on the stereo and turned the volume up and had "the drive of our life." About Ray's love of a good game of golf and about his frustration with his inability to sink a putt. About how Ray was probably, at this very minute, standing "outside the pearly gates having a smoke because you can't smoke inside." Lyn and the kids chose songs to play to remember their father. Raymond Jr. chose Eric

Clapton's "My Father's Eyes"; little Randy picked "I'll Never Break Your Heart." Everyone cried.

That service was all about Ray.

This — this was different. This service had been organized by Ray's mother. The priest didn't know Ray, so he fell back on all that standard-issue priest talk about closure and healing and, by the third time he said it, Lyn was sure she would scream. Randy seemed to know what was happening. He reached out, grabbed his mother's hand. "The only thing that kept me in that pew," Lyn would remember later, "was my kids. I had to stay for them." But at the end, she admits, she lost it.

Matt had to help her to the car. Matt and Moira knew Lyn hadn't been looking forward to this service, so they'd insisted on coming along. Just to be there, in case she needed them.

Now Matt drove the car. Moira was in the front seat, Lyn and the boys in the back. They drove in silence. Even Matt, usually the one to find some way to lighten a mood, couldn't think of anything to say.

Finally, it was Lyn herself who broke the spell. She turned to the boys. "I need you to do something for me," she said solemnly. "Okay?"

They nodded.

"I need you to yell this word as loud as you can for me. Okay?"

"Okay."

"SHIT!"

They looked at her, incredulous. "Shit." Tentatively.

"Again."

"SHIT!"

"And again!"

"SHIT!"

Soon the whole car was yelling in crazy unison. "SHIT! SHIT! SHIT!"

Monday, October 12, 1998

Redding

"We are still alive although I am not certain how we have made it," Judith Wilson wrote in her message to the Swissair families' web site Miles Gerety had just now discovered. "I felt certain that I could not live through that first terrible night," added Wilson, who had lost her 22-year-old son Jonathan in the crash. "It does not get easier. We are frustrated that no one keeps us informed. We have to search the Internet for any new information about the crash and investigation. Does anyone else feel this way?"

Gerety did. In Nova Scotia in the first days after the crash he and other family members had been swaddled in support. Not only did Swissair officials seem to anticipate the families' every need — grief counsellors, care partners and clergy were always on hand, always willing to talk, always willing to do their bidding — but the airline was also quick to organize regular briefings with all the top Canadian officials, from the head of the RCMP to the chief crash investigator. You could ask whatever questions you wanted and get answers immediately.

But after they'd returned to their homes around the world, it was as if the umbilical cord had suddenly, irrevocably been cut. While there were a few official communications to the designated next of kin — identifications made, "presumption of death" certificates sent out to sign, and so on — there was no longer anyone in authority keeping the families posted on the progress of the investigation or answering the many more questions they now had as the first shock of the accident began to recede.

What made them feel even more isolated was how quickly the international media had lost interest in the story. The American press, which had swooped in and out of Peggys Cove like a whirlwind in the week after the crash, was filled again with more than you ever wanted to know about the latest twists and turns in the Bill Clinton–Monica Lewinsky affair. Flight 111 was yesterday's news.

Swissair had set up a private Internet site for families to communicate with one another after the crash, but the airline hadn't done much to advertise the site's existence or use it as its own tool to keep families up to date on the latest developments in the crash investigation. Miles, in fact, had discovered the site only after a Delta representative mentioned it in passing.

Judith Wilson's electronic message not only reinforced Miles's own growing feeling of frustration with the lack of information being made available but also was "like an arrow to my heart. When I saw that, I thought, 'My God, this mother can't find anything out ... I've got to do something.'"

That something turned out to be what he does best — networking. The continuing coverage of the crash on the Halifax *Daily News* web site had become popular with family members wanting to find out the latest developments, so Miles emailed the editor of the paper, asking him to include on the newspaper's web site information about how to find the Swissair family web site. He also began to post his own links and messages to the Swissair web site, developing email and then telephone relationships with some of the other family members, including

Judith Wilson, who told him more about her son's plans to study in Europe, and Monica Hawkins, a New Jersey woman whose cousin had been killed in the crash and who posted whatever information about the disaster she could uncover. Gerety made contact with Lyn Romano, who'd taken it on herself to call the authorities in Nova Scotia every day to get updated figures on the number of passengers identified and the latest on the salvage operation, which she would then post to the web site so other family members would know what was going on. Gerety also talked with Nancy Wight, who, he says, was "feeling this tremendous guilt" about having argued with her daughter before the flight, and with Barbara Fetherolf, who'd "had a fight with her husband and took off for the Caribbean for a while" after her daughter's memorial service.

"I was hearing all these incredible, compelling stories of mothers and what they were going through, and I thought I have to do something to help." He should at least be able to help. He was, after all, a lawyer. His profession was to act as an advocate for others. And his brother had been one of the most prominent and well connected victims of the crash. Surely he could use that background and the heft of those connections to do something to help these people. But what could he actually do? He knew he could use some help in figuring out his next move, but he wasn't sure where to turn. Like other family members, he'd already begun to get messages from a number of individuals and groups "with their own agendas willing to exploit our grief for their own ends." He wanted no part of them. Finally, he emailed Anthony DePalma, a *New York Times* reporter who'd been in Nova Scotia to cover the crash. Gerety wrote in part to congratulate him on what he described as his "moving" article from Peggys Cove and in part to complain about the families' growing frustration with the lack of information they were getting. DePalma suggested he contact Matt Wald, the *Times'* Washington-based transportation reporter who'd been covering air disasters for 22 years. Wald, in turn, suggested he call a man who'd become synonymous with the rights of families in the aftermath of air disasters.

"You should talk to a man named Hans Ephraimson-Abt," Wald told him.

Ridgewood, New Jersey

Hans Ephraimson-Abt wasn't nearly as surprised to get the telephone call from Miles Gerety as he had been *not* to get a call from Korean Airlines on that awful September day 15 years ago.

As was his habit, Ephraimson-Abt had been the first person to arrive at his office that morning in 1983. On his way to work, as was usual too, he picked up a copy of the *New York Times*. In his office, he sat down at his desk, spread the paper out in front of him and began to read. Korean Airlines Flight 007, a 747 aircraft on its way from New York to Seoul, South Korea, had strayed into Soviet territory and been forced down by Soviet SU-15 interceptor jets. The plane had managed to land safely on Sakhalin Island in the Kamchatka Peninsula. Details were sketchy, the paper said, but initial reports indicated that all 266 people aboard had survived.

Ephraimson-Abt's eldest daughter, Alice, would have been one of those people. Although she was only 23, she was already an experienced world traveller. "We encouraged all our children to become citizens of the world," Ephraimson-Abt says proudly. When she was 18, Alice had taken a year off after New York's Catholic High School to travel. Later, she had studied in Taipei and

Shanghai, and Exeter in England. Now she was on her way back to China to teach English at the People's University of Beijing as well as to improve her own Chinese language skills. After changing planes in Seoul, she was scheduled to fly on to Hong Kong, where she would spend a night before entering China.

So Ephraimson-Abt, almost by rote, did what he does. He made arrangements. Since arriving in the U.S. from Germany by way of wartime Swiss labour camps in 1949, he'd run a highly successful business representing European business interests in America. He knew people all over the world, including the manager of the Peninsula Hotel in Hong Kong, where Alice was scheduled to stay. So he called his friend the hotel manager.

"I'm sorry," he explained, "but my daughter may not be able to honour her reservation for tonight." He explained what he'd read in the *Times* and then requested that, when Alice did arrive, the manager look after her for him. She might not be able to get her luggage, he explained, so she might need toiletries, perhaps some clothes. If he wouldn't mind. As a personal favour for him.

"That would be no problem," the manager replied, "but ..." How to say this? The latest information he had was different from what his friend had read in the *Times*. In Hong Kong, the media were reporting that the plane had been shot down, that it had crashed into the waters off Sakhalin Island, that there were no survivors.

No survivors! Ephraimson-Abt scanned the *Times* again, saw the name of a Congressman named MacDonald, whom the paper said was a passenger on the plane. He immediately called the man's office in Washington, spoke to his chief of staff.

"Don't worry," the man told Ephraimson-Abt. "I've just hung up from a conversation with Secretary of State Schultz. Everyone is okay. Your daughter is fine. The

State Department is on the case. Everyone should be released soon."

Twenty minutes later, the man called back. He was crying now. His information had been wrong, he told Ephraimson-Abt. The plane had indeed been shot down. There were no survivors.

Could this be? It all still seemed so improbable to Ephraimson-Abt that he immediately called the New York offices of Korean Airlines. Surely the airline would have phoned him by now if this was really true? He asked to speak to the station manager. The voice on the other end of the line was curt. The station manager was busy with a press conference, the voice said, and hung up.

"And that was the last time I heard from them," Ephraimson-Abt says today. "Except for one time a few days later," he adds with a sardonic smile. "They called and left a message on my machine to tell me there was going to be a service for the victims in Seoul. They said it was going to be 'a solid anti-Communist demonstration.' " He shakes his head. "My family has gone through several wars, the Holocaust; my daughter was a victim of the Cold War. For them to leave this message suggesting I'd be pleased it would be a solid anti-Communist demonstration still seems so incredibly insensitive to me."

It is 15 years now since Korean Airlines Flight 007 crashed into the sea, but there has been no closure for Ephraimson-Abt, nor for any of the others who lost loved ones in that disaster. Most of the wreckage has never been found, no bodies were ever recovered, and very few personal effects have been returned to the families.

Because the incident happened in the worst depths of the Cold War, authorities on all sides at first treated the families of the victims as little more than pawns in superpower diplomacy. Even after the Cold War ended, both Washington and Moscow seemed to regard the incident as embarrassing history and tried to shuffle the families away.

To rub sandpaper on the exposed nerves of the families' emotional wounds, the crash itself quickly became tangled in intrigue and innuendo. At least 15 books have been written about the tragedy. Some postulate the plane was on a secret spy mission for the CIA; others claim the plane somehow survived the two missiles fired at it and landed safely on Sakhalin. Its passengers, these so-called experts contend, have been held in secret prisons ever since.

The only important truth for family members like Hans Ephraimson-Abt, who lost their sons, daughters, husbands, wives, brothers, sisters when KAL 007 went down, was that everyone — government authorities, lawyers, the media and, perhaps most of all, Korean Airlines — treated them badly.

That is what made Ephraimson-Abt angry, what turned him into what he is today. What he is today is the chair of the American Association of Families of KAL 007, the first-ever support group for the families of the victims of a major airline crash. In the fall of 1998, the group, still active after all these years, staged small reunions around the United States to mark the fifteenth anniversary of the crash. Most people came, he marvels. "At the end, some-one asked, 'When will we get together again?' "

The association has also become Ephraimson-Abt's personal platform. He is 76 years old now, a short, delicate man with fine features and wispy white hair. He may be retired from his business but he hasn't slowed down. Truth to tell, he still does what he always did so well and so successfully. He talks, he lobbies, he cajoles, he occasionally even browbeats. But these days he no longer performs these roles on behalf of European business interests; his clients are now the families of those who die in plane crashes.

And not just the crash of Korean Airlines Flight 007. He is now one of the world's leading crusaders not only for better treatment for those left behind after airline crashes but also for improved regulation of the skies to prevent disasters.

It began slowly, almost accidentally, he explains. He attended a memorial service for the 61 American victims of KAL 007 at the National Cathedral in Washington. Later, he went to another packed service at St. John the Divine Church in New York. At both events, he met relatives and friends of other victims. They began to talk, and quickly discovered they shared not just the common grief of their own individual losses but also a frustration, already bordering on anger, at the lack of information and cooperation they were getting from the airline and the authorities.

"Finally," he recalls, "we looked at each other and somebody proposed, 'Why don't we go around the room and see what each other's resources are? Who are you? What do you to do?' " They found — as is often the case in international airline disasters — that they were a well-connected lot. One person turned out to be a neighbour of the American secretary of state; others worked for major media, including the *New York Times* and ABC television. One man even played golf with Vice-President George Bush's brother-in-law. Perhaps most crucial, however, one woman was a secretary at Columbia University and had access to a computer they could use to help produce a monthly newsletter so they could keep in touch.

"We mobilized our internal resources," explains Ephraimson-Abt. "At first, we offered primarily emotional support. But then, as the litigation dragged on and some families ran out of money — some were forced into bankruptcy, others were trying to educate their children — we became advocates too."

Korean Airlines took a hard line with them. Although

the 1929 Warsaw Convention provided for modest compensation for the families of victims of international air disasters, KAL claimed that, because the plane had crashed into the ocean rather than on land, the families weren't even entitled to that; the incident, the airline argued, was instead covered under the Death on the High Seas Act. Passed in 1920, that act was designed to award limited financial compensation to widows of seamen at a time when there was no workers' compensation. But, says Ephraimson-Abt, the act didn't contemplate a future of jumbo jet air crashes in the ocean in which children or the elderly would also be lost, so it didn't allow victims' family members to sue for damages beyond the direct loss of income that resulted from the death.

Financially, of course, none of that mattered much to Ephraimson-Abt. He didn't need, or much care about, compensation for himself. But he'd come to know the relatives of other victims, such as a New York City subway token clerk who'd lost her 40-year-old daughter. Since she couldn't demonstrate that she had suffered direct financial loss because of the crash, Ephraimson-Abt explains, she qualified for nothing under the Death on the High Seas Act. "So this elderly woman goes to church each day to pray for the soul of her daughter," he says bitterly, "but she gets nothing for the support her daughter would have given her had she lived."

For years, no one in authority listened. But then, on the evening of December 21, 1988, a bomb blew up a Pan Am Boeing 747 jumbo jet over Lockerbie, Scotland. All 259 passengers aboard Flight 103 were killed.

By that point, Ephraimson-Abt and others from KAL 007 had decided they were "emotionally ready" to do whatever they could to make sure the victims of this new disaster didn't have to suffer on their own through the same traumas they had. "There were 30 students from

Syracuse on board Flight 103," he recalls. "I happened to be on the parents' board at Syracuse University, which my son attended, so I knew some of those families. So it seemed natural for me to become involved."

The Syracuse students were among 189 Americans aboard Flight 103. Another was a Florida-based marketing executive named John Cummock, who had switched flights without telling his family so he could arrive home a day early and surprise his daughter on her birthday.

Like Ephraimson-Abt, Victoria Cummock didn't learn about her husband's death from the airline. She didn't even know anything was wrong until two o'clock in the morning of December 23 — 16 hours after the crash — when her husband's boss showed up at her door expecting to find a grieving widow. Later, when she tried to call Pan Am in New York to confirm what her husband's boss had told her, the lines were so overwhelmed with callers that she had to set the telephone to automatically redial the number over and over until someone finally answered. When she did get through, she was informed that Pan Am was still checking hospitals for survivors, and could she call back in a day or two?

"I have three children," she responded angrily. "They're going to be up in a couple of hours and they're waiting for their father to come home. I need to know whether my husband is dead. If you don't call me back within 10 minutes, I'm going to call every media organization in America."

Almost as soon as she hung up, a Pan Am vice-president returned her call. Yes, he said, John Cummock was on the flight. No, he informed her sadly, there were no survivors.

As the days turned into weeks, Cummock's frustration and anger grew, not only at what she saw as the airline's continuing inability to answer even her simplest questions but also at what seemed to her to be the cavalier, cost-benefit-analysis approach to passenger safety and security taken by the airlines and their government overseers.

Cummock became one of the first to join an organization called Families of Pan Am 103, Lockerbie. On Valentine's Day 1989, less than two months after the crash, Cummock and other family members gathered in Ohio to meet with a lobbyist whose role would be to make sure their voices were heard in the right places in Washington.

Victoria Cummock turned out to be the airline industry's worst nightmare. An articulate and strikingly attractive former model, she came across sympathetically on television. She was also well connected. Her children attended school in Coral Gables, Florida, with the children of Jeb Bush, whose father just happened to be the president of the U.S. at the time. She persuaded the younger Bush to tell his father about how the airline was treating the families of Flight 103 victims. And she traded on the influence of another neighbour, whose child's godparents were Senator Bob Dole and his wife, Elizabeth, to wangle a meeting with the senator to tell him about the airline's seeming disregard for the feelings of family members.

Together and separately, Cummock and Ephraimson-Abt became regulars on the Washington political and bureaucratic circuit, lobbying for improvements to airline safety and security procedures, for relaxation of rigid liability rules in the wake of airline accidents and even — or perhaps especially — for more humane treatment of families in the aftermath of a tragedy.

By the mid-1990s, their efforts had finally begun to bear fruit.

In 1995, the International Air Transport Association, which represents the world's major airlines, agreed to waive a provision in the Warsaw Convention that had dramatically limited financial liabilities in the event of a crash. Unless the families of the victims of a crash could

prove an airline had been guilty of "willful, wanton" misconduct, the maximum they had been able to collect in
damages under the convention was $75,000 per passen-
ger. Since such deliberate misconduct was difficult to
prove, litigation, expensive for everyone involved, tended
to drag on for years and years. To make matters worse for
the airlines, they more often than not ended up losing
their cases in court. It took lawyers for the families of
Korean Airlines 15 years of legal battles, for example,
but they eventually prevailed, proving the airline guilty of
wilful misconduct in that crash. In the case of Pan Am
103, the lawyers for the families also eventually met the
burden of proof for wilful misconduct, winning $500
million U.S. in damages, but only after 10 years of
contentious, high-profile litigation.

Because the bad publicity the lawsuits generated
proved almost as costly as the settlements, the airline
industry began to look for better ways to deal with legal
liabilities in the event of a crash. The voluntary 1995
agreement not only provided for an automatic payment of
up to $100,000 per passenger (worth $134,000 by 1998)
but also shifted the burden of proof for damages above
that limit. From now on, it would be up to the airline to
prove it took all reasonable precautions rather than to the
bereaved family member to show the airline had acted
recklessly.

Better still, Congress passed the Aviation Disaster
Family Assistance Act of 1996 to force airlines to come
up with detailed plans for dealing with a disaster,
including providing timely information, counselling
and assistance to families of passengers in the aftermath of a crash.

The ink was barely dry on that law — and many of
its provisions not yet put into practice — when TWA
Flight 800 went down off New York's Long Island on

July 17, 1996, killing all 230 people aboard. But even without the legal machinery in place, the families of TWA Flight 800 were able to draw on the resources of an informal support system of people who had lost their own loved ones in a crash.

They were all suddenly members in good standing of a community of sorrow and anger none of them had sought to join — but none of them could escape either.

When TWA set up a special centre for families at the Ramada Inn at John F. Kennedy Airport, it invited Victoria Cummock and Hans Ephraimson-Abt to come to the hotel to hold the hands of the victims' families, to listen to their disbelief and their shock and their rage, to understand in profound and profoundly sad ways no one else could contemplate just what they were going through.

When he heard on the news on September 2, 1998, that a Swissair flight had crashed off the coast of Nova Scotia, Hans Ephraimson-Abt knew he would be called on again. "I knew where my next cup of coffee was coming from," he says simply.

Wednesday, October 21, 1998

Halifax

Lyn Romano had flown back to Halifax again, this time to collect the one possession of Ray's that held the most meaning to her. As Ian Black, the Mountie from the identification squad who had become "the only one I would let call me" placed the object in her hands, Lyn suddenly wasn't sure she wanted it anymore.

"I'm not a religious man," Black told her as he delicately folded her fingers back over Ray's gold weddiing band, "but you willed this ring up, Lyn." Lyn was crying. Black had tears in his eyes too, she says.

It wasn't the first time they had cried together. Over the past few weeks, as authorities went about the gruesome business of attempting to identify the remains, she and Black had developed a strange, unlikely bond. They'd become so close that, when Black went on vacation for a few days, he continued to telephone Lyn every day, just to see how she was doing.

She was not doing well.

She wanted Ray's ring. She needed it. She insisted that they find it for her. *Now.* She was not above screaming at Black either.

Black had tried, as gently as he could, to make Lyn understand what the force of the impact had done to everything and everybody inside that plane, about the way in which the twisted, broken mingle of wreckage and human remains had spread out along the ocean floor, about the needle-in-a-haystack improbability of the divers finding one small wedding band in the middle of all of that —

"You have to find it," Lyn told him urgently. "You just have to."

"We'll do our best," he said.

"You have to find it," she repeated.

And they had. On his severed hand. It had been mixed up in a tangle of wires and plane parts hauled up from the bottom of the sea by the U.S. navy salvage ship *Grapple*. Black knew it was Lyn's ring as soon as he saw the letters engraved in it: 10-3-81. Their wedding day.

The ring was another piece in the puzzle of putting her Ray back together. The carry-on bag, the magazines, the legal pad, the shampoo, and now this ring, this precious band that she had placed on Ray's finger on their wedding day.

Lyn ran her fingers over it, trying to feel Ray in the gold.

She wanted it.

But she didn't want it.

If they'd found Ray's ring, it meant that Ray really had been aboard that plane. Part of her still didn't believe that. All of her still didn't want to believe that.

The day after she got the ring back, Lyn drove out to Peggys Cove for one last look. Unlike so many other family members who found comfort in the stark beauty of the rocks, Lyn saw only death. She would never go back, she told herself.

Back in her room at the Lord Nelson Hotel, she agreed to speak to a reporter from the Halifax *Chronicle-Herald*. She was crying. There were some people "I need to name," she told reporter Lois Legge. She singled out

Black, among several others. "I need the people in this country to know what wonderful, wonderful people they have here," she said. "Just everybody that I've come in contact with, from the customs agent to the coffee shop, even before they know anything. I mean, you should be so proud of your country."

And she needed them to know something else too. She had decided to sue Swissair, not for herself or her family, but so she could set up an organization to lobby for better airplane safety. "I am suing them because I fully intend to go after the airlines to implement safety," she explained through her sobs. "Because those people on that plane have to have died for a reason."

The world in general, and the airline industry in particular, would know soon enough that Ray Romano was more than just a name on a passenger list. They'd know too that Lyn Romano wasn't someone to mess with.

Thursday, October 29, 1998

Washington, D.C.

In Hans Ephraimson-Abt, Miles Gerety had finally found what he calls "a mentor for my over-talkative, hyperactive self." Almost from the moment he'd followed up on Matt Wald's suggestion to telephone the airline safety activist, Gerety had become caught up in the older man's whirlwind.

Ephraimson-Abt immediately invited Miles to join him for lunch that Sunday at his airy, plant-filled apartment in Ridgewood, New Jersey. The apartment was a curious mix: the rooms were filled with the finely crafted antique family furniture that Ephraimson-Abt's parents had brought with them to America from Europe after World War II, but the walls were covered with flimsy bookcases haphazardly filled with books — including at least two copies of Seymour Hersh's bestseller about the crash of KAL 007, *The Target Is Destroyed* — and stacks of official-looking reports, almost all of which had something to do with airline disasters.

Ephraimson-Abt, dressed formally as always in shirt and tie, served a sumptuous lunch followed by coffee, a variety of German cakes and sweets and plenty of conversation. "We just talked and talked," Gerety recalls. About the history of how families had been treated in the aftermath of air tragedies, about the improvements that had been made, about the need for even more changes in the future. Gerety told him about the Swissair families' growing frustration with the lack of information they were getting from everyone and asked about how to go about starting an organization similar to the American Association of Families of KAL 007. The biggest hurdle, he already knew, was that Swissair would not give out the names and addresses of next of kin: in part, of course, to protect their privacy but also to make sure no one besides the airline — such as litigation lawyers or safety lobbyists — would have direct access to the families as a group.

Perhaps, Hans suggested, there could be a way around at least part of that hurdle. He was planning to go to Washington the next day anyway. Why didn't Gerety come along? Gerety quickly agreed.

During the train trip to Washington, Ephraimson-Abt told Gerety more about his life, including how he'd gone to school in Switzerland as a child and had also spent World War II there as a refugee in Swiss-run camps where he was forced to earn his keep doing everything "from building roads and draining swamps to tilling fields and producing strawberry preserves."

"He is an inspiration to everyone," Gerety wrote in a message to the other families he posted on the private Swissair web site after he returned from what he called their "crazy trip" to the American capital.

Ephraimson-Abt almost instantly managed to line up meetings for Gerety with key senior State Department officials. "I told the heads of various consular and emergency offices that they had built a bridge to families with the 1996 Family Assistance Act," Gerety wrote to the families, "but that much of their effort was for naught because the final bridge to families collapsed upon our return from Halifax." He also read the officials some of the postings he'd saved from the web site, including the first one he'd read from Judith Wilson, "to soften them up because we knew we were going to need their help to get our message out to the families." The messages, he says, reduced several officials to tears.

That evening, Hans had arranged for Miles to meet and then have dinner with Assad Kotaite, the president of the International Civil Aviation Organization, a United Nations agency that helps foster cooperation among countries in order to promote and regulate the world's airline industry. After their meeting, as they travelled in a taxi on the way to a "a private dinner in the upstairs of a swank restaurant" Hans had also arranged, he and Kotaite, "the president of this international organization, [talked] about family, his family, my family and our international families on the plane. Somehow we connected."

At dinner, the other guests, Miles noted with admiration for Hans's connections, included the deputy assistant secretary of state for transportation, the head of the Air Transport Association, counsel for the Department of Transportation and others. "Hans was clearly in control as he steered every conversation towards victims' families," Gerety told the families in his message.

For his part, Gerety continued to schmooze with Kotaite, whom he discovered had a brother who was a doctor in New Haven, Connecticut. "I felt I had a bond with President Kotaite," he says. "I knew if I asked in front of the president for help with our mailing, they'd have to do it."

And they did. The larger plan was to enlist the help of the State Department, which had the names and addresses of all the U.S. citizens on the plane and could mail a letter from Gerety and his fledgling group, The Families of Swissair Flight 111, to the American next of kin inviting them to join the organization.

On Tuesday, Gerety continued his round of meetings,

including one at the National Transportation Safety Board, the American crash investigation agency, where he met with Gary Abe, the agency's deputy director of the office of family affairs. Abe agreed to email Swissair to suggest it make it easier for family members to contact each other, even though, as he conceded in his email, U.S. legislation on dealing with families didn't apply because the crash happened in Canada. Still, he suggested to the airline that "Mr. Gerety's suggestion is a normal and familiar request from family members" and he urged Swissair to do what it could, perhaps sending its own message to the families, including in it information on Gerety's group and how to contact it if they wished, "to meet the needs of family members ... I do hope you do consider this," he added in a thinly veiled warning, "because if the media becomes aware of this concern, it will tarnish what Swissair has so far successfully accomplished with the families."

While he waited for the airline to respond, Gerety spent much of the rest of the day scrambling to produce a letter to the families of the American victims. It took him several hours longer than expected because he had to redo the entire mailing after misspelling Nancy Wight's name as White on the letterhead. In the letterhead Gerety described himself as the acting chairperson of the steering committee, which included Monica Hawkins, who'd lost her cousin; Myron Ratnavelle, a European businessman whose parents died in the crash; Naomi Mann, the daughter of Jonathan, the AIDS researcher; Nancy Wight; Judy Wilson and Peggy Coburn's brother-in-law Nobby.

In the letter, Gerety explained that the group wanted to provide an opportunity for family members to share their feelings, to offer mutual support and to "plan a memorial appropriate to the extraordinary spirit of those who perished in Flight 111."

By the time he'd finished recopying the letters, taken a taxi through rush-hour traffic and arrived at the State Department, no one in the offices seemed to be answering calls from the front desk. There'd been a hurricane in the Caribbean and everyone was busy with that. Luckily for Gerety, the woman at the front desk knew Hans and remembered that Gerety had been with him earlier, so she went out of her way, making call after call to find a foreign service worker who would agree to take charge of the letters, envelopes and reply cards.

By the time he managed all of that Gerety had missed the early evening train he'd planned to take back to Connecticut. The one he caught didn't arrive at his station until early the next morning. "By 2:30 a.m., Silvia had picked me up at the train," Gerety wrote in his message to the web site. "She found me sitting in a police car bumming a cigarette (I don't usually smoke) and talking with an old cop about how he had notified relatives as a Marine after two tours in Vietnam. Incredibly ... his parents and siblings were born in Yarmouth, Nova Scotia. His father, grandfather and great-grandfather had fished the waters off Peggys Cove. He described the place to a 'T'. Ah, the people one meets in the middle of the night."

That afternoon, he added, "Hans was on the phone with more assignments!"

Shearwater

Larry Vance's cell phone rang. He slipped away to a corner of the room to answer it. It was Charlotte, his wife, calling from Ottawa. "You have to call the lawyer in the next five minutes," she told him urgently. "Otherwise, he says the deal will fall through."

Vance's stomach twisted. "I'm in the middle of a meeting I can't leave right now," he whispered into the phone. "I'll do it as soon as it's over. Promise."

The first few months of the Swissair investigation were, Larry Vance would say later, "as stressful as any I've ever experienced." Trying to balance the demands of establishing a new business from a thousand miles away with what he and Vic Gerden had begun to refer to as the "decisions-per-minute" stresses of running a complex, high-profile aircraft accident investigation were taking their toll.

He and Gerden had sat down together at the Holiday Inn that first night to iron out their working relationship. Though the two men knew each other professionally from crossing paths at conferences and courses, they had been based in different parts of the country and had never worked together on an investigation. In smaller accidents, the deputy chief investigator in charge usually looks after logistics — paying bills, keeping records and making sure the workload is fairly divided. But the Swissair accident was so big and the demands so great, the role of the deputy chief investigator essentially had to be the same as the chief investigator. "We didn't really define it but we knew we had to hit the ground running so we'd just have to keep filling in for each other as and where we were needed."

As the investigator in charge, they agreed that Gerden would handle the media while Vance would — after the first few joint briefings — take prime responsibility for briefing the families. During the first few weeks, that meant that after a day of continuous meetings and investigative work at Shearwater, Vance would swing by the Transportation Safety Board's operations centre at the Dartmouth Holiday Inn to pick up a briefing package the communications staff had put together throughout the day, read it over while being driven across the bridge to Halifax and then update, and answer questions from, often emotional, occasionally angry family members at the Lord Nelson Hotel.

"By the time it was over, I'd be absolutely zonked," he recalls. Sometimes, he'd grabbed a cab immediately and head back to Shearwater; sometimes, he'd take a slow, quiet ride on the Halifax–Dartmouth ferry "just to clear my head" and then hail a cab for the journey back to Shearwater and the 7 p.m. meeting.

In the beginning, he says, there were so many meetings that little time was left for anything else. The TSB's investigative team would meet for its morning briefing at 8 a.m. Three hours later, Vance or Gerden had to attend a major update meeting of all the key players — military, police, medical examiner, coast guard and volunteers — at the Maritime Command operations centre at CFB Halifax. At 4 p.m. there was the briefing for families; an hour later, the same information was given to the media. And then at 7 p.m., the TSB group met again for its end-of-day update. Even with all the meetings and briefings, the investigation was so huge and complex people sometimes ended up tripping over one another, with several people approaching Swissair from different angles for the same piece of information, for example, or straying into another team's specialty because the "lines aren't always as cut and dried as they should be." Part of Vance's job was to make sure all the investigators were "swimming in their own lane" and the investigation didn't bog down in turf wars.

Between meetings, he says, it was almost impossible to walk from one part of Hangar A to another without 10 or 12 people stopping him to ask this question or make that decision. "By the time you got where you were going, you'd forget why you were going there. You'd

always be taking notes but you'd never have time to refer
to them. You'd have to keep it all in your head and you'd
wonder sometimes if you could keep up the pace, if
you could stay half healthy and get through this thing in
one piece."

After a while, when it became clear that no one would
find the magic key that would instantly unlock the mys-
tery of what happened to Flight 111, the pace settled from
frantic to merely frenetic. Vance had gone home to
Ottawa once, long enough to pick up some fresh clothes
if not to be of much help to his wife with their business.
Luckily, she seemed to be coping well on her own. She
would probably have to do that for a long time.

Investigators had quickly — and logically, given what
they knew from the beginning about the conversations
between the pilots and air traffic controllers — zeroed in
on the plane's wiring, especially in the area of the cockpit.

Though they didn't ignore other possibilities, the
investigators did begin to look for signs of heat distress or
smoke in the cockpit. They'd found one section of burned
wiring in the cockpit ceiling that included pieces of wire
that connected to the aircraft's inflight entertainment
system. There were signs of arcing — a phenomenon in
which electricity travels along a wire like a lightning bolt,
vaporizing everything in its path — but no one could be
sure whether something in the entertainment system had
somehow caused the arcing or whether the cause of the
heat had come from somewhere else. That was one reason why TSB investigators travelled to Switzerland the
previous month to look more closely at the wiring for the
system aboard other Swissair MD-11s. Investigators
knew Swissair was the only airline to have installed this
particular entertainment system, and also that it had been
installed after the plane was manufactured under a special
permit issued by the FAA. Though investigators were

still far from certain what role, if any, the entertainment system had played in the crash, they immediately notified Swissair, the Swiss Federal Aircraft Investigation Bureau and the U.S. National Transportation Safety Board of their finding.

Swissair, for its part, wasted little time in announcing that it was pulling the plug on the entertainment systems on its aircraft "as a precautionary measure."

Personally, Vance thought the decision prudent — "You say to yourself, if the inflight entertainment system might have even possibly been involved in this and if this is something we can do without, that the plane can fly without it, then it only makes sense to be safe rather than sorry" — but he was curious to know what the amateur accident sleuths and self-proclaimed experts on the Internet would make of this latest development. Almost certainly much more than was warranted by the facts.

Vance occasionally checked in on some of the airplane accident chat groups to see what was being said with "absolute certainty" this week. One week, the cause was absolutely certainly Kapton coverings used to insulate aircraft wiring. Although still used on commercial airliners, Kapton had been banned for more than a decade from use in U.S. military jets because of concerns that it would break down in more adverse conditions aboard fighter aircraft. Critics say the military ban should have been seen as a "canary in the mine" — an early warning that the insulation eventually would break down in commercial aircraft, too. The next week, many of those same experts were blaming the pilots for supposedly abandoning the cockpit before the plane hit the water. Now, just as certainly, the cause would be the plane's inflight entertainment system. As he had often tried to tell families — many of whom were being contacted by lawyers and others who claimed to have figured out what caused the accident — the best way to tell whether a so-called air-craft accident expert was really what he claimed was to listen to what he had to say. If he claimed he knew what had happened without having done any real investigation, then he was a fake. "No one who is really an expert would come to conclusions like that without doing their own investigation," he told them.

He only wished it were as simple as the experts made it out to be. Then perhaps he'd be able to get back to Ottawa and his other responsibilities. As soon as the meeting ended, Vance picked up his cell phone and called the Ottawa lawyer who was handling the paperwork for the transfer of ownership of their learning centre fran-chise. He just hoped he wasn't too late.

Halifax

Truthfully, Lorne Clarke would explain later, he hadn't stopped to consider all the many and various "ramifications and complexities" that might flow from agreeing to ~~tions and complexities~~ ~~he might~~ have had second ~~thoughts~~. "But the process," confesses Clarke with a chuckle, "was as simple as the premier calling me up and asking if I would, and me saying yes."

Nova Scotia premier Russell MacLellan's choice of Clarke, the genial, white-haired, 70-year-old former chief justice of the province, to become a committee of one to determine how best to officially memorialize the tragedy of Swissair Flight 111 was an inspired one.

Clarke, who had been a highly regarded labour-management conciliator before being appointed to the bench, had a reputation for being able to achieve consensus even among his occasionally fractious judicial colleagues. During his time as chief justice, for example, Clarke, who believed passionately that the justice system must be publicly accountable, successfully championed such judiciously unpopular causes as opening up his court to video and still cameras and developing ways to grade the effectiveness of judges without losing the support of his fellow judges.

He'd surprised his colleagues that spring when he

announced his retirement six years ahead of the mandatory retirement age for federal judges, because he said he thought it was time for new blood in the system. But no one expected him to fade quietly into retirement, and he hadn't. He'd already been invited in by one side or another in a number of disputes to serve as an arbitrator, and the speaker of the legislature had asked him to head a provincial committee to look into the publicly thorny issue of how much members of the legislature should be paid.

He was still in the middle of that assignment when the premier had called him the week before to ask him to take on the Swissair project. The new task seemed straightforward enough: decide where the memorial should be, what it should look like, get it built and, oh, yes, figure out what to do with... be identified or returned to the families. And, shouldn't do all of that in time for the first anniversary of the crash the following September.

At the time of the call, Clarke had been little more than an interested spectator to media reports of the tragedy. The morning after it happened, he and his wife and two grown children had flown to St. John's, Newfoundland, for the wedding of their son. "I read about it in the newspaper," he says.

But certainly, he told the premier, he'd be happy to take on the job. He probably couldn't get started officially until after the beginning of the new year, Clarke warned him; he still had to figure out what an MLA should be paid. But that shouldn't be a problem. He'd start January 6. How complicated could it be?

Wednesday, November 18, 1998

East Brunswick

Peggy Coburn asked her late husband to give her "some kind of sign, something undeniable." The night before, she dreamed she was talking to him. It wasn't the first time either. The previous week, she'd been startled out of her sleep by the feel of someone "blowing hard in my ear, like blowing out candles. I shot up in bed. It was the ear that I had been lying on." Was it Rich? she asked herself. "It didn't feel like a dream. It felt real, from the outside, and it woke me up."

Peggy spent a lot of her time now — waking and sleeping — thinking about Rich. In the first days after she came back from Nova Scotia, she survived by focusing exclusively on the immediate tasks at hand. "I still had a family to take care of. I had to do laundry, go grocery shopping, feed the kids, plus give them attention." When she went to the grocery store, she says, "I was absolutely shocked that people weren't staring at me. Didn't they notice? I felt maimed. Didn't I look it?"

But as time went on, it had become harder and harder to keep up appearances. "I'm backed up on housework," she wrote in her journal. "Algae is growing in the toilet. I haven't cleaned since this thing happened. It's getting disgusting. I'm so busy all the time," she added almost plaintively, "I never have any time for anything, and I'm exhausted at the end of the day, well even before the end of the day."

A lot of what she was busy with was Rich's computer. Before the accident, she'd never used it. But then Rich's brother told her about an Internet site Swissair had set up for families. She logged on to that. A few weeks later, she called their Internet service provider for help sending and receiving email. On October 28, she downloaded messages — 2,704 of them, many of them from user groups Rich had belonged to — collecting in his email account since September 2. "Luckily," she says, "he had a cable modem."

On the Swissair family web site she met a couple of other family members, including Miles Gerety, whom she'd begun to email privately. She sent him a copy of the eulogy she'd written for Richard and later called him up. "I called him to tell him something, I think, but I just wanted to talk to him." When Gerety decided to set up a families group of his own, he asked her to handle a members' database, even though, she says, "I'm still not really computer literate."

It had been a conversation she'd had with Miles that touched off their latest plan, for some of the families to travel together back to Halifax on the American Thanksgiving weekend, in part to escape the holiday merriment but also to see whether she could get some answers to her request to have Richard's remains buried at Peggys Cove. Since her conversation the previous month with John Butt, she'd called a priest she'd met in Nova Scotia as well as several other officials to explain to them why she thought Richard would have wanted to be buried in that beautiful place. But she couldn't get any response from anyone. Until she called Miles. Miles had made some calls and then, suddenly, he and Peggy and about a half-dozen other family members were scheduled to fly to Nova Scotia the following week to stay with some local families, tour possible memorial and burial sites and meet with Lorne Clarke, the one-man Flight 111 Memorial Advisory Committee.

Something good would happen out of that, she was sure of it. Just as she was almost certain Richard was really still with her, even now. She just wished she could remember if she'd locked that door. Earlier, while she was feeding her daughter, Alea, in the kitchen, she'd stared hard at the apartment door, "wishing it would just open and Rich would walk in." Later, after dinner, when she came back into the kitchen, she noticed that the door was ajar. "I didn't remembered if I locked it. A possible explanation," she admits, "was that the door wasn't completely shut and when the downstairs neighbours opened their door, the wind pushed mine open too. But I just don't remember if the door was locked. If it was," she says, her voice hopeful, "I would know that Richard opened the door for me."

Monday, November 23, 1998

Haverford

"Miles," Barbara Fetherolf wrote in an email to Miles Gerety, "what on earth is going on?" It was a good question. Earlier in November, Miles's 13-year-old son, Paddy, had helped him set up an Internet club to serve as a meeting place for family members. Those who registered with the club could post messages, and there was also a chat room, where members could "chat" by typing messages to each other.

But the club, known as Families of Swissair Flight 111, had been operating for less than a month and already cracks were beginning to appear in the facade of unity among family members. It was probably inevitable. Hans Ephraimson-Abt, in fact, had warned Miles during their first lunch that it would be difficult, if not impossible, to keep all the grieving, confused, angry family members working together for long. The families of the victims of the Pan Am 103 crash over Lockerbie, for example, had ultimately split off into four often warring groups.

But Miles's own leadership style may have made the fissures occur even more quickly. He was uncomfortable with the free-wheeling ways of the Internet so he tended, lawyer-like, to be cautious to a fault about his legal responsibilities for anything controversial or untoward that was posted on the site. (At one point, he even deleted an innocuous message about the Death on the High Seas Act because he was concerned that, as a non-profit group, they shouldn't be seen as lobbying for legislative change.)

In the first few weeks, controversial postings were not a problem as family members migrated from the Swissair site — posting there, Monica Hawkins said, felt "kind of funny" because they knew Swissair officials would be reading their words — and began defining their new community of constant sorrows. And finding out about one another. "I am wondering if there are any other people out there around my age (19) who lost someone on the flight and would like to communicate," wrote one young woman whose father had died on Flight 111. Two days later, a woman who had lost both her parents posted an empathetic reply. "I'm not really sure what to write, but I really want to," began a post from a woman who'd lost her father as well and who had never participated in an Internet chat before. "Maybe writing to you all is a good way to deal with what has happened." Still another person came up with the idea of starting a Families newsletter and suggested she and anyone else who wanted to help could "set up a time to meet in the chat room and get rolling."

The mood began to sour, however, after Matt Wald wrote a story about the site in the *New York Times*. The publicity attracted not only new family members but also some people who had no direct connection with Flight 111 and some with an axe to grind. When a person who wasn't a family member, and who signed himself Aviator, began posting messages about the likelihood of pilot error or the role the inflight entertainment system may have played in the crash — sparking a sometimes heated debate — Miles responded by deleting his posts and removing him as a member of the club. "Many family members were very upset by these postings, since they saw the site as a place for emotional support, a personal place where they could post feelings," Miles explains.

But others were becoming just as upset with what they saw as Miles's controlling, paternalistic ways. In one message, for example, he issued a series of edicts about how members should conduct themselves on the site, ranging from posting no messages in all-capital letters ("This is the Internet equivalent of screaming and will not be tolerated here") to an admonition to members to "write posts about their difficulties coping" rather than getting into contentious discussions about the cause of the disaster. "Three violations of these rules may result in your denial of access to this site," he wrote, "especially if those violations appear to be intentional."

Mark Fetherolf, who quickly came to dismiss the unelected Miles as "the self-proclaimed leader" of the Families group, resented Miles's doctrinaire, "chain of command" approach to his role as webmaster. "On one hand, it's petty bullshit, hardly worthy," he allows. "On the other, it's a very interesting story about the formation of a community using the Internet as the basis for communication. There is a clash between the Internet culture — no rules, just people — and the more traditional view taken by Miles." But Mark's detached, Internet-savvy software developer's view of that cultural divide quickly changed when Miles deleted messages from Barbara Fetherolf and Lyn Romano.

The problem began when a family member from Georgia who, Miles says, was having a rough time, posted a message calling for the erection of a memorial at Peggys Cove on which the names of all of the victims of Flight 111 would be listed. Lyn and Barbara, who'd gone separately to Peggys Cove several weeks after the crash and after the first emotional visits to the site by groups of family members, opposed the idea. In messages they sent to the site, they argued that Peggys Cove could never be a place of beauty or peace for them and they didn't want their loved ones associated in any way with such a memorial. Barbara says now her point was that Tara "was young and too full of life to have her name on a stone. I also added that I didn't think that Peggys Cove was a beautiful place but one of pain and despair for our family."

Miles says he didn't object to what the two women had to say so much as to how they said it. "Our problem was with the tone of the remarks and that two people were piling on the poor woman." He immediately deleted both of their postings.

Though Miles had been one of the first family members to contact Barbara Fetherolf after the crash — "I liked him initially," she recalls. "He seemed to be a caring person" — she adds now: "I did notice that he did a lot of name-dropping and didn't allow you to say much." Miles, she says, was fond of invoking the name of Kofi Annan, the U.N. secretary-general, and brandishing condolence letters from such prominent people as former First Lady Barbara Bush.

After he deleted her messages, Barbara says, "he called my husband and explained in his crazy way that he wanted to be a judge in Connecticut and something about we were offending his mother. We were appalled. Why shouldn't we be allowed to express our feelings on this? We were already in tremendous pain and he was adding to it."

Miles's deletions quickly touched off a flame war — the Internet equivalent of a shouting match — with Miles and Monica Hawkins, the group's acting vice-chair, on one side, and Lyn and the Fetherolfs on the other, and non-combatants chipping in on one side or the other for good measure. For a week, the battle raged on the site and in private emails among the members.

Lyn declared that Miles and Monica hadn't simply deleted her postings, they had deleted "MY FEELINGS" and, in doing so, "MY RAY" too. Miles says the "threatening tone" of Lyn's angry emails "left Monica in tears and caused her to cease being active" with the group.

Admitting in a public message that he had made judgment calls "which I am willing to concede may have been bad calls," Miles urged everyone to cool out. "We owe our lost loved ones a better legacy than this." But he then closed his message with yet another I-know-what's-best postscript: "I am in the middle of a battle with Swissair," he noted. "Swissair has refused to let us contact non-U.S. families. Continue this debate and they win."

"What the hell are you doing?" an infuriated Mark fired back. "Do you really propose to censor this site based on your judgement only? I have been polite and sensitive. This is an outrage. I am livid."

After deleting one of Mark's public messages about the controversy, Miles emailed a warning to him: "This post is divisive, unhelpful and has nothing to do with support and grief. The rules are not debatable. If you post another message like this your access to the site will be denied."

A week later, after deciding enough was enough, Miles made the site private, meaning non-family members couldn't join and non-members couldn't read the postings at all. He also deleted Mark and Lyn from the group's membership list. Though Miles didn't remove Barbara, she quickly decided to drop out. "I am very disappointed in you," she wrote in her final email to Miles. "I guess there is a very simple answer to this. Don't be involved anymore. Frankly, when you look at the big picture, it certainly won't bring my wonderful daughter back and it does nothing for this family ... so time to quit."

Mark then set up a new web site, SR111, which was

open to anyone who was interested in discussing any aspect of the crash. Its stated purpose was broader than that of the Families site — "This club is an open forum about Swissair 111: the crash, investigation, victims, survivors, what went wrong, why, who is responsible and how will such tragedies be prevented in the future" — and Mark made it clear from the outset that no one's posting would be censored.

At the same time, Mark and Barbara settled on their own, not-carved-in-cold-stone memorial for Tara. They established the Tara Maritza Fetherolf Memorial Endowment, a scholarship fund at the Johns Hopkins University Institute for the Academic Advancement of Youth, which Tara had attended.

Friday, November 27, 1998

Halifax International Airport

This is *not* going to be a good weekend, Rob Gordon thought. He had come to the airport — along with what seemed like every other journalist in town — to meet a group of a half dozen Swissair family members arriving to spend the American Thanksgiving weekend in Nova Scotia. The group, led by Miles Gerety, had come to Nova Scotia for a number of reasons: to meet and say thank you to some of the fishermen and others who'd risked their own lives to look for survivors in the immediate aftermath of the crash; to have a memorial service aboard a Canadian military ship at the site of the crash; to look at possible locations for a permanent memorial; and, not at all incidentally, to escape what would almost certainly be now-painful memories of Thanksgivings past.

While they were waiting for the luggage to arrive on the carousel, Gordon had managed to arrange an interview with a young mother named Peggy Coburn. The usual thing. Why have you come? What are you hoping to accomplish? His cameraman, Dave Laughlin, was just beginning to film when a white-haired man beside them interrupted loudly.

Gordon recognized him immediately from pictures in the newspapers. Miles Gerety. Though they'd never met, they had talked several times on the telephone. Gerety talked a lot. Gordon had already seen him in action once this morning, ordering cameramen to stop filming the families as they milled about waiting for their luggage. As Rob Gordon saw it, it wasn't so much that Gerety didn't want them filming the families as he didn't seem to want his wife to know he was smoking.

"My name is Miles Gerety," he said in a booming voice, "and I'm in charge here." He was addressing the reporters, instructing them that they were to be sensitive to the families or he wouldn't let them take any pictures or talk to anyone at all. And then he launched into a loud monologue. Laughlin looked at Gordon. There really was no choice. He swung the camera around to begin recording Gerety. So did others. Gerety spoke for so long without pausing that Laughlin had to change video cassettes in his camera. Gordon knew he would use almost none of the film, and he motioned to Laughlin to step back and get some cutaways they could use when they edited the item.

Gerety saw Laughlin turn off the camera. "No, no," he told Laughlin, "this is serious. You should be getting this. I'm going to say something important."

Gordon was shocked. "I'd never seen anyone before in my whole life who was such an unbelievable control freak," he would say later.

Still, there was no doubting Gerety was clearly very much in control. Gordon had discovered that for himself earlier that day when he'd called the navy's public affairs office to make arrangements to accompany the family members on their trip to the crash site aboard HMCS *Goose Bay*. The only TV reporter being allowed to make the voyage, the officer told Gordon, was a reporter with the CBC's French-language service.

"How come?"

"Mr. Gerety's orders." Gerety! The navy, for whatever reasons, had given Gerety virtual veto power over who could accompany them. He had apparently said yes to the French reporter because Jonathan Mann's daughters had spoken with him several times since the crash and had specifically asked Gerety to include him.

Now Gordon had to beg Gerety, a man he was quickly coming to dislike intensely, for permission to accompany them. Gerety borrowed Gordon's cell phone and called the navy, asking to speak to "the Flag." Gordon was even more surprised when he realized that Gerety appeared to have a direct line to the admiral's chief aide.

"I have a revision for the names on the list for the warship," Gerety announced without preamble. He was "real abrupt," Gordon remembers.

Less than a minute after Gerety had hung up, Gordon's cell phone rang. It was the navy's public affairs office. He had been cleared to accompany the families, he was told without explanation.

Gordon was still marvelling at this turn of events when he overheard Laughlin trying to make small talk with a local fisherman they'd met during the first few weeks at Peggys Cove. The man was driving around one of the families that was spending the weekend at his home.

"What's going on with you?" Laughlin asked casually.

The vehemence of the man's response stunned them both. "How many fuckin' times am I going to have to do this?" he demanded. "They come up here, they eat our food, they drink our beer, they use our gas. And not even a word of thanks for any of it."

Families of the victims had been almost continuous visitors at his home since mid-September, he told them. The visits had been organized by local church groups who saw them as an opportunity for the families of crash victims to get to know the people who'd tried to help their loved ones. But it wasn't working out for everyone. For this fisherman, at least, the visitors had long since worn out their welcome. "There was one fuckin' group of them last weekend. They spent the whole weekend with us. Drive 'em here. Drive 'em there. Feed 'em. Give 'em beer. And all they do is hang around the kitchen table crying while their kids run around and make a mess. They don't take care of 'em at all. And then when they was gettin' set to go, one of 'em offers me $50. Fifty bucks! These guys had buckets of money and what do they do? Offer me $50. I mean, why offer me any money at all if you're going to offer me $50?"

The man turned away in disgust and went to gather the bags for his designated family.

Wow, thought Gordon, the warm, fuzzy feelings of the first weeks were evaporating faster than ice on a hot radiator. It was inevitable, of course. The families and the fishermen did come from very different worlds. Perhaps there could be a story there. In the end, it turned out that this particular fisherman's views weren't representative, either of his fellow fishing family hosts or of the community at large, which was still almost universally sympathetic to the grieving families. But his flash of resentment showed how fragile the bonds between these two very different groups could turn out to be.

For now, however, Gordon was less concerned about those larger long-term questions than about how to keep in touch with Miles Gerety, the man in control of the events of this weekend. Gerety had said he didn't want reporters bothering the family he would be staying with by tying up their phone with calls to him, so the local correspondents for the CBC's French television network and CTV had given Gerety their cell phones and asked him to call them with his plans as they evolved. Gordon felt he had no choice. He turned over his cell phone too, asking only that Gerety limit himself to local calls.

"I won't be limited," Gerety insisted. "I can't. I don't know who's going to be calling me or who I'll have to call. I can't be limited."

This is not going to be a good weekend, Gordon said to himself again, not good at all.

Saturday, November 28, 1998

CFB Halifax Dockyard

The next day did not appear to be starting out any more auspiciously than the one before had ended. Rob Gordon and a dozen other journalists — had they all had to beg for Miles's permission to be here? he wondered — were standing around in the late-fall, wind-off-the-harbour early-morning chill beside the gangway of HMCS *Goose Bay*. They'd been here for the past half hour, waiting for Miles Gerety to show up.

The day before, the navy had instructed the reporters to be at the dock and ready to set sail at 7:30 a.m. But when they got there, they'd been told they weren't allowed to board until Miles arrived. He wanted to talk to them first, they were told.

And so they waited. And grumbled. Finally, a few minutes past eight, a procession of cabs and limos pulled up a hundred feet from where the reporters were standing. As the family groups made their way toward the vessel, Gerety rushed ahead to speak to the reporters.

"Here are the rules," he began. He told them who they could shoot and where they could shoot and when they could shoot. "I don't want anyone talking to family members unless I say so. If you're not respectful, you'll be put ashore."

For his part, Gerety would explain later, he was simply

doing what the families had asked him to do. "Before agreeing to make the trip, the Wilsons wanted assurance that the press would leave their kids alone," he says. "Most had real reservations about having the press along at all."

The *Goose Bay*, one of the navy's newest ships, commissioned only in July 1998, had been built for fisheries patrols, drug interception, coastal surveillance and search and rescue, and was designed to be crewed primarily by reservists. Many of the crew today had taken part in the Swissair recovery operation and were looking forward to the opportunity to take the families to the scene of the tragedy.

As the ship pulled away from the jetty and made its way out of the harbour, many of the family and reporters gathered on the bridge to look back at downtown Halifax. Despite Gerety's injunction, Gordon struck up a casual conversation with Jonathan Mann's two daughters. "You see that clock up there on the hill," he said, pointing to the historic Old Town Clock on Citadel Hill, the fortress that overlooked the harbour. "It was designed by Edward, the Duke of Kent, back in—"

Suddenly, Gerety stepped between Gordon and the two young women. "Are you okay with this?" he demanded of the women.

They were. But Gordon wasn't, not anymore. Gerety's constant presence made him feel like he was back in school.

Conversation became a moot issue soon enough. As the *Goose Bay* passed MacNabs Island and out of the mouth of the harbour, the sea turned nasty. With the winds blowing at 40 knots and the swells reaching six to eight feet, the vessel bounced up and down as it plowed through the chop on a five-and-a-half-hour steam to the site of the crash.

Most of the families and more than a few of the reporters — not to mention some of the crew — became seasick, and many of the passengers retreated below deck to wait out the weather. The families had been assigned to the officers' mess, the press to the seamen's quarters. There was a galley between the two messes serving lasagna to those brave enough to eat.

"We'd be standing in the line for the food with family members, and Miles would be watching everyone like a hawk," Gordon recalled later. "It was very uncomfortable."

As the ship drew closer to the crash site, family members began drifting back up to the deck, huddling together in small groups. Many of them, ill prepared for the bitterly cold winds, were now dressed in bits and pieces of sailors' uniforms the crew had given them. Dave Archibald, Gordon's cameraman aboard the *Goose Bay*, took some shots of that, close-ups of the petty officers' stripes on a uniform, then pulled back discreetly to show the back of a woman's head as she stared out to sea.

At first, Gerety had ordered that there be no cameras at all on the bridge when they reached the crash area. Later, he modified that, saying he would allow some cameras but would determine where they should be placed. Then they could be anywhere — but with no microphones recording anything. Finally, he just gave up and said they could do what they wanted. "From my perspective, we gave reporters an awful lot of access on a very emotional boat trip," Gerety said later. "It doesn't take all that much imagination to figure out what may have happened if there had been no control at all."

Gordon wondered what Gerety thought they were going to do. Stick the cameras in the the faces of the grieving family members so they could film the tears and hear the wails? If so, he thought, Gerety had not been paying attention to the respectful way reporters — especially local reporters — had treated the families.

Gordon noticed the Wilsons — Tim and his wife,

Judith, and their two youngest children, Blair, 13, and Joshua, 11 — standing together along the starboard side of the vessel. The family had lost their 22-year-old-son, Jonathan, in the crash. Gordon knew from things he'd heard that the family was very religious; the father was a minister or something in Florida. He approached them tentatively.

"Mr. and Mrs. Wilson," he said, "my name is Rob Gordon and I'm a reporter with CBC. I'm not sure if you want to know this, but one of our cameramen, Dave Archibald, was the one who found your son's Bible."

Tim Wilson seemed interested. "How do you know it was my son's?" he asked.

"It had a white cover," Gordon explained, "and inside the cover, there was an inscription: 'From Mother and Father Wilson.' "

"He would have been reading it when the plane went down," Judy Wilson said. "I'm sure he would —"

Miles stepped between Gordon and the Wilsons.

"What are you doing?" he demanded of Gordon.

Gordon tried to explain, to talk past Gerety to the Wilsons, explaining that he would be happy to introduce them to Archibald if they were interested in talking to him or getting a copy of the videotape he had shot.

"I don't think this is the right time," Gerety interrupted. "Not now." He paused. "Go from us now," he told Gordon.

Go from us now! "I wanted to fucking kill him," Gordon would tell friends later, "just fucking kill him."

But he had no choice. He looked at Mrs. Wilson. She looked at him. "Here's my card," Gordon said. "If you want to know any more, you can call me."

And then he walked away.

"We're approximately two minutes from the spot where the plane went down," the ship's captain, Lt. Cmdr. Tim Guzan, announced over the loudspeaker.

The ship became eerily quiet now as everyone —

family members, crew members, reporters — retreated into their private thoughts.

From the bridge, Gordon and the other reporters and crew kept a respectful watch as the families gathered on the *Goose Bay*'s aft deck. The Wilsons, Peggy Coburn and her sister and her kids, the Mann sisters, Miles and his son, Nancy Wight. Huddled together. They held each other as Tim Wilson offered up a few words of prayer and then they all tossed red flowers and a memorial wreath into the roiling waters.

As the flowers drifted away in the wake, Gordon heard a low, soft whimpering sound, a mournful wail of such deep distress, he would say, "it's never been successfully faked in the movies." As they all watched, a sliver of sunlight suddenly cut through the clouds and played over the wreath as it slipped beneath the surface of the ocean.

"Beautiful," Tim Wilson said to no one in particular. "Beautiful."

Pearl Island was beautiful too. In its own desolate, stark, windswept way, the tiny sanctuary and nesting area for rare seabirds — the closest piece of land to the spot where Flight 111 went down — might have made a meaningful memorial to those who died. Some had already suggested it. That was another reason they'd wanted to come out here today. They would be meeting with Lorne Clarke that next day to discuss what would be an appropriate memorial. But it was clear as the *Goose Bay* sailed close by the shore of the uninhabited island that it was not what most of the families had in mind as a memorial site. They would need to look elsewhere for a more accessible place people could come to remember what they had lost.

Tuesday, December 1, 1998

Haverford

"Can I speak to Tara, please?"

He was an old boyfriend from the Johns Hopkins summer school program. He didn't know. Why should he? He and Tara had kept in touch in the haphazard way kids do when they meet in such circumstances, with calls around the holidays and birthdays. Tara's birthday was the previous Friday. She would have been 17. He was probably calling to wish her a belated happy birthday.

"Tara's dead."

"What?"

"Dead." Barbara Fetherolf had to tell him, had to tell the whole awful story all over again. He was shocked, speechless. He was only a kid too. Barbara tried to be gentle. It wasn't his fault. When she got off the phone, she could feel the familiar anger bubble up again. This was all so unfair, she thought. Why wasn't Tara here? Why couldn't things be the way they were before September 2?

She went back to her computer and wrote a message to the members of the SR111 group, telling them what had happened, explaining how she felt. "This is what we hope to address on this site," she wrote. "Why did this happen to these 229 people?"

Tuesday, December 15, 1998

Halifax

It was strange how things had turned out. Despite her initial fears when the *Daily News* had published her address along with her letter about Rowenna in late September, Nancy Wight had received only one other telephone call, from a housewife who called a few weeks afterward and who just wanted to chat about Swissair. In contrast, Nancy had been deluged with kind letters — 70 from Nova Scotians, 400 from around the world — most just thanking her for thanking them and telling her they were thinking of her.

Ellen Haynes and her husband, Eric, who had taken the CBC reporters to the scene and later served as coast guard auxiliary members in the recovery effort, were among the first to write. "In a way, we felt we had failed [Rowenna and the other passengers] because we had not found survivors. We are truly sorry for the loss of your daughter ... We appreciate your gracious thank you."

David King, an officer aboard HMCS *Halifax*, which was involved in the recovery operation, wrote: "Over the course of the past three weeks I was unable to personalize the tragedy or comprehend the scope of loss due to the hectic pace of operations until three days ago when I read your published letter in a local newspaper. Thank you. I have kept a copy as a sombre reminder of just how precious and fragile life is. Tomorrow, I will return to my wife and children with a renewed sense of appreciation of what they offer."

"I would like you to know that your letter had helped me more than any of the counselling," added one of the volunteer ground search and rescue workers who'd helped scour the shoreline for human remains.

The first letter to arrive was from a Dartmouth teenager, Alissa Dawson, who'd enclosed four little angel pins for Wight to wear. It was, says Wight, "a most beautiful letter and, interestingly, not about herself at all." When Wight had decided to return to Nova Scotia the month before, she'd called Alissa and arranged to take her to lunch. They talked about all sorts of things, Wight says, including Alissa's ambition to become a hairdresser. She also told Wight about some friends of hers who'd been killed in a car crash a few months before. After their lunch, she and Wight continued to correspond.

Like the unexpected letters from strangers, coming back to Nova Scotia had turned out to be a comfort for Wight.

Greg McMullin, a young Anglican priest she'd met at the Lord Nelson Hotel that first weekend, arranged for her to stay in a bed and breakfast in Halifax. She'd wanted to get away from New York during the holidays, in part because there were too many reminders there, and in part, she says, because "I didn't have anything to keep me there any longer." After Rowenna's death, she'd taken a year's leave of absence from her job teaching English as a second language at Pace University in New York. In Halifax, she spent her time helping out on the computer at Trinity Church, where McMullin was the rector, and also did some cooking at the bed and breakfast where she stayed. The couple who owned it had gone away on vacation themselves for the entire month of December, leaving her in charge. Though the owners had told her she didn't need to take in paying guests, she preferred the company. She even became an unofficial guide to Nova Scotia, helping one couple from Düsseldorf find out where they could go square dancing in Nova Scotia.

On this day, like most mornings, Wight had gotten up at six o'clock to make muffins and watch "the sun rise over the graveyard" across the street while she listened to the "imaginative programming on CBC Radio. This was the best part of the day," she would say later.

The woman who owned the bed and breakfast had helped hook Wight up with a local grief group, where she met other parents who'd lost children to sudden death. Listening to them talk about how their sons or daughters had died in accidents or been murdered or committed suicide offered a poignant reminder both that she was not alone in her suffering and also that others' situations seemed even more difficult to cope with than her own.

While in Halifax, she finally met face to face with Dr. Butt — a planned 15-minute meeting to talk about Rowenna's remains lasted for more than an hour — and attended a symposium at Dalhousie University titled "The Swissair 111: Lessons Learned," which featured many of those who'd taken part in the rescue and recovery operation.

Wight went to the symposium with Robert and Peggy Conrad. Since the day they'd spent together with the Wilkinses back in September, Wight and the Conrads had continued to be in touch, exchanging emails and even gifts. Robert says he sent her "a lovely hymn. I wanted her to read the lyrics." She sent him a leather-bound edition of the Psalms. Robert was one of the invited participants at the symposium, offering a fisherman's perspective on the crash and its aftermath.

Rob Gordon was a panellist that day too. After the endless round of live reports he'd done during the first few days of the tragedy, Gordon had essentially adopted Swissair as his full-time beat. He estimated that he'd probably done 50 to 60 television news reports about the crash, on everything from the families' return visit to Peggys Cove in November to the attempts by "shark New York lawyers to make hay out of grief." In the spring of 1999, CBC Halifax's *First Edition* newsroom would win an Atlantic Journalism Award for its spot news coverage of the Swissair disaster and Gordon himself would be a finalist for the annual Journalistic Achievement Award for his work on the story. But at the time, Gordon could sense that his bosses at the CBC were "concerned that the daily grind of reporting the tiny developments of the investigation might be getting a little tedious." Though Gordon agreed that there were fewer and fewer significant scoops to report as the investigators settled in for the long haul of trying to figure out what had gone wrong, he also knew such scoops would be even more unlikely if he wasn't allowed to focus on the story.

Wight saw Gordon on the panel that day, but she didn't pay much attention. They'd never met and, despite the inadvertent positive things that had happened as a result of the publication of her letter and address, she still wasn't all that well disposed to the press.

She was, on the other hand, instantly enchanted by Ceiline Griffiths, a "dear, warm-hearted, emotional half-Irish lady" whose husband, David, a research fellow at the university, was one of the symposium's panellists. After the crash, Ceiline had used her own furniture to set up a lounge area at the Shearwater morgue for the staff and families of the victims. Later, she and her husband collected bottles of water from Peggys Cove for the families to take home if they wanted it. When she returned home from Peggys Cove that day, she told Wight, she had "collapsed in total exhaustion." Several weeks later, her husband showed her Wight's letter in the newspaper "and she wept." Ceiline not only invited Wight home for dinner but also urged her to come to England and stay in their home there for a while.

As comforting as all of this was, it was impossible for Wight to ever forget how it had all begun and why she had ended up in Nova Scotia in the first place. Despite all the kindness shown to her, in the end she would write of the month and a half she spent in the province that fall: "It was not a very happy time for me."

Halifax

It was done. It had taken just over three months. Remarkable, really, thought John Butt. He had expected the task of recovering and identifying the remains of the 229 passengers to take much longer. But that day, his office had issued a press release announcing that "the recovery of human remains is essentially complete. To date, 228 passengers have been positively identified." The discrepancy was accounted for by the simple fact that two of the passengers were identical twins; they carried the same DNA.

It wouldn't have been possible to identify the remains so quickly — or to identify many of them at all — if not for advances in DNA technology. It certainly wouldn't have been possible to unite arms and legs and other body parts belonging to the same person if Butt hadn't been able to call on the assistance of RCMP labs in Halifax, Ottawa, Regina and Vancouver as well as the Centre of Forensic Sciences in Toronto to process the approximately 1,500 DNA samples his teams had collected.

That's not to say mistakes weren't made — one victim ended up, briefly, with three feet because of cataloguing carelessness, and 17 small pieces of dental remains, which were being stored until further testing could be done on them, were inadvertently discarded and then incinerated — or that all of the remains had been recovered or, more important to some families, identified.

After mid-November, most of the few remains still

being brought to the surface either contained none of the soft tissue normally used for DNA sampling — "The flesh," Butt says, "had been cleaned off the bone" — or the soft tissue itself was now too decomposed to be of use for DNA testing. Even among the smallest pieces of soft tissue the labs had tried to identify, there were often problems. The impact had driven some of the bodies together with such force that what appeared to be a single piece of a body might contain DNA from two different people.

To determine the DNA of the bones would mean sending them to U.S. labs, where they would need to be pulverized in a sterile atmosphere for testing that might take months to produce results. "It's a different type of technique, very time consuming and expensive," Butt explains. "We had to ask ourselves if that was our job."

Lyn Romano certainly thought it was someone's job. After she discovered in late fall that the 2,300 pounds of small, mostly bony, unidentified human remains would probably end up being buried together in a mass grave, perhaps as part of a memorial site she also objected to, she began a vocal campaign to force authorities — Swissair, in particular, which she had come to believe was ultimately responsible for the crash — to complete the DNA identification process, regardless of the cost. After a while, Butt says, her calls became so frequent and so hostile that he refused to speak with her on the telephone.

"He told me to put my request in writing," she says now. In her posts to the Fetherolfs' web site, she began to refer to Butt as "THAT MONSTER ... that man they call 'doctor.' "

Romano also took her objections to Lorne Clarke, the chair of the one-person committee that was dealing with both the memorial and the treatment of the human remains. Clarke's hope that those tricky issues would be resolved easily and quickly was now smacking up against the strong-willed Lyn Romano.

Wednesday, February 10, 1999

Goldens Bridge

"You actually got a smile out of me on a WEDNES-DAY," Lyn Romano emailed Doug Johnson at the SR111 web site, "and I can assure you THAT IS NO EASY TASK!"

It had, in fact, been a good morning. Lyn had begun making arrangements for the founding meeting of the International Aviation Safety Association, the flight safety lobby she was creating.

The founding group of close to a dozen were all people she'd met through the Internet, a curious mix of aviation safety experts, government whistle-blowers, tagalong journalists and a few assorted unlikelies, such as Aart van der Wal, a Rotterdam businessman who'd lost his 19-year-old son in a car crash in July 1998. He and Lyn had met when Lyn "ripped his lips off" in an email message after he speculated about the cause of the Swissair crash on an Internet chat group. Inexplicably, the two had become allies, and Lyn had asked him — despite his lack of any connection with airline safety — to be the vice-chair and European head of her new organization. "He has an incredible business mind," she says, "and he understood the loss I felt."

Some of the other members of her fledgling organization were more predictable: experts, some of them self-proclaimed, who posted regularly to airline safety web sites. These days, many of them were being quoted in news accounts speculating on the cause of the crash of Swissair Flight 111. Ed Block, a freelance consultant who had served as the U.S. Defense Department's wire-and-cable expert when Kapton wiring insulation was banned from military aircraft in 1987 and was now investigating the TWA 800 disaster, had become, in Lyn's description, "my wire guy." John King, a 30-year veteran aircraft mechanic who'd made it his mission to expose FAA malfeasance, was her "database guy."

Lyn soaked up everything they had to offer, then did her own research besides, becoming fluent in all the buzz-words and phrases of the air safety business: air worthiness directives, three men in a cockpit, emergency check-lists, resetting tripped circuit-breakers, and so on. Her plan was to devote whatever she earned from her $175-million lawsuit against Swissair to funding IASA. The organization would underwrite lobbying and research to promote airline safety. As its chair, she would use her own clout as the "grieving widow" who refuses to take no for an answer as a kind of club to bludgeon those in power into doing something to clean up the dangerous cesspool she believed the international airline industry had become.

She would take the first leap into that brave new world of high-profile lobbying in two weeks' time when van der Wal, Block, King and a dozen others came to her home in Goldens — along with a number of reporters — for the one-day founding meeting of the IASA. She was even planning to cook lasagna for the whole crowd, the first time since the accident that she'd felt like entertaining. But this was different. This was entertaining with a purpose.

Later that week, after the meeting, she'd fly to Halifax, no longer simply Lyn Romano, the grieving widow of one of the 229 passengers aboard Flight 111, but Lyn Romano, the chair of the International Aviation Safety Organization. She'd meet with Vic Gerden and other top officials of the Transportation Safety Board for a personal briefing on the latest in the investigation and then let him know, in no uncertain terms, that IASA intended to become a focal point for future efforts to make the skies safer. That would be her personal memorial to Ray, not some marker on a cold rock at even colder Peggys Cove.

But that was later. Now, as she scanned the SR111 web site, she noticed that a woman named Liz Benteau had written in "as a Canadian" to make the point that the best hope anyone had of finding out what had really caused the accident was to wait for the TSB to issue its report. (Many critics believe, for instance, that the American Federal Aviation Administration is too closely aligned with the airline industry to be fully objective.) In her message, Benteau took a light swipe at the supposedly more politicized U.S. aviation authorities: "As this disaster does NOT involve a Canadian plane or airline, nor is there any Canadian in any jeopardy what so ever of having any blame put on them, then why would Mr. Gerden have any fear of 'covering' anything up?" she demanded. "That is why I am quite confident they will not 'miss' anything ... we will know the truth."

Lyn couldn't help herself. "Maybe you are right ... and of course you are entitled to say whatever you feel," she replied, using her email name, Rosebush. "But I do love my country as well as you love yours. We do have our problems," she conceded, but then added pointedly but obliquely: "I know of a few 'professionals' in Canada that leave much to be desired and that will be told in my book." (In December, Lyn had bought a six-hectare farm in Nova Scotia where she planned to spend the summer of 1999 with her two sons while she wrote her own book about her husband and her experiences with Swissair Flight 111.)

There were all sorts of other messages Lyn read as well, many having to do with the recent revelation that Aviator, who'd migrated to the SR111 site with disaffected family members, was a fraud. He's claimed to be a former commercial pilot and offered his take on many of the technical issues behind the crash. Far from being a pilot, he apparently worked in a travel agency and had a history of posting to airline-related web groups under a variety of names.

Many of the SR111 regulars, including Doug Johnson, an aviation accident buff, were angry about Aviator's intrusion into their site; it had led to confusion and many pointless arguments as he challenged the views of some of the real aviation experts on the site. But Johnson had a plan for dealing with him: "I think we ought to sic the Italian Stallion on him," he suggested in a posting, referring to Lyn, "and Rosebush him to a quivering pulp."

Lyn couldn't help but smile. "Just point me in the right direction," she replied, "and this ITALIAN STAL-LIONESS (hope you don't mind I prefer the female status (smile)) will do her thing."

She'd barely hit the Send button on the computer when the telephone rang. It was nine-year-old Randy calling from school. He was in tears.

"I miss Daddy," he said.

Lyn hurried to the school to get him and bring him home.

When she got back, she emailed the SR111 site to explain what had happened. "I go offline now ... to be with him," she wrote simply.

Tuesday, March 2, 1999

Haverford

"On this horrible anniversary, that marks six months of severe pain and loss for this family and all the other 228 families, I just want to say that my daughter should be in the village of Chesières-Villars growing into the fine young woman she was on her way to becoming," Barbara Fetherolf wrote in a bitter time-marking message to the SR111 web site.

It wasn't getting any easier. Even though she did her best to be a good mother for Amy — who needed her now more than ever — she still found it impossible not to find echoes of Tara everywhere. A few days before, for example, when Amy had attended her first semi-formal dance, "I put my small strand of pearls on her like I always did for Tara for a special event." Then, she says, "I had to very discreetly leave the room to just sob."

Her relationship with Mark was deteriorating too. After clashing with Miles Gerety and launching their own web site in November 1998, Mark and Barbara had become increasingly isolated from other families — and from each other. By Mother's Day 1999, the couple had separated.

"We put Tara on that plane that fateful day excited about the great new life she would be having, happy that she would be meeting other children from all over the world," her anniversary message continued. "We had total faith in Swissair delivering her to her destination safely. One child never arrived at the school called Aiglon that she was to attend. One plane out of 30,000 flights that day didn't make it to its destination. I should be on the phone with her right now, discussing plans for our next visit with her ... listening to her excitedly telling me about all the great people she is meeting. Instead she and 228 other human beings were destroyed. Swissair's reaction is to try and throw money at the families," she noted in reference to the airline's offer of ex gratia payments of $135,000 U.S., "and to continue to boast that their ticket sales are brisk. They have demonstrated over and over again that they don't begin to understand the scope of the pain that they have caused these families. If Swissair is found to be responsible for the deaths of these 229 amazing souls, at the very least the CEO should step down out of respect for the families.

"To my daughter I just want to say we continue to be so very proud of you and the courage and effort you put into everything that you did during your short but amazing lifetime. We miss your beautiful smile, your laughter and everything that made you so unique and special to us. Life will NEVER be the same without you.

"To all of the families, we express our deepest sympathy."

Wednesday, March 3, 1999

Zurich

It was almost as if the night of September 2, 1998, had never happened at all. In its annual report in January, the U.S. Federal Aviation Administration had declared 1998 to have been a fatality-free year in American aviation, a convenient fiction based on the fact that Swissair Flight 111 was a foreign air carrier and that the aircraft had crashed in Canadian waters. And now, in Zurich, at SAirGroup's annual meeting, CEO Philippe Bruggisser announced that 1998 had been a banner year for the company's business. Net profit was up 11 per cent, to $246 million U.S. The crash, as Swissair president Jeffrey Katz had insisted all along to reporters, "has had only a small impact, if any at all," on the company's bottom line.

Mention of the crash of Flight 111 was kept to a minimum. In an otherwise upbeat corporate annual report, there was a simple, tasteful two-page tribute to the passengers and crew. "I deeply believe our soul is indestructible by nature," it quoted Goethe. "Living on from eternity to eternity it appears to our earthly eyes that it may set as does the sun. Yet like the sun it never sets, but continues to glow forever."

While Beatrice Tshcanz, Swissair's head of PR, had already quietly begun preparing the company's top executives to deal with the possibility that investigators would conclude that Swissair had been responsible for the accident — "We don't want to think so but we don't know so we must be prepared," she says — there was little downbeat talk in public.

But back in Canada, it was certainly clear that something awful — and awfully expensive — had happened in Nova Scotia that night. Even as Bruggisser was delivering his financial good news to shareholders in Zurich, officials at the Transportation Safety Board in Ottawa were checking and rechecking their calculations for a report slated to be released in two days. The report would outline just how much the investigation and recovery of Swissair Flight 111 had cost Canadian taxpayers so far: nearly $63 million, and the costs were still mounting.

A spokesperson for the TSB said it was unlikely that Canada would attempt to recover any of those costs from Swissair. The rule in the international air disaster business is that the country that takes the lead in investigating the accident also takes responsibility for paying the full bill. It wasn't necessarily fair or logical, but it was the way things worked.

Monday, May 17, 1999

Cambridge Suites Hotel, Halifax

"I'll be right down." Larry Vance had completely forgotten our appointment, even though he'd agreed to meet me only a few hours before. It's easy to forget the small stuff; there are still so many, far weightier issues to occupy his thoughts and his days. Nevertheless, he says he is grateful for the chance to spend an evening with someone different, even if it is a journalist and the conversation is going to be about the same investigation that takes up the rest of his waking hours. "It's cheaper than talking to a psychologist," he jokes, "and it's nice to see a new face once in a while."

Larry Vance has been seeing the same faces 12 hours and more each day seven days a week for eight and a half months. In all that time, he's been home to Ottawa only four times: two fleeting visits to pick up necessities, once for Christmas and then for 10 days in late April.

The good news is that the tutoring franchise he and his wife bought last fall is doing well. "My wife has been a real trooper," Vance says of Charlotte, who has had to take on her own intended role running the operation as well as Larry's duties handling the business side of the venture. "She had to do absolutely everything herself," he says, "and since neither of us had ever been in business before, it was like jumping off the deep end. I'm really proud of her."

The bad news, of course, is that he's still here. When he first arrived last fall, Vance thought he'd be in Nova Scotia until Christmas. Now he refuses to even think about a possible end date for the Transportation Safety Board's investigation. "Whenever I've put a date on it in my mind, I've ended up feeling depressed when we didn't hit it," he explains. He just knows he's in it for the long haul, however long that haul ends up being.

How long it will take to complete the critical hauling process itself — bringing up to the surface the thousands more pieces of aircraft still on the ocean floor — may be answered soon. To this point, authorities have used almost everything — from divers to USS *Grapple*, an American navy salvage ship capable of winching 300-ton chunks of twisted metal to the surface — to bring up as many pieces of the wreck as they can. In April, a converted fishing vessel began plying the waters over the site, using a trawl to scoop up more of the smallest pieces.

Remarkably, given the depths and the effects of tide and current, they've recovered more than a million pieces of the plane, close to 90 per cent of the weight of the aircraft. The problem is that the 10 per cent still on the ocean floor — about 28,000 pounds' worth — is the most critical for investigators because it includes much of what was left of the cockpit after the impact shattered it into the smallest, most difficult to salvage pieces.

Investigators have so far catalogued 16,000 individual pieces of the aircraft — the prime focus of their investigation — and they have used what they have recovered to try to reconstruct the cockpit on a special life-size wire jig on which they can place each of the pieces. Swissair has provided investigators with full-sized colour photos of every nook and cranny of the inside and outside of an MD-11 cockpit to help them piece together exactly what goes where. Investigators are also using those photographs, taken at 10-degree angles from one another, to create a 360-degree 3D computer model of the cockpit that ultimately — once they recover more of the pieces — will help them detect any patterns of heat and fire damage in the cockpit area.

"It's not unlike how you investigate a house fire," Vance says. Once you have the pieces in place, you try to figure out the areas of most heat and least heat, and then determine how the fire spread, which should lead you back to where it began. What in that area could have triggered the fire? And did that — whatever that turns out to be — cause the fire to ignite, or was it merely the result of another problem sometime before and somewhere else in the plane that was the real triggering event for the disaster? To help determine that, he says, you have to go back to all the other information you've already gathered from instruments such as flight data recorders and attempt to integrate that data with the physical evidence to see if it matches up. And then — but still far from finally — you begin to develop and test scenarios to determine whether you're right about the cause and the effect you hypothesize. Finally, after all of that, you get to the real purpose of the whole exercise: coming up with recommendations to make sure the same thing doesn't happen again.

But it's hard to do any of that without having the first key pieces of the puzzle in hand: the missing parts of the cockpit. If investigators have to depend on conventional methods of gathering up the rest of those pieces, Vance knows it could take all of the summer and part of the fall just to complete the slow and painstaking job. But that evening, sitting in his hotel room — the third he's occupied in the past eight months — Vance is hopeful that, with a little luck and some bad weather on Newfoundland's Grand Banks, the recovery could be sped up dramatically.

The consortium developing the Terra Nova oil field in the North Atlantic just over 200 miles southeast of St. John's is using a specially designed vessel, *The Queen of the Netherlands*, to excavate glory holes — massive depressions in the seafloor to protect well heads from iceberg damage. The vessel, built in 1998, is one of the few ships in the world, and the largest of them, using what's known as suction-dredging technology.

Put to work off Peggys Cove, the vessel could quickly and efficiently suck up everything from the seabed, Vance says, including virtually all the salvageable pieces of the wreck. "That would compress our time down considerably." But only if the seas are too rough in the North Atlantic off Newfoundland in the spring for the vessel to complete its work will it be available for the Swissair salvage. "If we can get that vessel over here ..."

He pauses, considers. Better to talk about how well the investigation has been handled to date, than the uncertainties down the road. "It's very important for everyone that the TSB gets this right," Vance says, adding: "I am very proud of what we've accomplished so far." He credits Vic Gerden for that. "Vic comes across as what he is, which is calculating and careful. On an investigation like this, you need someone like him rather than a charismatic free-wheeler. You don't want some guy who is too loose, who starts to like the attention and then begins saying things to get it. Vic is a conservative guy who isn't looking for glory or attention, and that's the face he's put on the entire organization. Some people may find that boring, but that's what you have to do in a job like this to get credibility."

Getting and maintaining credibility, and dampening expectations that there will be quick answers to the question of what caused the crash, have become even more important as the investigation has dragged on and others, possibly with vested interests or axes to grind, have begun to leak selected information to American journalists. While no one knows for sure who has been behind the leaks, suspicion has quickly fallen on Boeing, the aircraft's manufacturer, which has its own officials helping out in the investigation, because the leaked material led away from blaming the crash on a failure of the aircraft itself and focused instead on the possibility of pilot error. Shortly after the crash, for example, ABC-TV News reported details of conversations between the pilot and co-pilot inside the cockpit, information that's banned by law from publication in Canada and that could only have come from someone with access to what the investigators were uncovering. Later, the *Wall Street Journal*, also using leaked notes of those same conversations, reported that the two pilots had been arguing over what course of action they should take during the flight's fateful final minutes. In each case, Gerden was at pains to cast doubt on the significance of such information even as he refused to confirm its authenticity. That careful approach frustrated reporters. Canadian Press reporter Stephen Thorne, who has been covering the Swissair story since September, says he admires Gerden for his carefulness but calls him the "world's most unexciting interview. You come back from talking to him and you have to sit down and analyze your notes to try and figure out if he told you anything." But Vance says his approach has been absolutely essential in keeping the investigation from getting derailed by public pressure.

The TSB's mandate — "to advance transportation safety through the investigation of transportation occurrences" — doesn't include dealing with the families of those killed in air crashes, but Larry Vance says he doesn't think anyone could have done more to treat family members with "dignity and respect" than Vic Gerden. "I don't know what happened in TWA 800 because I wasn't around for that investigation, but I don't know how anyone could do more for the families than we have. It began at the very beginning with the coroner and the RCMP. They acted with dignity and grace, and I think we've continued that when it comes to dealing with the families."

The family members, who often can't agree about much else, do agree about that. In March, a delegation from Miles Gerety's Families of Swissair Flight 111 came to Halifax to stage a thank-you dinner at a local hotel for Gerden, Vance and other key players in the recovery and investigation. Just a week ago, Lyn Romano came to town, too, fresh from the founding meeting of her International Aviation Safety Association and, in her words, "loaded for bear" to put the investigators on notice that she and her group would be carefully monitoring everything they did. At one point during her two-hour meeting, she even took Gerden's face in her hands and made him look her in the eye. "I want you to find me a cause," she said urgently. "Don't come up with a probable cause. I want a cause." Still, after the session, Romano would tell reporters she thanked God the plane "didn't go down in my country" because she had faith the Canadian investigators would do a thorough, honest job.

Vance credits Gerden for buying the investigators the time they will need — with the families, Swissair, Boeing, other regulatory agencies, their bosses at the TSB, the politicians and the public — to do the job that needs to be done, not only to find the cause, if one is findable, but also to come up with the concrete recommendations to make sure it doesn't happen again.

How much time? Vance doesn't need reminding that U.S. investigators are still looking into the cause of the 1994 crash of USAir Flight 427 in Pennsylvania that killed 132 people and the 1996 TWA 800 explosion that took

230 lives. Will the investigation of Swissair Flight 111 take that long?

Larry Vance would rather not think of that now. He'd rather talk about how his three grown children are driving down from Ottawa to visit him for the day on Friday. His oldest daughter is getting married in the fall so she's taking her fiancé to Moncton to introduce him to her relatives there. His other daughter and his son decided to come along for the drive in dad's car — "I haven't been using it lately" — to visit with him as well.

Vance says he'll take them on a tour through the hangar at Shearwater "just so they know what it is I'm doing here. Sometimes, I don't think they really have a clue what I actually do; just that I live in a hotel and get to order room service." He glances around at the antiseptic hotel room, at the bottle of laundry detergent on the dresser. "It's not quite as glamorous as they imagine," he says.

Tuesday, May 18, 1999

Flight 111 Secretariat, Halifax

After several months on the job, Lorne Clarke appreciated much better what he called "the ramifications and complexities" of dealing with the issue of Flight 111 memorials. By the time he and his small staff finally moved into the spare, temporary downtown office suite furnished with mismatched desks and chairs borrowed from other government departments on January 6, 1999, he had begun to understand the strong — sometimes conflicted and often conflicting — views so many people had about the best way to memorialize the tragedy of Swissair Flight 111.

There were all the different interest groups: the families, of course, whom everyone agreed must be first among equals in deciding what, if anything, to do; the dozens of St. Margarets Bay fishermen who'd rushed out that first night to search for survivors, many of whom still weren't able to go back to fishing because of the continuing recovery operations on their fishing grounds; the 30 or so do-good organizations and the thousands of local volunteers who'd done whatever good they could in the days and weeks after the crash; the communities nearest the crash site, which had already been turned upside down by the disaster and which would have to live every day with whatever memorial was erected; the tourist

operators along the province's South Shore, who ago-
nized over the effect on their businesses of turning the
province's most photographed tourist destination into a
symbol of grief and despair; the military; the Mounties;
the chief medical examiner; Swissair; and, of course, the
provincial government, which had asked him to take on
this thankless unpaid task in the first place and would, in
the end, have to foot the bill and deal with whatever flak
followed whatever recommendation he would make.

And coming up with recommendations on where the
memorial should be and what it should look like — yet
another issue — would only dispense with the first part
of his mandate. There would still be the even trickier
matter of what to do with the more than a ton of bone and
flesh and muscle the medical examiner had not been able
to identify or return. While the consensus among almost
all the families was that they wanted any such mass burial to take place at Peggys Cove — the place that had
been the emotional ground zero for their grieving — the
residents there were far less keen on that idea, and the
tourist operators were downright hostile.

And, since those unidentified human remains could
include Christians, Jews, Muslims, Hindus and Greek
Orthodox adherents, as well as the usual mix of agnos-
tics, atheists and even a few who would probably have
classified themselves as none of the above, Clarke says
that, "denominationalism became an issue we had to deal
with." Jews and Muslims, as Clarke had discovered in
meetings with their spiritual leaders — "I've learned a
lot," he says — have strict rules about dealing with the
dead that would have to be taken into account.

To further complicate the task he had taken on,
Premier Russell MacLellan wanted Clarke not only to tell
him what he should do about these weighty issues but
also to make his recommendations in plenty of time for

the memorial to be built and the burial planned for September 2, 1999, the first anniversary of the crash. And, of course, he had to do it all in a way that would promote reconciliation and healing instead of division and pain for those affected by the disaster.

If anyone could do it, Lorne Clarke could.

As a judge, he was used to weighing evidence and making decisions. "That didn't intimidate me," he says, though he admits the issues here were more complex and personal than even he was used to dealing with. Perhaps more important, as an arbitrator he had honed the ability to bring people with different interests together to forge a consensus. His folksy, self-deprecating style — "I don't like using the upright pronoun," he is fond of saying — made him an empathetic listener. The key, he says, is simply "to engage oneself in one's human feelings, then sit and be quiet and listen to what people have to say, showing as much compassion and understanding for them as possible."

Even though he'd been inundated with unsolicited pleadings, suggestions and arguments from all quarters after his appointment, he decided in January to formalize the consultation process, holding community meetings in Indian Harbour, near Peggys Cove, in Blandford and in Halifax, where many of the volunteers lived. He quickly realized that each of the St. Margarets Bay communities, on opposite sides of the bay and almost equidistant from each other and the crash site, had compelling claims as the real centre of the tragedy. Peggys Cove was the world media centre as well as where the families came to grieve in public, but Blandford was where the military search effort was based and where wreckage and remains were brought ashore. From both places, you could look out on the spot where the plane had gone down.

Clarke included a list of six potential memorial sites

around the Bay in a questionnaire that he distributed at his community meetings. The questionnaire, which was mailed out to all the next of kin as well, also listed a range of possibilities for types of memorials, ranging from monuments to scholarships, and a question about whether the human remains should be interred at the memorial site or somewhere else.

Besides the community meetings, Clarke met individually with dozens of people, from spokespersons like Miles Gerety and Lyn Romano — separately, of course — to a "young woman who lost her father and stepmother. There were a lot of very sad people," he says.

In the end, Clarke's recommendation to the premier — quickly endorsed by all three political parties — was a Nova Scotia–style compromise: three separate memorials, all on Crown land and therefore available at no cost, one at Bayswater near Blandford (there was no Crown land available in Blandford), one at Whalesback, a spot 500 yards west of Peggys Cove, and a third, unmarked memorial to be designated at the exact latitude and longitude where the plane went down.

On the question of where to bury the human remains, Clarke eventually came down on the side of Bayswater instead of the more touristy Peggys Cove. "We don't want to turn this into Coney Island," he explains.

The nature of the memorials themselves would depend on the choice a jury would make from among submissions local architects and designers had been invited to make. But whatever form the memorial would take, he decided it would not include the names of those passengers whose families objected to having their names on the memorial.

The decisions weren't going to please everyone, of course, but there were remarkably few public complaints. Even Lyn Romano — who objected to the idea of the memorial, to her husband's name being on it and to there being any mass burial of unidentified human remains — was remarkably circumspect in her criticism of Clarke, whom she'd earlier publicly thanked for giving her a fair hearing. In a message to the SR111 web site before the decision was announced, she wrote: "I feel so sorry for Judge Clarke and what he must decide. He is between the largest rock and hard place of anyone I know. I've met with him, I respect him and I've said from the start: Whatever decision he must come to, I know it will be what he feels he must."

Clarke is pleased by that, pleased too that the planning for the first-anniversary dedication of the memorials and interment of the remains is going so smoothly. Helping organize that wasn't initially part of his mandate, but it "followed logically," he says. Swissair has already booked 1,000 hotel rooms it expects will be needed to accommodate the family members it has offered to fly back to Nova Scotia for the event. They'll almost certainly be joined by several thousand Nova Scotians who were involved in September's recovery operations, as well as a host of what Clarke calls "high-profile foreign visitors."

Clarke thinks the event will be an important one. "I don't like to use the word closure. I know it's overworked. But this will definitely be part of the healing process — for the families and for our own people too, who need this to finally come to an end so everyone can begin to get on with their lives."

Lives that, in many cases, have been changed forever by September 2, 1998.

Epilogue

Monday, April 26, 1999

Vancouver, British Columbia

It was oddly appropriate, or perhaps appropriately odd, that the four of us — a one-time New York ballet dancer who had become a teacher of English as a second language; a Fox Point, Nova Scotia, tuna fisherman who'd taken a mid-career break to earn a degree in theology; a transplanted westerner who'd taken on the seemingly thankless job of professionalizing the business of sudden death in Nova Scotia; and me — would end up sitting together at a round table in 900 West, the elegant dining room of Canadian Pacific's venerable Hotel Vancouver, chatting over lunch like old friends who hadn't seen each other for a while.

None of us had heard of any of the others a year ago. We were all in Vancouver to appear on *Gabereau*, a nationally syndicated television talk show, to share our very different perspectives of last September's crash of Swissair Flight 111: Nancy Wight, the mother who'd lost her only daughter in the crash; Robert Conrad, the fisherman who'd risked his life to look for survivors; Dr. John Butt, the pathologist who'd been in charge of identifying the dead; and me, the journalist who was writing the book about all of them.

The crash was our only shared experience, but — for a few hours one day far from any of our homes and 3,000 miles from where it had all happened — it seemed more than enough.

Nancy Wight, a gentle, thoughtful woman who seems both delicately fragile and incredibly resilient all in the same moment, was the connecting link among us. Her letter to the editor thanking John and Robert was what had initially led me to each of them. They, in turn, were meeting face to face for the first time that day, but already they had exchanged phone numbers and made plans to meet again when they were both back in Halifax.

When I'd learned that Butt was going to be in Vancouver for this taping, I called to ask if we could schedule the conclusion of a long-delayed interview while we were both in the same city at the same time. Sure, he said, then hedged. He didn't want to commit to getting together immediately after the show. "I don't want to leave Nancy alone in a strange city after something like that," he said, almost protectively.

In the end, he didn't have to worry. The show's host, Vicki Gabereau, and its producer, Ruth Anderson, took us all out to lunch. Nancy ordered Digby scallops and Robert, normally a vegetarian, indulged in a busman's holiday sampler of fresh west coast tuna. Nancy brought out pictures of Rowenna for us to admire. Robert showed us the envelope from a letter he'd received, a symbol of his notoriety as a result of having been interviewed in the days after the crash by journalists from around the world. It was simply addressed to "Robert Conrad, FISHER-MAN, Nova Scotia." "Somehow, the post office figured it out," he says in amazement. Butt, who had earlier introduced us to his grown daughter who lives in Vancouver and had come to the studio for the taping, told us how he'd been spending his West Coast holiday. Someone asked him about rumours that he was about to get yet another award for his work in the Flight 111 tragedy. It turned out he was: having already been named to *Maclean's* magazine's Honour Roll of the 12 Canadians who'd "made a difference" in 1998, he was scheduled to get the President's Award from the Association of Nova Scotia Psychologists in May, as well as an honorary degree from Dalhousie University. We also talked about all the usual stuff — places we'd been, books we'd read, summer plans. It all seemed so ordinary. And yet so extraordinary.

The crash of Swissair Flight 111 was a horrific event. It is tricky to look for — let alone claim to discern — anything good that might have come of such a profound tragedy. But some good has. People who should somehow have connected have met, friendships have been forged. Robert Conrad and Nancy Wight, Lyn Romano and Barbara Fetherolf, Miles Gerety and Peggy Coburn. Life does go on. For those who have lost so much, it is woefully small consolation. But at least it is that.